THE NEW

San Francisco
at Your Feet

THE NEW

San Francisco
at Your Feet

Best Walks in a Walker's City

THIRD REVISED AND UPDATED EDITION

Margot Patterson Doss

Photos by John Whinham Doss, M.D.
Compiled from the *San Francisco Chronicle* Series

Grove Weidenfeld
NEW YORK

Published by Grove Weidenfeld
A division of Grove Press, Inc.
841 Broadway
New York, NY 10003-4793

Introduction reprinted courtesy of *American West Magazine*.
Maps courtesy of the *San Francisco Chronicle*.

Library of Congress Cataloging-in-Publication Data

Doss, Margot Patterson.
    The new San Francisco at your feet : best walks in a walker's
city / by Margot Patterson Doss : maps courtesy of the San Francisco
Chronicle ; photos by John Whinham Doss. — 3rd rev. and updated ed.
        p.   cm.
    "Compiled from the San Francisco Chronicle series."
    Previous eds. published under title: San Francisco at your feet.
    Includes index.
    ISBN 0-8021-1145-9 (alk. paper) : $12.95
        1. Walking—California—San Francisco—Guide-books. 2. San
Francisco (Calif.)—Description and travel—Guide-books. 3. San
Francisco (Calif.)—Description—Tours. I. Doss, Margot Patterson.
San Francisco at your feet. II. San Francisco Chronicle.
III. Title.
GV199.42.C22S2694   1991
917.94'610453—dc20   90-21803
                                                            CIP

Manufactured in the United States of America

Printed on acid-free paper

Design and maps by Irving Perkins Associates

First Evergreen Edition 1974
First Printing, Second Revised and Updated Edition 1980
First Printing, Third Revised and Updated Edition 1991

10   9   8   7   6   5   4   3   2   1

CONTENTS

INTRODUCTION

"Make no mistake, Stranger, San Francisco is West as all Hell!" Bernard De Voto's caution, in the form of a bumper sticker, hangs on a bulletin board over my desk. The Camelot-city, born each day anew on her approximately forty hills, is so cosmopolitan, magical, exotic, and intriguing that it seems forever like a faraway place. For romance, it easily ranks with Istanbul, Paris, Singapore, or Rio. Yet go any farther west than San Francisco's three-mile-long Ocean Beach and either your feet will be wet by the blue Pacific, or you will be twenty-two miles offshore on the lonely Farallon Islands.

Reminders of our Western heritage are everywhere. Along Montgomery Street, for example, there is a plaque indicating that Pony Express riders used to pull up there. Pick up your newspaper on the right day and you'll discover that the Grand National Rodeo is being held at the Cow Palace.

Not that I need reminding.

From my office window, I can see that spectacular confluence of land and water where old Mama Sacramento and fourteen other rivers reach the sea. This is the gap in the Coast Range of mountains that pathfinder John Frémont, the Oliver North of his day, named the Golden Gate.

I have walked much of it. Sage, coyote brush, poison oak, and star thorn make up the chaparral on the north side of the Golden Gate Strait where Mount Tamalpais, elevation 2,572 feet, dips a toe into the water. On old Cantil Blanco, the south side of the gate, there are shooting stars, milkmaids, seaside daisies, Douglas iris, and lizardtail blooming in the springtime as they have since long "before the gringo came."

The Golden Gate is an historic place. The earliest non–Native American visitors recognized the splendor of the site immediately. In a diary entry dated March 28, 1776, Fray Pedro Font wrote of Juan Bautista de Anza: "The commander decided to erect the holy cross on the extremity of the white cliff (Cantil Blanco) at the inner point of the entrance to the port, and we went there at eight o'clock in the morning. We ascended a small low hill and then entered a tableland, entirely clear, of considerable extent, and flat, with a slight slope toward the port. It must be about half a league in width and little more in length and keeps

The Golden Gate Bridge, as day breaks over San Francisco. At left, the Bay Bridge and Telegraph Hill. *San Francisco Convention and Visitors' Bureau.*

narrowing until it ends in a white cliff. This tableland [*mesa* in the original Spanish, of course] commands a most wonderful view, as from it a great part of the port is visible, with its islands and entrance, and the ocean as far as the eye can reach—even farther than the Farallon Islands.

"The commander marked this tableland as the site of the new settlement, and the fort which is to be established at this port can be defended by musket fire, and at the distance of musket shot, there is water for the people. . . ."

People have been admiring the view ever since. There has also been a fort at that location ever after. Not the same one, unfortunately. It would be fun to have the first fort, El Castillo de San Joaquin, the horseshoe-shaped Spanish fort, there today. Think of the horse operas and advertising commercials that could be filmed in it! Alas, wind, rain, and earthquakes leveled El Castillo as is their wont with adobe buildings. By the time Frémont and his men swam their stolen horses across Golden Gate Strait to storm El Castillo, even the eleven cannons they spiked were lying about on the ground, already useless. Two of the cannons guard the Presidio Officers' Club today, and two are located at the Main Gate of the fifteen-hundred-acre post.

The U.S. Army Corps of Engineers cut the tip of Cantil Blanco down to the water's edge around 1853. Old Fort Point, a brick counterpart of Fort Sumter, has what remains of Cantil Blanco's cliff as a pediment. Now a Civil War museum "where never a shot was fired in anger," Fort Point's military use was soon outdated. It also lay in the path of the Golden Gate Bridge. Thanks to the goodwill of bridgebuilders Joseph B. Strauss and Clifford Paine, who redesigned their masterpiece, Fort Point still stands. A beautiful arch of steel built into the south pediment frames Fort Point—an engineer's appreciation of earlier engineering expertise.

The beautiful bridge, which is really painted rust-resistant international orange rather than gold, as many people expect, has always been a walkers' bridge. (Strangely enough, the suicides arrive by car, frequently by taxi. One would think jumpers would go off the scenic west side, where the setting sun slinks slowly into the sea in classy travelogue style. But no! It's off the east side they go, facing the city and the cozy Marin and East Bay suburbs.)

On May 27, 1937, when the Golden Gate Bridge was opened to pedestrians for the first time, 202,000 people flocked across it. Fifty years later, more than three million people walked across it on the anniversary, a pedestrian traffic jam that lasted ten hours.

Most visitors, and certainly every San Francisco walker, intends to cross the over-one-mile-long Golden Gate Bridge on foot; every month about five thousand of them do it, lured by the incomparable vistas of sea, sky, bay, mountains, city, villages, islands, and nearby fortifications. Since the Golden Gate National Recreation Area became landlord of the bridge, as well as of the Presidio and other military lands on either side of the Golden Gate, walkers no longer have to pay to cross.

Looking toward the Golden Gate from the west-facing windows of our old townhouse on the slope of Russian Hill, superficially nothing seems changed. We could take a snapshot from a window today, as we did thirty years ago when we bought the house, and the two photos would look much the same. Off to the left is that vast amphitheater of

Pacific Heights, with its mansions, many bay windows, and well-preserved Victorian homes.

In the middleground stands the graceful rotunda and dome of the Palace of Fine Arts, a legacy from the Panama-Pacific International Exposition of 1915. Behind it sweeps the deep green of the Presidio's eucalyptus groves, planted in 1880, and now being replanted.

Remarkable are the missing things—what is not there. There is no freeway, for one thing. Nor is there an identical twin bridge. There are no highrise towers. Not that there haven't been efforts to ram such things into the area. I cannot remember a time when the citizens of San Francisco have not been embattled with one or another of the greedy, big-money monsters of that dubious condition sometimes mislabeled "progress." There are land fights reminiscent of the range wars of the Old West, fought with words instead of guns.

I like that scrappy quality. This happy land we call San Francisco is so precious to its residents, it seems to demand and get protectors. It is no accident that the Russian Hill Neighborhood Association, for example, has become a band of savvy and experienced guerilla-fighters in their never-ending struggle to keep the community from being despoiled. Russian Hill was the first such group to employ a lawyer, digging into their own pockets to pay his fee. To give an idea of how long ago that happened, the lawyer was Caspar "Cap" Weinberger, later Ronald Reagan's Secretary of Defense. Russian Hill, which has been called the most livable urban neighborhood in any American city in more than one national survey, was also the first to employ an architect to speak for the association before the city planning commission. He was Sim Van der Ryn, later state architect under Governor Jerry Brown.

The "wins" of such citizens' groups have been many. Most recently an outraged and thorny group "ran up the Bear Flag," to use a local idiom for "taking on" the federal government, to defeat an effort by the U.S. Army to put a post office distribution center adjacent to the Golden Gate Promenade, the most popular trail within the Golden Gate National Recreational Area. It goes between Hyde Street Pier and Fort Point, within fifty feet of the Bay all the way.

Tourism today is San Francisco's biggest business and every one of those environmental successes has helped to make San Francisco a tremendous tourist attraction. Outraged citizens have squelched a freeway that would have destroyed Fisherman's Wharf, the Hyde Street cable car, our movable national landmark, Aquatic Park, Fort Mason, three yacht harbors, the Marina Green, and at least a dozen other famous places. They have prevented the "Manhattanization" of highrise hotels and apartments, like those in Rio or Miami, along the northern waterfront, and stopped a third bridge that would have placed one pediment in Aquatic Park and another on Alcatraz.

If this sounds as if San Franciscans do nothing but stop "progress," think again. Its citizens have created some remarkable solutions and innovations, such as the recycling of historic buildings. Factories like the Pioneer Woolen Mill and Ghirardelli Chocolate have been transformed into Ghirardelli Square, a rabbit-warren of boutiques and restaurants. The Cannery, which really was a cannery, is comparable. The pattern of recycling historic buildings has been successfully copied worldwide. For that matter, at least two new "pseudo-places" in San Francisco, Pier 39 and the Anchorage, have tried to build in the illusion of antiquity to pick up on the success of Ghirardelli Square and The Cannery.

Creative recycling doesn't stop with shops. The Palace of Fine Arts, a huge rococo rotunda and dome-shaped building, now houses the Exploratorium, one of the most imaginative hands-on scientific museums in the world.

The former Fort Mason Port of Embarkation, where soldiers sailed off to Manila in 1898 and later to the South Pacific and Korea, now houses Fort Mason Center. This lively cultural resource has within its old piers fifty-two separate organizations, including the Mexican Museum, the Italian Museum, the African-American Museum, a folk-art museum, five theaters, several art galleries, the distinguished Porter Shaw Maritime Library, such remarkable conservation groups as Friends of the River and Women in the Wilderness, the Media Alliance, and the celebrated Zen vegetarian restaurant Greens.

On an even vaster scale, creative re-use is represented by the Golden Gate National Recreation Area (GGNRA), which encompasses nine former military installations, stretching from the Presidio and Fort Mason south around the peninsula of San Francisco to Sweeney Ridge in San Mateo County. It also crosses the Golden Gate Bridge and extends from Sausalito north to Point Reyes. The citizens' group we can thank for it is People for a Golden Gate National Recreation Area, locally nicknamed PFGGNRA and pronounced "piffganura." It also came up with a creative way to finance our most popular national park. Written into enabling legislation is permission for the National Park Service to purchase land as private citizens do—with a down payment and the rest to come. Previously, parks had to await congressional appropriations—giving land speculators plenty of time to send prices skyrocketing on land designated for parks. Last year thirty million people visited the GGNRA, far outnumbering Yosemite, Yellowstone, and Disneyland combined.

Change, however paradoxical this may seem from what I have written thus far, is the essence of San Francisco. Like Paris, the more it changes, the more it remains the same.

The very nobility of its placement, colors (Oh, that Mediterranean blue sky!), scale, and mild climate seems to spawn a subtle and humane way of life. We are still the West of strangers, where everyone came from somewhere else. As it has always been, if early accounts by Charles Dickens, Mark Twain, and Robert Louis Stevenson are to be believed, the city is tolerant. We manage to accommodate diverse multitudes in a very small space.

One sees this especially in the neighborhoods. Outside San Francisco, perhaps our best-known neighborhood is Chinatown. To give an idea how compact the city is, suppose you are staying on Union Square, at the Hyatt, for example, or the St. Francis. It is possible to stroll from either hotel through Union Square, with its talented street musicians, mimes, and other entertainers, to Maiden Lane. This swank, two-block-long, pedestrian-only shopping street boasts a Frank Lloyd Wright building, the circular interior of which was a prototype for New York's Guggenheim Museum.

Make a left turn after walking one block on Maiden Lane and you will be on Grant Avenue, where the formal Chinatown Gate, with its guardian "foo dogs," is visible two blocks north. Step through the gate and you are in a different world, the largest Chinese village outside of China. It is bursting at the seams. Grant Avenue, the tourist trinket trail, has a counterpart shopping street one block north where the Chinese do their own marketing. This is Stockton Street. Near Broadway, where the corner is locally called "Little Hong Kong," the daily crowds are so deep that an unwary walker can be forced off the sidewalk.

Not surprisingly, satellite Chinatowns have sprung up. One is Clement Street, four miles west. Another, largely composed of Southeast Asians—the Cambodians, Thais, Hmongs, Miens, Vietnamese—is materializing along Larkin Street, in the lee of Civic Center. Long a depressed area of drunks and dopers known as the Tenderloin, its old fleabag hotels are being repaired and remodeled to house Southeast Asian families. Tiny kids play in the once-mean streets. There are now new little parks there, and on two days of the week, the Heart of the City Farmers' Market, which allows only produce from California, springs up outdoors in United Nations Plaza. Near the equestrian statue of Simón Bolívar, the market is often like a little United Nations. One is as apt to see a towering Samoan in a *puletasi,* or a tiny Bengali in a *longgi,* as a Yuppie in designer sweats buying the chanterelles or baby pattypan squash.

Just a few years ago, the new park called Potrero del Sol in the Mission neighborhood was a paved parking lot full of broken glass under the Army Street Interchange. Now it is green, well gardened, and alive with children. Another of San Francisco's ever-growing immigrant populations lives nearby. On its shopping street, 24th Street, you can find Salvadoran, Nicaraguan, Colombian, Peruvian, Mexican, Bolivian, and Chilean specialty foods for sale, and half a dozen restaurants serving a variety of South-of-the-Border cuisines. The Mission also has other communities many cities would consider exotic—Tongans, Samoans, Sikhs, Ethiopians, and several I have yet to discover.

North Beach, which hasn't had a beach for a hundred years, has traditionally been "Little Italy," even when North Beach Beat poets brought the focus of the literary world to it in 1959. One still finds espresso at Trieste and Malvinas, but there are also so many other coffeehouses and trattorias that a first-time visitor might wonder, "Is this Paris? Is this Rome?"

You think you have a handle on the city, but blink once and things are different. I wouldn't have it any other way. Looking south from my windows toward Civic Center, that exemplary Beaux Arts epitome of the "city beautiful" ideal, our state bird, the building crane, catches my eye on the horizon line. The completion of Louise M. Davies Performing Arts Center, home of San Francisco's symphony orchestra, started a remarkable "ripple effect" in the surrounding blocks. New restaurants, art galleries, and other things cultural have revitalized an area that became depressed more than thirty years ago when a tentacle of the "Bloody Bayshore" freeway, Route 101 South, writhed through the Western Addition.

Not far from it, the old Western Addition parts known as Redevelopment Areas A-1 and A-2 have had a different kind of renaissance. Under the guidance of the late M. Justin Herman, a genius among planners, another sore spot has been healed. Instead of slums, we have the Japan Center, a three-block-long segment of the new Japan, alongside Nihonmachi, a vignette of Old Japan. A few blocks farther down Post Street, at Fillmore, is a group of fine old Victorian houses, all moved to one location and rehabilitated. In their old location are new apartments, nicely scaled to the fabric of the nearby buildings. Interior courts, some created by shutting off through streets, make these apartments livable and provide common green space for children.

Those of us who lived through the stormy years of his efforts also thank Justin Herman for the stunning new face of downtown San Francisco. Moscone Center and the emerging new Yerba Buena Gardens beside it had their genesis in Justin Herman's office. So did that remarkable complex the Embarcadero Center, site of the old produce district. Colorful as it was, the old produce district had nowhere near the charm of Sidney Walton Park, Golden Gateway Commons, the Golden Gateway Towers, the Alcoa Building, and Embarcadero Center that have replaced it. Who today would trade the waterfront dives that once stood at the foot of Market Street for the Hyatt Regency and Embarcadero Center's skybridges over the streets below? They allow a walker to stroll from Sidney Walton Park to the Ferry Building safely removed from traffic. En route, the stroller can enjoy a collection of municipally owned sculpture that can't be equaled this side of Paris's Galerie de Plein Arts. Herb Caen, our preeminent newspaper gossip columnist, may not like the Vaillancourt Fountain, but I love it. A celebration of water, it has big square concrete stepping stones under the fountain's many spouts, where one can walk without getting wet. Mr. Caen has hard words for the Transamerica Pyramid, too. Not I. It gives our boxy downtown skyline a much-needed spire shape, like the church steeple in a country town.

Artists trigger the transformations in some neighborhoods. South of Market, nicknamed SoMa, is one example. Once a dreary, light industrial area, today it has some of the liveliest chic night clubs and restaurants to be found.

The east cliff of Telegraph Hill has also had resurgence. Formerly a collection of godowns, as warehouses designed for holding goods near Embarcadero piers were called, it now has radio and television studios, advertising agencies, and, most impressive of all, the two-block-square home offices of the West's favorite blue jeans—Levi's Plaza. Follow the waterfront south and another promenade reaches Pier 7 and then South Beach, which fronts a community of new apartments.

"Oh, give me the simple life!" is a tune most San Franciscans pretend to march to. "Given a choice between a simple life with fewer material possessions and reaching a higher standard of living, we favor the simple life by almost 3 to 1," according to a *San Francisco Chronicle* poll taken October 2, 1986. Yet our city has more gourmet restaurants, and more diners out, more frequently, than any other place in the United States, New York included. California Cuisine started here. There are upward of fifty culinary schools in which to learn it, or any other kind of cooking. The simple life! Gulp!

How does one reconcile these opposing facts? One doesn't even try. We watched the Beats come and go. We watched the Flower Children. We chuckled when photographer Imogen Cunningham defined a hippy as "a young person you don't like." Many of those hippies have turned into entrepreneurs—music mogul Bill Graham, Dr. Larry Brilliant, founder of the SEVA Foundation, and Stewart Brand, creator of *The Whole Earth Catalog*, for example.

We watched the Gay Revolution produce the bachelor city called "The Castro." We weathered the assassinations of a mayor and supervisor. The homeless and the epidemic called AIDS are with us now, and we shiver about that fact, but the city never loses its perspective.

San Francisco is surrounded on three sides by water, making it a mecca for mariners. *San Francisco Convention and Visitors' Bureau.*

When San Francisco's worst previous catastrophe, the Fire and Earthquake of 1906, struck, some irreverent rhymester wrote:

If, as they say, God spanked the town
For being overfrisky
Why did He burn the churches down
And spare Hotaling's whiskey?

No one as yet has come up with a quatrain that captures at once the insouciance of the Castro and poignancy of its disintegration, the recent shake of 1989, or the plight of the unhoused, but give us time.

These are only hints of San Francisco's personality, pleasures, places, and possibilities. If I tried to tell them all, like Marco Polo, I might be accused of exaggeration, except by people who have come to see the city with their own eyes and cameras. They all return home to stun their friends with the wonders of our air-conditioned city. Why don't they stay? As in so many other things, the cost of housing in San Francisco is second to none. Those of us who already live here and love it think it's worth the cost.

—Margot Patterson Doss
Russian Hill, San Francisco
April 1989

THE NEW

San Francisco
at Your Feet

PRESIDIO

The Presidio, which contains nearly two thousand acres, although not under the jurisdiction of the municipal authorities, may be properly regarded as part of San Francisco's park system.

—JOHN P. YOUNG, *San Francisco,
a History of the Pacific Coast
Metropolis* (S. J. Clarke,
Publishers, 1912).

Situated at the dramatic meeting place of the San Francisco Bay and the Pacific Ocean, the fifteen-hundred-acre Presidio of San Francisco is so spectacular that it could be a candidate for "best park location in the world." It has all the necessary qualities—unique beauty of site, rare and endangered flora and fauna, and significant historical importance.

For more than two hundred years, reveille has sounded through its gentle glades. The flags of three nations have flown over this venerable military post. Within its mellow old stone walls stand relics of this long use: skillfully engraved cannons forged for the king of Spain that were one hundred twenty years old when the Declaration of Independence was signed, half-remembered bivouacs where soldiers camped during the Spanish-American War, headstones of heroes of the battles that shaped our nation and even of the camp followers, such as "The Great Western," the toast of two regiments.

There is a lake on whose shores Juan Bautista de Anza camped, a reputedly aphrodisiac spring from which Indians drank, three museums—one inside the most significant Civil War fort this side of Fort Sumter—and recognizably early bits of brickwork, including commendable military architecture from every period of American history. There are children's playgrounds, graceful trees, the only free-flowing creeks in San Francisco, three romantic beaches, excellent walking trails and footpaths, several plants that grow nowhere else in the world, and some of the last wild animals in the city.

By being its own authentic self, the Presidio manages to make history and geography both believable and understandable in a way that textbooks, television, the movies, or Disney-style amusement parks cannot.

First-time visitors to the Presidio are amazed to discover that it was already well founded in 1776 when our nation was being born. "San Francisco doesn't look old enough!" I once heard a man from Mary-

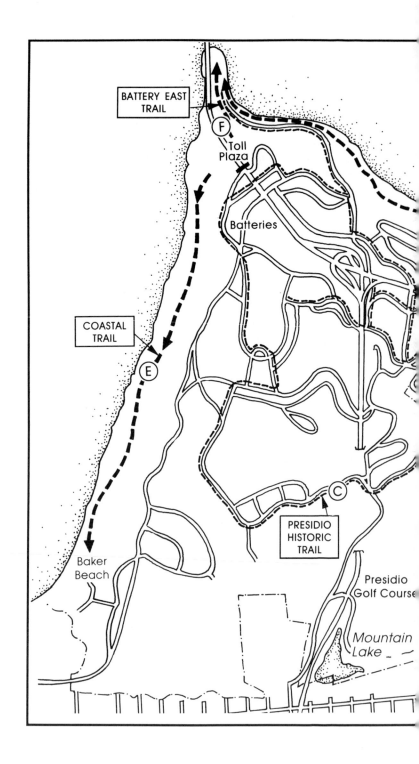

BATTERY EAST TRAIL

F

Toll Plaza

Batteries

COASTAL TRAIL

E

Baker Beach

PRESIDIO HISTORIC TRAIL

C

Presidio Golf Course

Mountain Lake

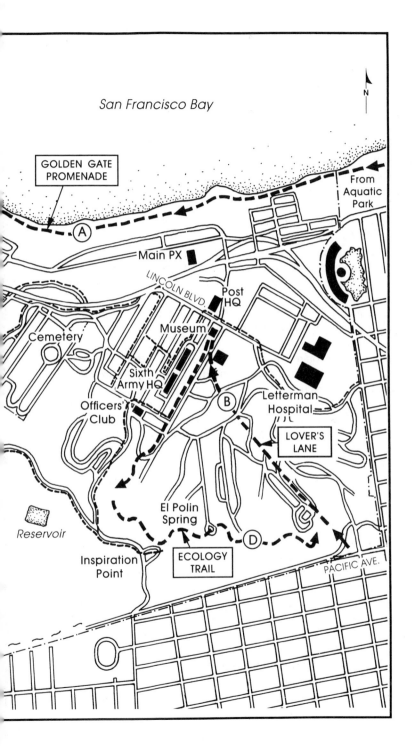

San Francisco Bay

GOLDEN GATE
PROMENADE

From
Aquatic
Park

N

Ⓐ

Main PX

LINCOLN BLVD.

Post
HQ

Museum

Cemetery

Sixth
Army HQ

Officers'
Club

Letterman
Hospital

Ⓑ

LOVER'S
LANE

Reservoir

El Polin
Spring

Ⓓ

Inspiration
Point

ECOLOGY
TRAIL

PACIFIC AVE.

land protest after reading the date on one of the pillars of the Lombard Street gate, then swinging around to look again at the city visible east of Lyon Street. His instincts were sound.

The Presidio was established as a Spanish garrison fifty-nine years before the first city lot in the Mexican El Paraje de Yerba Buena (the original name given to what is now San Francisco) was granted to an adventurer and trader, Don William Antonio Richardson.

The señorita whom Richardson wooed and won, Doña María Antonía Martínez, was born in what is now the Presidio Officers' Mess, while her father, Ignacio Martínez, was the commandant. Mission San Francisco de Asis, as Mission Dolores is correctly called, is also older than Richardson's pueblo. In those days, long before the automobile, the three places were a good hour's walk from one another.

Parts of the routes from the Presidio to the mission and the budding city were incorporated into a seven-mile Historic Trail for walkers in 1965 by Brigadier General Charles "Monk" Meyer. This remarkable trail makes an irregular loop that touches on every geographical section of the Presidio.

Although it is the longest and most comprehensive, the Historic Trail is only one of many walking trails within the Presidio. There are dozens more used by schoolchildren, soldiers and their wives, visiting dog walkers, and other citizens in search of a respite from the crowded urban scenes. The oldest of all the Presidio's trails may well be Lover's Lane. It is, for anyone who grew up in the city's less frantic and crowded years, the semisylvan stroll from everyone's seventeenth summer.

The Sixth Army Engineers, based at the Presidio, has maps identifying Lover's Lane by this name for the past ninety years and possibly longer. It is shown on the U.S. Coast Survey map of 1868 as part of the old Spanish Trail between the Presidio and Mission Dolores. How long the Indians may have used it before the Spaniards arrived in 1774 is anybody's guess, for it rambles from a high point once used as a lookout to a lower one near a stream, not far from El Polin Spring.

Lover's Lane may not be on your map, and there is but one street sign to identify it, but walkers will find it at the northwest corner of Presidio and Pacific avenues, just inside the pedestrian gate of the Presidio. It goes as the crow flies, along a gentle downhill grade to Tennessee Hollow, and was well worn when the infantrymen of the First Tennessee Regiment camped here, waiting to be shipped off to Manila in 1898. At Tennessee Hollow, it crosses a brick footbridge, the oldest in the city, and stops at Barnard Avenue, east of the parade ground.

At the beginning of the lane, look at the north side of the steep 3200 block of Pacific, a group of compatible houses abutting one another and the Presidio wall in close harmony. Bruce Porter, Willis Polk, William Knowles, Ernest Coxhead, and Bernard Maybeck are the architects of this unique composition, which was built between 1901 and 1913. The unmarked site of the old Indian lookout is one block uphill, at the southeast corner of Pacific Avenue and Lyon Street.

Lover's Lane in Presidio.

Step through the gate at Lover's Lane and you are in a different world, a place of bucolic enchantment where songbirds sing and motes float. It is so civilized and well curried that no alien thistle or poison oak intrudes. There is a quality of timelessness here and the result is sublimely refreshing.

Lover's Lane crosses three roads, a battalion of eucalyptus trees planted in 1880, a row of Georgian houses, and a meadow without a swerve in its course. Near its lowest elevation, it passes an all-enveloping weeping willow tree bending over one of the last free-running streams within the city limits.

When you reach the footbridge, pause a moment to look around Tennessee Hollow. It was here that the First Tennessee and Thirteenth Minnesota regiments camped during the Spanish-American War. Look west along the stream, which was trenched at one side to provide dry foundations for tents. Old concrete about three hundred yards upstream from the bridge still traces the location of the tents.

At Barnard Avenue, Lover's Lane ends, or loses its identity. You are now at Presidio Boulevard, once the entry road to the Presidio's workaday compound. Turn left, uphill, and walk past historic officers' housing of the Victorian era to Funston Avenue.

At Funston Avenue, pause to look both left and right. This old company street, whose houses were built in 1862, is the finest of its kind still in existence, a living museum where people still live. Turn right on Funston to reach, at Lincoln Boulevard, the Presidio Army Museum, housed in the oldest building built by the U.S. Army on the post.

It opened as the Wright General Hospital in 1857 and functioned as the post dispensary from 1899 (when Letterman Army Medical Center opened) until 1969. Since 1973, it has been a museum dedicated to the military history of San Francisco.

If you arrive at the museum—which is free to the public—between 10 A.M. and 4 P.M. any Tuesday through Sunday, go in to see an early model of the Spanish Presidio and the Presidio's first fort, El Castillo de San Joaquin, among more recent exhibits.

The Presidio Army Museum is also the starting point for the seven-mile Presidio Historic Trail and for the shorter Presidio Ecology Trail, created in 1976, which is devoted to the plants of the Presidio. Its route passes thirty different kinds of trees. Along the way, it stops at El Polin Spring (at the end of MacArthur Avenue), visits Inspiration Point, then swings back behind Pershing Hall and the Funston Avenue company street to return to the museum. Hundreds of San Francisco schoolchildren have made this two-mile loop as part of their classwork.

Among less-known trails within the Presidio is the old bridle path, which connects Park Presidio Boulevard with the stables and mule barns at McDowell Avenue, passing the U.S. Public Health Service Hospital and Mountain Lake.

Horsemen in our time have urged the reopening of this link between Golden Gate Park and the Golden Gate Bridge as part of the natural route for the Bay Area Ridge Trail and the longer De Anza Trail from Yuma, Arizona.

The best-known and most widely used of the Presidio trails are within the areas that were first transferred to the Golden Gate National Recreation Area (GGNRA), which has been the landlord of the entire Presidio since the sprawling park was established.

Prime among the GGNRA trails is the Golden Gate Promenade, which begins at Hyde Street. It follows the edge of San Francisco Bay within fifty feet of the water for its entire length and enters the Presidio at Lyon Street, passing Crissy Field to end at Fort Point. One of the most scenic trails in the world, it is used daily by hundreds of walkers, runners, joggers, bicyclists, wind surfers, and fishermen; their eyes are filled with a westerly view of the Golden Gate Bridge and the Marin Headlands. On the return trip east along the three-mile trail, San Francisco's downtown skyline is the eye-filler.

Park rangers conduct a Bay Marine Ecowalk along the Promenade for the San Francisco Unified Schools' environmental science department. Golden Gate Audubon Society and Chevron have also created a Bay Shore Study Guide for the Promenade.

Fort Point, the sentinel of the Bay, from which never a shot has been fired in anger, is a good walk in itself, but high on the cliff above it there is another fine trail around Battery East and Andrews Road, once the lane that led to the home of Colonel René de Russy, builder of Fort Point. Its terrain and wooded area are so different from that of the beach below that the San Francisco School District Environmental Science Center has created another project for science classes—The Fort Point Ecowalk.

A length of the Coastal Trail linking the San Francisco and Marin parts of the GGNRA has existed within the Presidio for the past sixteen years. It will one day also connect the southern part of the GGNRA, tying Marin and San Mateo counties together for walkers and, it is hoped, for horse riders and bicyclists as well.

For now, the Presidio section of the Coastal Trail goes west from the Golden Gate Bridge, passes through Battery Marcus Miller, an old coastal fortification, then skirts Lincoln Boulevard to swing down to Baker Beach.

A state park before it came into the GGNRA, Baker Beach has a unique demonstration exhibit that includes a "disappearing" six-inch gun at Battery Chamberlain. The old Point Lobos Pumping Station and a free-running portion of Lobos Creek can also be seen at Baker Beach. The Coastal Trail leaves the Presidio at 25th Avenue.

Two locations in the Presidio are among the parks under the jurisdiction of the San Francisco Recreation and Park Department. The larger and more historically significant of these is Mountain Lake Park, which lies north of Lake Street between Seventh and Funston avenues. A marker on the sunny south shore of Mountain Lake commemorates the occasion on March 27, 1776, when Juan Bautista de Anza and his exploring party camped beside this spring-fed lake.

Anza called it Laguna de Presidio and decided it held enough water to supply the garrison. It did. From this shore, he went on to erect a cross on the promontory he called Cantil Blanco, overlooking the Golden Gate Strait. It was on Cantil Blanco that the Spanish erected El Castillo de San Joaquin, fitting it with eleven cannons.

Eighty years later, on July 1, 1856, Captain John Charles Frémont and his men crossed the Golden Gate Strait from what is now East Fort Baker and spiked the cannons, putting them out of commission. Among them were the two cannons that now guard the Presidio Officers' Club, one at Fort Point and the pair at the Lombard Street gate. (The other cannons are in the Smithsonian Institution in Washington.)

Cantil Blanco has a trail over what is left of it (after being sliced into twice, first to accommodate Fort Point and later to admit the Golden Gate Bridge toll plaza) and descends to Fort Point.

Running from Mountain Lake along the Presidio's south wall is West Pacific Avenue, well used by joggers who begin with the warm-up offered by the Mountain Lake Parcourse, the first exercise course of its kind when it was built.

When they reach the Presidio wall within the park, many head east on West Pacific Avenue, leaving Mountain Lake sidewalk. The trail then continues unpaved for part of the way along the Lobos Creek watershed, skirts the Presidio Golf Course, passes Arguello Gate, and ultimately reaches Julius Kahn Playground, the second of the city parks within the Presidio.

Of all the Presidio walks, the most serene is within the National Military Cemetery. It is a hillside stroll dear to the nation, valuable to all who seek perspective in this topsy-scurvy world and precious to those whom the heroes have left behind.

If you feel a thrill of pride when the flag of the United States "yet waves," go some sunny day to the cemetery, entering it at Lincoln Boulevard and Sheridan Avenue. Its great wrought-iron gate is open from 5 A.M. to 5 P.M. On the left, as you walk in, is a rostrum where Abraham Lincoln's address, made at Gettysburg in 1863, is carved on a cenotaph and enjoins us, the living, "that from these honored dead we take increased devotion to that cause for which they gave the last full measure." On the east side, near the gate to the Post Chapel, is the plot dedicated by the Grand Army of the Republic to pioneer G. H. Thomes. At its dedication in 1893, the program expressed the hope that here our country's defenders "may rest undisturbed by the march of local improvements, or the 'vandalism of avarice' through the generations to come."

A FEW PRESIDIO FACTS

- When the Spaniards arrived in 1776, the land that has been the Presidio ever after was as bare as the Marin Headlands visible just across Golden Gate Strait. The first forestation project began in 1880. Soldiers planted the eucalyptus and pine trees in military style, row upon row.
- The original Spanish Presidio was a walled camp approximately two hundred yards square, surrounded by palisade walls. The old quadrangle of the Spanish Presidio is marked by bronze plaques placed by the Daughters of the American Revolution in 1928. The Post Chapel and the Officers' Club both survive from the Spanish time. A section of the original adobe wall of the commandant's house, now the Officers' Club, is preserved for viewing under glass on the club's stage.
- The Presidio was used by the Spanish until it was taken over by the Mexicans when they gained their independence from Spain and a republic was declared in 1823; it was occupied by the Mexicans until the United States took forcible possession in 1846. Formal occupation of the Presidio by U.S. troops was on March 27, 1847, with Major James A. Hardie in command.
- On February 25, 1963, the Presidio of San Francisco was designated a Registered National Historic Landmark for "exceptional value in commemorating and illustrating the history of the United States."

Walks for an Hour or a Day

Whatever amount of time is available to you for walking, the Presidio has a trail to fit it. If you have only an hour, consider:

LOVER'S LANE. Served by Muni bus 43, this romantic trail begins in Pacific Heights at the intersection of Presidio and Pacific avenues and runs straight downhill to Barnard Avenue. (See walk Ⓑ on map, page 5.)

MOUNTAIN LAKE. In Presidio Heights. A secret trail, it hides behind Lake Street houses and is best approached from the north end of Funston Avenue. Muni bus 28 is handy to it. (See map, page 4.)

If you have a morning to enjoy walking, try:

BATTERY EAST TRAIL AND ANDREWS ROAD. Overlooking the Golden Gate Bridge and the entrance to the Bay, this spectacular trail is easily approached from the toll plaza, where Golden Gate Transit buses stop, as does Muni bus 28. There is good free parking and a trailhead at Battery East Road and the Presidio's Lincoln Boulevard. Once you're on the trail, Andrews Road is the first left. (See walk Ⓕ on map, page 4.)

PRESIDIO ECOLOGY TRAIL. Two miles long, the Presidio Ecology Trail begins and ends at the Presidio Museum and loops around Lover's Lane, El Polin Spring, Inspiration Point, the historic central parade ground, and the Post Chapel. Take Muni bus 29 to the museum, at the Presidio's Lincoln Boulevard and Funston Avenue. (See walk Ⓓ on map, page 5.)

To spend a whole day:

THE PRESIDIO HISTORIC TRAIL. A challenging choice with a startling variety of terrain. Trail maps are available at the Presidio Museum. Muni bus 29 will take you to the museum. (See walk Ⓒ on map, pages 4–5.)

THE COASTAL TRAIL. Take this link of a longer trail from the Golden Gate Bridge south to Baker Beach for dramatic views of the Marin Headlands, including Hawk Hill, Bonita Light, Mile Rock, and the Golden Gate Strait. Battery Chamberlain at Baker Beach has a small museum. The trail leaves the Presidio at Seacliff, takes to the city streets, then re-enters the woods at 33rd Avenue and El Camino del Mar. From there, it swings around Eagles' Point and Lands End to the Cliff House. (See walk Ⓔ on map, page 4.)

GOLDEN GATE PROMENADE. Take a Hyde Street cable car to the Aquatic Park turntable and begin walking the trail west from the Hyde Street Pier. It passes Fort Mason and Marina Green before entering the Presidio at Lyon Street. Plan to enjoy your brown-bag lunch at Crissy Field beach, especially if you like to watch wind surfers. The trail ends at Fort Point's museum, which will take at least an hour to explore. The trail is three miles long, or six miles round-trip. For a quicker return, climb above Fort Point to the Golden Gate Bridge toll plaza to catch a Muni bus 28 to Beach and Laguna streets, and walk to the Hyde Street Pier through Fort Mason from there. (See walk Ⓐ on map, pages 4–5.)

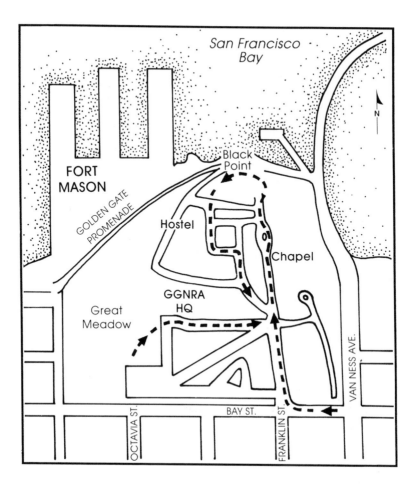

FORT MASON

WALKING TIME: A morning, if you relax.

DISTANCE: A mile.

PUBLIC TRANSPORTATION: Muni buses 30, 42, and 47.

PARKING: Free and ample.

CLOTHES: Easy does it.

San Francisco, ever a seductress, reveals her secrets a little at a time. One of the more charming of these is an old wood-and-brick "temporary" Civil War battery in Fort Mason, headquarters of the Golden Gate

National Recreation Area. Situated high on Black Point, the woodsy northernmost tip of the city, the battery has been restored by the GGNRA to its 1864 glory and enhanced with wayside exhibits, lawns, picnic tables, and barbecues.

To make the walk, start at Van Ness Avenue at Bay Street. Once there, walk west along the winding park pathway that fronts Fort Mason parallel to Bay Street. Turn right on Franklin Street and walk toward the Post Chapel, a Mission Revival–style building easily identified by its carillon tower.

Using your own wheels, drive into Fort Mason from Franklin Street. Turn left sharply at the Post Chapel and go past the large white building that houses the Golden Gate National Recreation Area headquarters and Visitors' Center. Continue west, and just beyond the red tile-roofed park police station, turn left. Drive south to the end of this short park road to find a large parking lot parallel to Bay Street.

Once parked, walk north on the path that continues from Octavia Street leading over a berm to reach the Great Meadow, a large lawn that slopes toward the Marina.

If the day is clear, the view toward the Golden Gate opens like a flower as you walk. (Those who arrived on foot may want to walk west to this spot to enjoy the view before returning to the chapel.)

Bear right on the Great Meadow peripheral trail and right again at the unimposing San Francisco Conservation Corps building, a vestige of the temporary military buildings that occupied this whole area until 1972, when the park was created.

The area to the left will be the site of a memorial to the late Representative Phillip Burton, credited by his colleagues as having done more for parks in our lifetime than any other person. Continue east to the Post Chapel. Cross Franklin Street and pause a moment near the big round-topped post box to look about. The stately frame building beyond the circle of lawn to the east is known to historians as Brook House No. 1, built in 1855. To men who served in the U.S. Army at Fort Mason, it was McDowell Hall. Generals Irvin McDowell (for whom it was named), P. H. Sheridan, and Arthur MacArthur are among those who served here.

When Fort Mason was headquarters for the San Francisco Port of Embarkation, a cannon stood nearby, and sunset and sunrise salutes were fired daily over Aquatic Park. Now McDowell Hall, an officers' club, has a dining room opened to the public for lunch.

As you walk north, you are on the company street of the original quarters created on orders issued November 6, 1850, by President Millard Fillmore to Colonel Richard Mason, then military governor of California. Officers once lived on the east side, enlisted men on the west of the street.

The first house you reach on your right, notable for its steep red roof and circular window, is the youngest house on the street, built in 1880. The next three are elegant Greek Revival homes built soon after the Gold Rush by San Francisco businessmen: Brook House No. 2; the Leonidas Haskell House, where Senator David Broderick died in 1859 after his duel with the terrible-tempered Justice Terry; and the Joseph Palmer House.

The more modest houses on the west side and two around the corner on Funston Road date from 1863, when Black Point, named for the dark-leafed laurel trees that grew on it, was pressed into service against the threat of Confederate raids on the Bay. Together, the houses of the little company street comprise a fine museum of pre-earthquake San Francisco architecture.

When you reach the carriage turnaround, follow the sidewalk to your right beyond Palmer House on to a shady lawn accessible only on foot. Within a few steps, you are at the site of Porter's Lodge. The one-story cottage was razed in 1863 when the recently rediscovered Civil War battery was originally built.

Climb the stairs to your left to reach the location of the first fortification to stand on Black Point, Bateria San José. When the Spanish placed bronze cannons here in 1797, Black Point was called Point San José.

For a fine overview of the later Civil War battery, walk to the northwest corner of this little terrace. Then descend the stairs to the next lower level, where picnic tables have been placed on the sheltered east side. "Uncle John" McLaren of the San Francisco park system contributed many of the trees here to dress up the Fort for the Panama-Pacific International Exhibition of 1915.

It was Park Ranger John Martini who discovered the old Civil War battery, which had been covered by tons of earth during construction of a nearby powerhouse in 1911. In doing research on Fort Mason, John had read of a temporary Civil War battery with a dozen ten-inch Rodman cannons. In the 1970s he went looking for them. While clearing a clogged passage leading into the hillside, John found an underground concrete powder magazine, which was installed in 1898, and, near it, a section of brick wall that he recognized as construction from the Civil War era.

Archaeologists excavated small parts of the area, tracing the brick wall to reveal intact walls outlining two gun pits. Later, San Francisco Conservation Corps members, supervised by archaeologists, dug out thousands of cubic yards of soil. In the process, they recovered several thousand artifacts, which eventually will be put on display at Fort Mason.

In time, a Rodman cannon weighing twenty-four thousand pounds will arrive from the Smithsonian Institution in Washington, D.C., for display at one of the gun mounts.

To see how Black Point looked when San Francisco was still a frontier town, take a good look at the wayside exhibit. Greg Moore, director of the Golden Gate National Parks Association, said the wayside exhibits are part of a five-year project in which volunteers in his organization raised $100,000 to excavate, document, and restore the Black Point Civil War battery.

When it is time for you to go, walk across the grass within the battery toward the nearest building, originally built as a barracks for the soldiers who manned the battery. It is now the San Francisco International Youth Hostel.

Turn onto the first street you encounter, Magazine Street, then turn right onto Battery Street. Digress downhill for a moment to the Golden Gate Promenade to seek out two more wayside exhibits, one about the Liberty ship *Jeremiah O'Brien* visible below and the other on the history of Fort Mason's Port of Embarkation, whose old piers and forepiers now contain the lively Fort Mason Center.

If you are still game for walking, the Golden Gate Promenade continues for three miles to Fort Point. If this is more walking than you care to do today, retrace your steps to the International Youth Hostel and follow the road around to the lawn, originally the Fort Mason parade ground, in front of it. A Greek Revival front porch once ran from end to end of the barracks building.

Cross this lawn toward the fence to find the prize-winning Fort Mason community garden, originally the site of the post orchard and vegetable garden. Then, using the Post Chapel carillon tower as a landmark once again, continue to the left to complete this loop walk of Black Point.

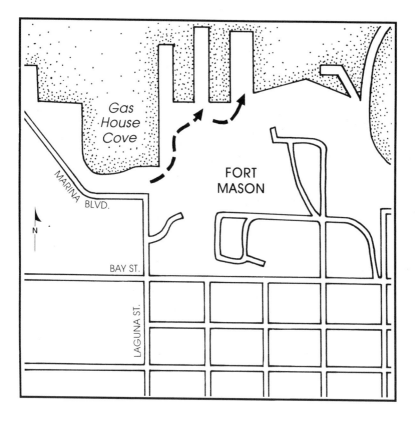

FORT MASON CENTER

WALKING TIME: Allow two to three hours.

DISTANCE: From here to creativity.

PUBLIC TRANSPORTATION: Muni buses 22, 28, 30, 42, 47, and 49; 28 is best.

PARKING: So-so.

CLOTHES: Chic but comfortable.

FEES: Modest.

Fort Mason Center for the Arts, Humanities, Recreation, Education and Ecology has been likened to "a cultural vortex," a "garden of the mind," and "a visit to Utopia." Wordy as its whole name seems, no one ever calls Fort Mason Center dull.

The brainchild of the Golden Gate National Recreation Area's first superintendent, William J. Whalen, it has become one of the prime civilizing influences of the Bay Area in the few years since its establishment. Marc Kasky, executive director of the Fort Mason Center, who likes to point out that the center is self-supporting, rarely makes a point of the $27 million it contributes annually to the city's economy. Instead, quoting architect Zach Stewart, one of his mentors, Kasky likes to think of Fort Mason Center as "a work in progress of becoming."

If you haven't discovered this contemporary treasure, which was once an Army port of embarkation, walk around it. At almost any time, one can find plenty of diversion. Fort Mason Center's entry gate is at the watery end of Laguna Street, across from the Marina Safeway, which was once Gas House Cove.

Look beyond to see the white sails of yachts, the blue of the Bay, the green of the hills, and the orange of the Golden Gate Bridge. Heading east, walk through a gap in the wall alongside Building A, and turn left. When you reach the simple swinging board that announces the Fort Mason Center offices, you'll discover that its lobby is the Perception Gallery.

Pick up a copy of the free monthly calendar and look at its back cover for a map of the thirteen-acre center and directory of its fifty permanent residents. Another 450 nonresident groups use the center each year.

Next stop for art buffs is the San Francisco Museum of Modern Art Rental Gallery. Its neighbor museum in Building A is the San Francisco Craft and Folk Art Museum, which has a small, well-supplied shop offering folk art for purchase.

Unless the prize-winning Zen restaurant Greens entices you for lunch, walk east about forty feet to Building B. Enter its midblock door, where the Cooks & Company counter in the wide corridor is usually jumping with students of the San Francisco Community College Art Center. They often carry their cups along the corridor to reach the Coffee Gallery, formerly a big storage room, where works by students and faculty adorn the walls. After you have admired the local work, climb the staircase just across the corridor to reach the Life on the Water Theater.

As you leave the theater, walk east again, this time on the indoor bridge that crosses to Building C. It will bring you out alongside the Young Performers' Theater, which may be offering a performance for kids.

Descend to the first floor to reach the ground-level location of the Children's Art Center, which teaches kids from two to twelve years old.

When you have peeked in on this productive group of budding Picassos, continue down the corridor of Building C to reach the Museo Italo-Americano. After you have absorbed the current show, continue around to the farthest gallery to see a festive Sicilian horse cart and, on the wall near it, paintings by two San Francisco painters of Italian extraction, Giuseppe Cadenasso and Rinaldo Cuneo.

Go across the hall to find the San Francisco African-American Historical Society Museum. The Wajumbi Dance Group often performs African dances here.

Leave Building C by the east door, cross the broad street just below what was once a military loading platform and now makes a nice walkway, to reach Building D. Once inside the door, a tremendous mural will alert you to the Mexican Museum. Go in and be prepared to marvel. The dance troupe Grupo Folklorico Mexicano sometimes stars here.

When you have enjoyed the museum, go out the same door through

Liberty ship *Jeremiah O'Brien*, viewed from the Fort Mason Civil War battery. The walker is on the Golden Gate Promenade.

which you entered and walk bayward to find Pier 2, which now houses both the Herbst Pavilion and the new Cowell Theater. Audiences have the fun of stepping out from lobbies during intermission onto the pier, where lights at night on the Golden Gate Bridge make a romantic backdrop.

Return to shore, noticing the easternmost forepier, Building E, which is largely devoted to things maritime, including the Oceanic Society, the Marine Mammal Center, Lifeline Mammal Research, and the J. Porter Shaw Library.

The last museum of your visit to Fort Mason can also be maritime, the National Liberty Ship *Jeremiah O'Brien*, which moors alongside Pier 3 and welcomes visitors aboard on Sunday for a pittance.

If you'd rather look at her than climb aboard, walk past the little firehouse, Building F, to find an ornate memorial bench at the water's edge, ideally placed for dreaming, gull watching, or musing. The rugged cliffs beyond it are an unspoiled bit of the original Bay shoreline.

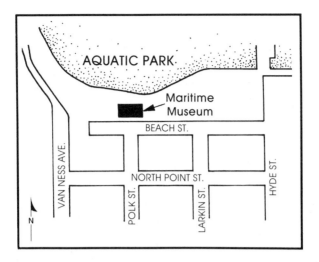

MARITIME MUSEUM

WALKING TIME: Allow an hour.

PUBLIC TRANSPORTATION: Muni bus 19 takes you to the door.

PARKING: Only fair.

CLOTHES: Rubber-soled shoes.

"The call of the running tide . . . a wild call and a clear call that may not be denied," as described by John Masefield, hits many San Franciscans whenever there's a salty onshore breeze.

When it does, those who have boats go sailing on the Bay. Those who have time and money take a cruise. The rest of us "hoist up the John B. sails and see how the mainsail sets" at the National Maritime Museum. Vicarious sailing in the concrete ship at the foot of Polk Street is one of the choice walks in the city.

The location of the Maritime Museum within the Aquatic Park Casino is a marriage made in heaven. It is difficult to believe the building was not created for the purpose, yet architect William Mooser III designed it in 1935, long before the museum was a mote in curator Karl Kortum's long glass. A restaurant and later a USO center dallied in the casino, but these were shipboard romances.

It is rare to see the work of three generations of architects from one family in one glance, yet this was possible from the doorstep of the casino until just recently. William Mooser II designed many of the

Aquatic Park—Hyde Street Pier, with historic ship, is on the right.

Ghirardelli buildings. His father created the handsome old Fontana warehouse, now razed and replaced by two apartment buildings.

Before entering, look west toward the colorful canopy on the boccie ball court. A tall ivy-covered brick chimney of the San Francisco Waterworks, a favorite landmark of old sea captains, stood there until the thirties. Face east to see the bright pavilion at the Hyde Street cable car turnaround, part of the Victorian, gas-lighted plaza in Aquatic Park, and the Haslett warehouse.

Gallant old craft that might have moldered to ghostliness on some forgotten Rotten Row are anchored at the foot of Hyde Street for the public to visit. They have names that would excite a folklaureate: the ferryboat *Eureka*, the lumber schooner *C. A. Thayer*, the steam schooner *Wapama*, the scow-schooner *Alma*. The better-known *Balclutha*, the beautiful full-rigger that rounded Cape Horn seventeen times under sail, the seagoing ferry *Eppleton Hall*, the Liberty Ship *Jeremiah O'Brien*, and the submarine USS *Pampanito* are also part of the Maritime Museum. There is a modest fee to go aboard them.

A red buoy just inside the door of the Maritime Museum welcomes contributions, but there is no fee. The great anchor of the *Constitution* vies with figureheads of Lord Clive, who once adorned the *Himalaya*, and Mary, Queen of Scots, from the bow of the *Star of Scotland*, and other salty artifacts. Great ship models stand proudly under sail as they once stood out through the Golden Gate. Downeasters, deep-watermen, clippers, bumboats, barges, and tugs are all captured here in legend, record, and photograph. Upstairs the saga of the seas swells with romance. It reaches a factual crest in the little oval pilot room on the third floor, where an excellent research room and staff for serious marine historians is located in the museum's office.

On the starboard side of the casino is a locker room. (To find it, go around the Senior Center until you parallel the beach, where the white sand, incidentally, was imported from Monterey.) Worth seeking out is the eight-oared shell overhead in which Coach Ky Ebright's University of California team brought home an Olympic championship in 1928.

If Able and Baker mean Cain's brother and chocolate to you, watch which doors you walk through. An old salt occasionally tells visitors that the ship's flags painted on the lintels spell out an old sea chantey with the refrain: "Blow ye winds of morning, oh, blow ye winds heigh-ho." He's taking poetic liberties. The flags are nothing but the locker-room signs, rigged out in a disguise.

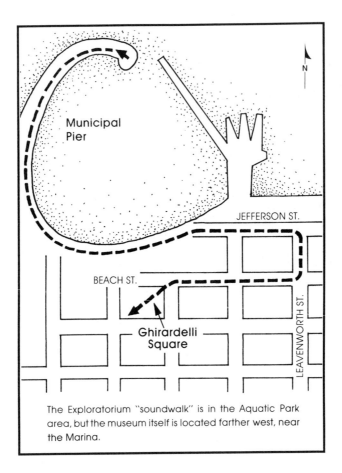

The Exploratorium "soundwalk" is in the Aquatic Park area, but the museum itself is located farther west, near the Marina.

A SOUNDWALK

WALKING TIME: Allow a morning.

DISTANCE: Three city blocks.

PUBLIC TRANSPORTATION: Muni bus 42, 47, or 49.

PARKING: Very little.

CLOTHES: Comfortable.

"Snick snick snick snick snick" comes the rhythmic rush of footsteps of a weimaraner approaching in the grass. Over it is the "sussur-russurrus" of wind in the trees.

24

"Beeeeeeeeeeeeee" sounds a deep foghorn, to be answered in a few seconds by the restrained "OOOOOOOOO" of another near it. "Ah ha hahahahaha," a lady cascades out a laugh in the middle distance. "Sputter sputter sputter sputter." A nervous lawn mower up the hill? No, it's a little yellow service vehicle coming this way. "Gurgle ga-gurgle swoosh spash." Water surges around the sea stack just below us. Beyond a pilot boat goes purring by almost as silently as the Phantom of the Opera.

Consider yourself tuned in to the soundscapes of the city if you can identify from these few clues where we are in San Francisco. Waterfront. Right! It is about 11 A.M. Monday on that length of the Golden Gate Promenade within Fort Mason. We are walking east toward Muni Pier. The occasion is a "soundwalk," suggested by the Exploratorium in its bimonthly magazine.*

"Sightseeing is what attracts most tourists to the San Francisco wharf area, but there's a very different way to tour this popular part of the city—sound-hearing," suggested editor Diane Hales, who accompanied me on the walk she had described "as an experiment in raised *aural* consciousness . . .

"All you really need to make this walk," she said, "is two ears and two feet." Thus equipped, transport yourself to the watery end of Van Ness Avenue, that curved hook on the far end of Municipal Pier.

"We start at Municipal Pier, where waves break against the rocks. Wind blowing hard from the west intermittently swooshes past our ears. In between the swooshes the afternoon is quiet, and our feet make the loudest sounds we hear."

After duplicating the walk on a sunny morning, my own notes say: Add the mewling of gulls, the efficient snicker of a fisherman's reel tossing out a baited line, the happy squeals of children, mellowed across the sheltered water from the apron of sand in Aquatic Park.

The Exploratorium's soundwalk goes on to suggest that, as an experiment, we put on blindfolds. It is amazing how all sounds become exaggerated once the sense of sight is blocked. (Don't try it unless you have a friend along to steer you away from that raised curbing behind the benches.) Diane tied a scarf around my eyes. Suddenly, the volume seemed amplified for every sound. A poptop-can opened was frightening, a little thundering out of proportion to its size. Gull conversation that had seemed casual emerged as a wrangling argument—the peck order jockeying for a favorite piling on the nearby Alcatraz pier. Happiest sound of all was the song of the Hyde Street cable car bells across the water.

* The Exploratorium, Vol. 2, No. 3, August/September 1978.

"You can hear fog," Diane said. "It is different from wind, a strange sound." To me it seems most audible by the changes it makes in muffling other sounds.

As we walked, she explained that all the world was an Exploratorium to the founder, Dr. Frank Oppenheimer, who developed a whole new museum section on language and sound, including "The Vidium," in which one can see patterns of one's own speech, and the tree that lights up when one stands nearby and claps hands or speaks. "Little kids say 'I love you' a lot to that tree," Diane commented, "but my favorite experience with the sound exhibits was to come upon a deaf boy teaching himself to modulate sounds with The Vidium."

Another popular display at the museum is The Cocktail Party, in which two conversations are happening, one at either ear; when one presses a button, they mesh, resulting in total aural confusion. You can speak into the exhibit, turn a dial different ways, and hear yourself as a cackling witch or a low-moaning monster.

We went past the National Maritime Museum, with its whipping flag, past the bleachers where a steel-drummer often holds forth, and were passed, in turn, by the clickety clickety clickety click of a skateboard with increasing, then diminishing, music. At the Cannery's Jefferson Street entrance, we turned into the mall. A juggler dropped a soft, gray, felt top hat with an interesting hollow sound. There was a heavy contrast of the natural noises we had heard out over the water and the surge of man-made crowd noises in the mall.

Coming out on Beach Street we turned right toward Hyde Street and picked up the humming of the cable under the cobbles and metal plates, the snort of buses, the noisy click of a Hasselblad camera lens as a tourist snapped a picture. As we mounted the Larkin Street steps to Ghirardelli Square, we could sort out the splashes of five jets of water in the Ruth Asawa fountain while a string quartet played Haydn in the background.

By then, tuned in to the sounds of our environment, we were ready for a noisy lunch. The Exploratorium's soundwalk ends at Polk and North Point with the disagreeable snorts and coughs of municipal buses lined up like circus elephants holding one another's tails. We ended instead at Gaylords, to the happy slapping of *paratha*, the baked Indian bread, to the sizzle of tandoori hot from the oven, the rhythmic chopping of vegetables, and the soothing sound of a raga.

If that isn't your dish of tea, one of the most interesting sounds in all of San Francisco is available under the rotunda back at the Palace of Fine Arts. Stand exactly in the middle and clap your hands. You should hear at least four (count 'em, four) echoes of that hand clapping.

PALACE OF FINE ARTS
AND EXPLORATORIUM

NOTE: *For map, see Wave Organ, page 30.*

WALKING TIME: One half a day.

DISTANCE: From here to infinity.

PUBLIC TRANSPORTATION: Muni bus 30.

PARKING: Very little.

CLOTHES: Comfortable.

I love the Christmastide, and yet . . .

CAROLYN WELLS

It's that "and yet . . ." that gets many of us down at Christmas. The realities somehow never live up to the expectations.

If this feeling threatens to overwhelm you, consider a walk to renew your childhood wonderment. The place to do it is in San Francisco's biggest toybox, the Exploratorium, in the Palace of Fine Arts. Here, within one of San Francisco's finest restored and recycled architectural treasures, Science, with a little help from the late Dr. Frank Oppenheimer, has provided more magic, marvels, and mysteries than one can comprehend in a day, a week, or a month.

"I intended a kind of woods of natural phenomena that were organized and selected in some way so that people could take many constructive paths," Dr. Oppenheimer said of his collection of four hundred hands-on exhibits. "This is not a museum, it's a curriculum." It has also been called "a large, highly sophisticated school . . . in which the surface offers the appearance of random activity but is actually undergirded with a dense web of interrelated stimuli."

Don't be put off by this high-flown rhetoric. First and foremost, as the lucky kids who have discovered since the museum opened in 1969 can tell you, it is FUN! Where else can you shake hands with yourself, elude your shadow, bend your voice, walk on tiles that make musical notes, light up a tree with the clap of a hand, see yourself multiplied into infinity, jump into a ton of birdseed, or crawl sightless through a score of textures almost as though being reborn?

To experience some of these sensations, transport yourself to North Point and Broderick streets. For openers, walk west one block to Baker Street to view the Palace of Fine Arts as its architect, Bernard Maybeck, intended, mirrored in its own reflecting pond. The largest structure remaining from the Panama-Pacific International Exposition of 1915, it was so loved that philanthropist Walter Johnson, and hundreds of other local citizens, refused to let it disintegrate. According to Hans Gerson, who directed the reconstruction and who was formerly Maybeck's partner, the architect took Böcklin's painting *The Island of the Dead* as his inspiration.

Pause a moment to enjoy the view, the rosy dome surmounting a semicircle fronted by a handsome colonnade, surrounded by trees, shrubs, green lawns, fountain, and mirroring water. If you had come this way in the late 1800s, a steam dummy traveling along tracks in the street would be taking picnickers to pioneer Rudolph Herman's Harbor View Park and Baths at the waterfront. The line of eucalyptus trees that borders Lyon Street at the end of the Marina was planted originally by Herman. Harbor View, the first of several recreational endeavors to occupy this land, once gave its name to the entire area, a site that had only recreational uses after the time it became an Indian shell mound.

The south end of the Palace of Fine Arts is occupied by a theater, often used for film premieres and the annual film festival. Walk to the shore of the pond and bear right on the paved walkway that borders it. Come this way by night during the holidays and traditionally *son et lumière* lighting transforms the whole sweetly melancholy scene into a deliciously romantic nighttime confection.

Swing with the path to the north end of the building (locate the exterior rest rooms in case you have a child or two along) and go between them through the main entrance into the museum. As you enter, the workshops where exhibits are created will be on either hand, with work in progress visible for all to see. Immediately within, look up over the door to the clock that has lighted mirrors for hands. ''Meet me under the clock'' is an old San Francisco tradition.

Patterns are the clue to the first exhibits. The sun is the key to the next one, where a beam from an opening in the roof goes through prisms. Stand in front of the fractured light, and you find the separated colors change as you move. Concerts, films, lectures, and such are often under way in the theater just beyond the Exploratorium office.

Christmas shoppers may find themselves attracted by the store on the opposite wall, but save its goodies for your return trip. Old or young, you are sure to leave it burdened with a bag of scientific playthings. Instead, make your way along the right aisle to the far end.

When you reach the Tactile Dome, come back along the left, or east, aisle.

Humming a happy little tune when he walked me through the museum some years ago, Dr. Oppenheimer paused to point to a group of children at one exhibit playing in colored shadows. "It always makes the kids dance," he said.

At another exhibit, a cluster of boys were trying to "stop the differential." Farther along, young people were taking the temperature of their hands on a block of ice. At another gallerylike area, the work of cartoonist Saul Steinberg has been dissected with overlay panels to show how artistic balance suffers if one component of the drawing is elided.

We stood a while beside a giant kaleidoscope that people duck under to get into. "This would be a great way to film a movie without extras," a man said as he emerged. "Go on in, it's a party," a woman told us.

Don't be disappointed if you can't get into the Tactile Dome. It is so much in demand, it must be reserved months ahead. If this is your first visit to the Exploratorium, you won't even care that you've missed it. You'll want to come back again anyway. Again and again and again.

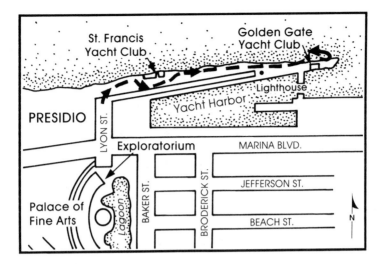

WAVE ORGAN

Walking Time: A lazy half day.

Distance: One-half mile.

Public Transportation: Muni bus 30 line ends at Beach and Broderick streets.

Parking: Good at the end of Lyon Street.

Clothes: Your best designer sweats.

"What are the wild waves saying?" poet J. W. Carpenter asked, about a hundred years ago. Since the dawn of time, it's a question everyone who ever stood on a shoreline has pondered.

The answer is revealed on San Francisco's Marina breakwater, of all unlikely places, where stonemasons George Gonzales and Tomas Lipps have created a "Wave Organ" out of recycled granite, using the skill of a craft that is almost extinct.

Like the miniature lighthouse that stands midway along the breakwater, this voice of the sea is made from rubble—old street-crossing blocks, curbstones, and headstones dumped long ago from the four pioneer cemeteries that once stood on Lone Mountain.

Other changes have taken place along this narrow man-made spit of land that juts east from Lyon Street. Given good weather, the views in all directions are superlative. When the weather is desultory, things close at hand make this walk interesting.

30

To make this walk, begin at Marina Boulevard and Lyon Street and turn north for one long block. At the outset, notice the classic dome of the Exploratorium, whose artists-in-residence program sponsored the Wave Organ. Project Director Peter Richards, who conceived the idea, piped the music of the Wave Organ into the Exploratorium. Save your visit to the Exploratorium for last, and walk to the exact place where Lyon Street ends at San Francisco Bay. The line of eucalyptus trees that borders this northernmost sea-level block of Lyon was planted by pioneer Rudolph Herman before the Gold Rush. Long ago a steam dummy railroad car brought picnickers to Herman's Harbor View gardens, complete with a restaurant, shooting gallery, and hot saltwater baths.

Look east just inshore of the seawall to a beautiful garden—a memorial given by friends of the late Lita Vietor, one of San Francisco's "beautiful people." The garden boasts lawns, colorful flowers, and shrubs that surround three half-moon-shaped viewing spots with benches. Start walking east on the bayward side of it. Try out one of those curving benches, if you choose, to drink in the beauty of the green Marin Headlands, framed by the Golden Gate Bridge, the Bay and its islands, and far off on the eastern horizon, the Coast Range hills of the East Bay.

Continue on the short walkway, repaired since the storm damage of 1982 and '83, until you reach the private St. Francis Yacht Club, whose red-tiled roof and Spanish architecture have been a landmark here since 1928. Damage incurred in the 1989 quake has been repaired. Sometimes, a great Hiroshige wave slaps at the windows of the big glass-enclosed lounge, visible at the corner of the building.

When you reach this point, turn right and follow the wall south. Cross in the crosswalk outlined underfoot in yellow paint when you reach Yacht Road. In a few steps you will be on an island of fine old cypress trees. Pause here and look straight ahead to see plastic sailboats, not moored but parked inside their trailers. To accommodate this storage, the Yacht Harbor walkway has been moved south six or eight feet over the water. Turn left within the trees and follow another small path that meanders through this little island.

Walk toward the Bay for another surprise, immediately at the water's edge: The San Francisco Recreation and Park Department's little card-room shelter.

Fisherman Leo Lembi, who was pulling a sand dab out of the Bay when I came along, said he has spent almost every weekend and many other days for fifteen years fishing at this site. "But that's nothing," he said. "Some of the men have been coming here for thirty years."

Walk along the restored walkway, cracking under the continual onslaught of water, until you reach the little lighthouse. This was once publicized by Robert "Believe It or Not" Ripley as the only municipally owned lighthouse in the world chartered by a national government. As late as the 1960s, the thirty-foot-high tower was surrounded by a small grassy park guarded by stone lions. Once this park was the eastern end of the breakwater. Now the breakwater is almost double in length and may get longer.

The ambiance immediately becomes rougher as you pass Yacht Road's NOT A THROUGH STREET sign. Old riprap, some of it beautifully wave-worn, replaces the more formal cobbled and stepped seawall. Look along the left especially for tafoni, the veined sandstone pieces fashioned by erosion into designs as intricate as lace.

Within a few steps, you will be parallel to the Golden Gate Yacht Club. On your right, the handsome houses of Pacific Heights, and below them, those fronting Marina Boulevard, are in turn fronted by the sleek yachts in the harbor. Ahead are the towers of Russian Hill and Nob Hill, with red-bordered Marina Green looking like an elegant carpet leading toward the city.

Soon the breakwater takes a northerly jog. When you reach the fenced area, designed to keep out cars but not walkers, you are almost at the Wave Organ, an imposing composition that captures the dignity of the stone itself. Other beautifully placed examples of the stonecutter's art serve as benches.

Within the Wave Organ, there are three granite "listening posts." From the topmost station, when the tide is high—say 4.5 feet or more—issue the soothing harmonic sounds of the water. As the tide goes out, the listener can go to the next lower terrace to hear it, then even lower for ebb tide.

How does this organ work? Stonemason George Gonzales says that pipes going into the stone chambers beneath the water act like compressors to produce the harmonic sounds.

Listen a while to the restful cooing, dipping, gurgling, swooshing music and you may never want to leave this seductive undersea voice.

When you must return to the mundane world, make your way back to Marina Boulevard at Lyon Street to the Exploratorium, the wonderful science museum in the Palace of Fine Arts building. Listening to the water music here is a totally different experience.

GOLDEN GATE PROMENADE

NOTE: *For map, see Presidio, pages 4–5.*

WALKING TIME: Allow two hours.

DISTANCE: 3.5 miles.

PUBLIC TRANSPORTATION: Muni bus 30 to go. Golden Gate Transit bus from Marin to return.

PARKING: Good.

CLOTHES: Flat shoes, a sweater.

As spectacular as any walk in the world, the Golden Gate Promenade, a three-and-a-half-mile waterside ramble from Aquatic Park to Fort Point, is a natural escape hatch. Part of the Golden Gate National Recreation Area, opened October 14, 1973, by Mayor Joseph L. Alioto, this writer, and three thousand or more stalwart walkers, it follows the shoreline of San Francisco's Northern Waterfront within fifty feet of the Bay all the way. Walking west, one faces the lyric sweep of the Golden Gate Bridge. Walking east, the hills and towers of San Francisco lie ahead. Either way, at your feet is sand and surf. Sailboats, fishing boats, tour boats, container ships, and tankers pass within a stone's throw of the walker, yet there is a wide expanse of open space over water. Pinch me, the unbelieving minds seem to say, am I really in a city?

The entire length of the promenade is a half-day's outing one way. For the walker who would like to skim the cream of it in less time or who isn't in shape to make the round trip, there is a fine shorter section convenient to public transportation. This is the length at the end of Marina Green between Lyon Street and Fort Point.

To make this lap of the walk, transport yourself to the end of the number 30 bus line at Broderick and Jefferson streets. Walk north toward the water on Broderick, through that Mediterranean village known as the Marina. It blossomed here on fifty of the one hundred blocks vacated by the Panama-Pacific International Exposition of 1915. Since most of it was built on fill, the marina suffered greatly in the earthquake of 1989. At the Yacht Harbor, skirting the boats, go west two blocks to Lyon Street. This brings one alongside a handsome lane of eucalyptus trees that divides Marina Green from the Presidio. Walk exactly to the water's edge through the patio of the municipal pumping station. Here, to your surprise, there is a sidewalk that initiates this lap of the promenade.

Follow the water west. Soon you reach the finest surf-sailing beach in the world. Abreast of Crissy Field, an emergency helicopter landing field only, you reach a driftwood beach, complete with dunes, wildflowers, starfish, and shells, ideal for sunbathing and surf fishing. Continue a little farther and there is the trim red-roofed building of the Fort Point Coast Guard station, flanked by fine old palms. A ramp crosses the dock for the convenience of walkers on the Promenade. Next landmark is the Fort Point Mine Dock, often elbow-to-elbow with fishermen, especially when the black bass are running. Veer south around the offices of the National Park Service and continue walking under the cliff to complete this walk at historic Fort Point, now a museum. Here the bugle calls sound as they did in the Civil War, guards wear the Hardie hat, complete with plume, and the great anchor chain festoons the water's edge.

After you have dreamed away a lazy hour, climb the cliff behind the pediment of the Golden Gate Bridge to find transportation back. Or better still, hoof it. The views are every bit as dramatic on a return trip.

Author Margot Patterson Doss and Mayor Joe Alioto cross the Golden Gate Promenade, along with three to four thousand other walkers, on opening day.

LOVER'S LANE

NOTE: *For map, see Presidio, pages 4–5.*

WALKING TIME: A brisk ten minutes or a leisurely half hour.

DISTANCE: An easy quarter mile.

PUBLIC TRANSPORTATION: Muni bus 3 to Jackson and Presidio. Return via Muni bus 45 from Lincoln Boulevard.

PARKING: So-so.

CLOTHES: Comfortable shoes, sweater.

Sanguine, sentimental old San Francisco has among her secret places a walk that's in the mood for love. It's a beautiful two-hundred-year-old byway built for two through the second-act set from *A Midsummer Night's Dream*, or a sequence of full-color backgrounds for the furniture ads.

For those of us who grew up in the unfrantic, uncrowded years, it's the semisylvan stroll out of memory from everyone's seventeenth summer. It's a place where you can go home again and it must be seen to be believed. So must its name, which is almost too deuced lucid to print.

The name is Lover's Lane. The Sixth Army Engineers, U.S. Army, Presidio of San Francisco, has maps identifying it by this name for the last ninety years and possibly longer. It is shown on the U.S. Coast Survey map of 1868 as part of the old Spanish Trail between the Presidio and Mission Dolores. How long the Indians used it before the Spaniards arrived is anybody's guess, for it ends near El Polin Spring.

No one remembers the lovers who were responsible for the name. Were they the Russian Rezanov and his Concha? Were they an infantryman from the First Tennessee Regiment and his sweetheart, dreading seeing him go off to Manila in 1898?

Lover's Lane may not be on your map, and there is only one street sign identifying it, but walkers will find it at the northwest corner of Presidio and Pacific avenues, just inside the pedestrian gate of the Presidio. It goes as the hawk soars, along a gentle downhill grade to Tennessee Hollow, where it crosses a brick footbridge and stops at Barnard Avenue, just short of the Presidio parade ground.

It exists to be walked, so bring your walking stick, tot's stroller, or sweetheart some sun-drenched afternoon. At the outset, look at the north side of the steep 3200 block of Pacific, which seems to be a house of a different structure: long, shingled, and singularly skinny. It is not one but a group of compatible houses abutting the Presidio wall and one another in close harmony. Bruce Porter, Willis Polk, Ernest Coxhead, and Bernard Maybeck, creator of the Palace of Fine Arts, were the architects who contrived this turn-of-the-century confection. Just inside the pedestrian gate is the high point of Lover's Lane. Look about you. This is a different world, a place of bucolic enchantment, where ground squirrels scurry and songbirds sing, trilliums thrill and motes float. It is so civilized and well curried that no alien thistle or poison oak intrudes. There is a quality of timelessness here. The stop signs, don't-drop signs, the go signs, the slow signs, the billboards, electrical spillboards, neons, and come-ons: the hundred million subliminal stimuli of the pushy present have been edited out of the landscape.

Lover's Lane crosses two more roads, passing a tree with a knotted rope swing and another with a tree house, a row of Georgian houses and a meadow. At Tennessee Hollow, where the First Tennessee and Thirteenth Minnesota regiments camped during the Spanish-American War, it passes under an all-enveloping weeping willow tree of just the right leafiness to let sunbeams ravel through on a head of curls or a tip-tilted nose. The footbridge is the right height on which to sit. At Barnard Avenue, the lane ends or loses its identity. Depending on your point of view, Lover's Lane either goes nowhere or it goes out of this world.

EL POLIN SPRING

NOTE: For map, see Presidio, pages 4–5.
WALKING TIME: Twenty minutes.
DISTANCE: About half a mile.
PUBLIC TRANSPORTATION: Muni bus 45 Presidio.
PARKING: Great.
CLOTHES: Warm.

Within the Presidio reservation of San Francisco is a spring called El Polin to whose marvelous virtues were attributed the large families of the garrisons. Its existence and peculiar qualities were known to the Indian from a remote period and its fame was spread throughout California.

This provocative suggestion comes from Volume 1 of Zoeth S. Eldredge's *The Beginnings of San Francisco*, and is supported by a manuscript written by General Mariano Vallejo titled *Discurso Histórico*, dated 1876, which said:

It gave very good water, and experience afterward demonstrated that it has excellent and miraculous qualities. In proof of my assertion, I appeal to the families of Miramontes, Martínez, Sanches, Soto, Briones, and others; all of whom several times had twins; and public opinion, not without reason, attributed these salutary effects to the virtues of the water of El Polin, which still exists.

Neither the files of Planned Parenthood nor most guidebooks to San Francisco will tell you where to find El Polin, yet Vallejo's words are valid today. The legendary spring still exists. A walker can follow the route the Spanish señoras of the garrison once walked daily, their ollas balanced on their heads.

El Polin lies, where logic says it should, about half a mile from what was once the Spanish Presidio compound. The Officers' Mess, which claims to be the oldest adobe building in San Francisco, incorporates an adobe wall reputed to be part of the *comandancia*, or headquarters, of the Presidio in 1776 when Juan Bautista de Anza occupied it.

Beginning at the "old adobe," stroll southeast past Pershing Hall and across the Presidio's Funston Avenue. There you'll find a flight of steps that leads down to Barnard Avenue. Once across it, the walk skirts

Tennessee Hollow. If you see the marker that says, "In the ravines of the southeast of this point were camped the Thirteenth Minnesota and First Tennessee Volunteers regiments of infantry and other units which participated in the War with Spain," you have gone too far.

At the bottom of the steps, and just across the road, five cypress trees whose lower trunks are painted white lead the walker to the corner of MacArthur Avenue, where a yellow sign says SLOW, CHILDREN AT PLAY. MacArthur is a quiet street, suburban in flavor, which lies in a valley. The homes are ranch-style, out of barracks, by General Issue and occupied by sergeants and their families. On a fair day, only a wind-eroded hillside that lies at the intersection halfway to the end of the street reveals why it is locally known as "Pneumonia Gulch."

The seeker of El Polin should continue, past hordes of children, to the end of MacArthur. There, in a road-enclosed circle of willow trees, one so old its trunk heaves out of the ground like the Loch Ness monster, is a little park with picnic tables. In its center is a cobbled reservoir, fed by two small streams. A marker proclaims: "El Polin Spring. From the spring in this clump of willow trees the early Spanish Garrison attained its water supply. According to the Spanish legend, all maidens who drank from this spring during the full of the moon were assured of many children and eternal bliss."

Neither the City Health Department nor the Army will vouch for the purity of the water today. Maidens who go at the full moon drink from El Polin at their own risk. No one today seems to remember how rare is any source of eternal bliss.

NATIONAL CEMETERY

NOTE: *For map, see Presidio, pages 4–5.*

WALKING TIME: Allow a morning.

DISTANCE: The circumnavigation of twenty-five acres.

PUBLIC TRANSPORTATION: Muni buses 41 and 45 to Presidio Parade Ground stop.

PARKING: Good on weekdays.

CLOTHES: Sober.

TIMES: Open 5 A.M. till 5 P.M.

There is a sad and sacred walk in San Francisco where a bugle-note echoes through tall trees the eloquent promise that "All is well. . . ." It is not a walk for the callous, nor for the "penny wise, ground foolish"; but if you feel a thrill of pride when the flag of the United States "yet waves," come some Veterans Day or Memorial Day to the San Francisco National Cemetery. Come before 11 A.M. and let the silver-throated requiem as it sounds "Safely rest . . ." lead you through Time and to Eternity.

The National Cemetery stands, appropriately, within the Presidio, that irreplaceable preserve that, with Golden Gate Park, has saved San Francisco from headlong congestion, the curse of less fortunate cities. Beginning at the Lombard Street gate, follow Lincoln Boulevard, part of the transcontinental Lincoln Highway, past the parade ground toward the Golden Gate Bridge. It reaches the great wrought-iron main gate of the cemetery at Sheridan Terrace.

Left, as you walk in, is the rostrum. Abraham Lincoln's address made at Gettysburg in 1863 is carved on the cenotaph and enjoins us, the living, to take increased devotion to "that cause for which they gave the last full measure. . . ." On the right is a little white building housing burial records.

Pause for a moment and look about. Is it a trick of the imagination, or does the sunlight seem softer here? The groping fog more protective?

Look west along the first row of marble tablets where a disproportionately boyish sandstone soldier commemorates Thomas Thompson, killed in the Spanish-American War at the age of twenty years, seven months. "Sleep on brave Tommy and take thy rest," the inscription

National Cemetery.

says, "God took thee home when He thought best." Close your eyes and the shadow armies of Lexington, Cumberland, San Pasqual, Chickamauga, Ball's Bluff, Morro Bay, Ypres, Anzio, Iwo, and the Mekong Delta pass the reviewing stand of the mind.

Look uphill toward the circle where Old Glory waves over the monuments. In row 46 (look along the curbstone for row numbers), near a marker that looks like a great granite bathtub, is the headstone of "Laughing Breeze," the glamorous woman "Spy of the Cumberland." The carving says, "Pauline C. Fryer, Union Spy." What it does not say on her modest tablet can be found in Harnett Thomas Kane's book, *Spies of the Blue and Gray*. Brevet Major Pauline Cushman Dickinson Fichtner Fryer was an actress when this word was spoken with a knowing lift of the *supercili*. As the first woman commissioned by the U.S. Army, Pauline is probably the great grand dame of the WAC. Her perils included alcohol, narcotics, three husbands, capture by the Confederates, court-martial, and a sentence to be hanged.

Walk on past the circle to row 68, to the grave of Two Bits, Indian Guide, dated October 5, 1875. Although the burial ground did not become a national cemetery until 1884, it contained two hundred seventeen known and thirteen unknown dead at that time. Indians had used it as a burial place long before the Spaniards came. Two Bits, however, was brought from Fort Klamath when a cemetery there was abandoned. Fort Colville in Washington, Old Camp Grand in Arizona, and the Modoc Lava Beds have also given up their dead for transshipment here.

Generals McDowell, Shafter, Funston, and "Machine Gun" Parker, the orator "Gray Eagle," as Colonel Edward Dickinson Baker was known, four soldiers whose obelisk claims they were "Murdered by Strikers," and Sarah Bowman, the toast and intimate companion of more than one regiment, can all be found here. There is also a grave that contains two wives of one soldier.

Captain Abraham Johnston, aide-de-camp to General Stephan Watts Kearny and known to historians as "Old Stove Bolts," may be one of the 408 Unknown Soldiers whose monument is on the west side. Johnston, killed in the Battle of San Pasqual in 1864, was exhumed for shipment and his simple pine box confused with boxes of iron stove bolts during a fire. A merchant who later ordered government salvage got the surprise of his life when he opened a box expecting stove bolts and found instead one very faded old soldier.

On the east side, near the gate to the Post Chapel, is the G. H. Thomes plot of the Grand Army of the Republic. When it was dedicated in 1893, the program announced that here the comrades in arms and our country's defenders "may rest undisturbed by the march of local improvements, or the 'vandalism of avarice' through the generations to come."

"God is nigh" comes the lingering reprise of "Taps," and the walker, bemused, may wonder if generations of the future will respect this monument to the past.

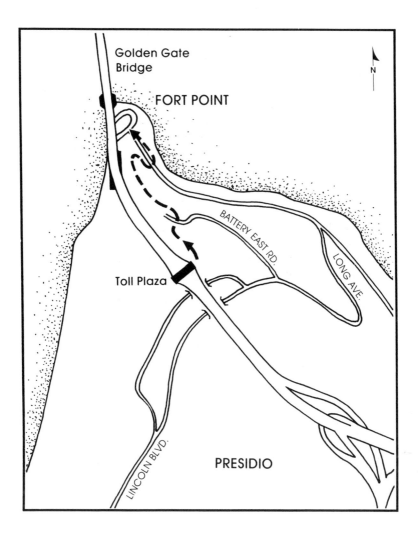

FORT POINT

WALKING TIME: Allow two hours.

DISTANCE: Two miles round-trip.

PUBLIC TRANSPORTATION: Muni bus 28.

PARKING: Good off Battery East Road.

CLOTHES: Sturdy shoes and a sweater.

"This tableland commands a most wonderful view," wrote Fray Pedro Font in his diary on March 28, 1776, "as from it a great part of the port is visible, with its islands and entrance, and the ocean as far as the eye can reach—even farther than the Farallon Islands."

He stood there with Juan Bautista de Anza. "The commander," he reported, "marked this tableland as the site of a new settlement, and the fort which is to be established at this point can be defended by musket fire, and at the distance of a musket shot, there is water for the people."

Fort Point stands there today—four stories lower than its predecessor, the Spanish fort El Castillo de San Joaquin. Cantil Blanco, the white cliff that supported the earlier fort, was cut down at the time Fort Point was built.

Now the "Sentinel of the Bay," the fine old Civil War fort "where never a shot was fired in anger," is part of the Golden Gate National Recreation Area.

Outside the fort are wayside exhibits and, in the sheltered, sunny lee of the eastern salient, two benches dedicated by the Fort Point Gang of walkers as a modest memorial to one of its members, well-known labor leader Lou Goldblatt, who died in 1983.

Inside, in the Fort Point Museum, is a sutler's store where one can purchase hardtack, the soldier's ration, or antique military gear, as well as books on the fort itself.

A big garrison gin—a jig to hoist cannons—and a remarkable renovated Rodman gun stand in the parade, as military people call the central court. Rooms on upper levels have been fitted with appropriate furniture of the time.

Best of all is the barbette, on roof tier, about the level at which Fray Font was standing when he made what may be the earliest paean to a San Francisco view. From this level, the outlook is breathtaking.

Begin this walk at the toll plaza of the Golden Gate Bridge. Nearby is the statue of Joseph B. Strauss, builder of the bridge. Walk past the statue into the flower garden maintained by the bridge district. Turn right at the fork in the garden path and go through the open chain link gate.

You are now on Battery East Road, where the surroundings are suddenly semiwilderness. Walk left, or north. The massive substructure of the bridge is so overwhelming that first-time visitors often stop in awe when they discover it from the clifftop intersection.

Before heading on, look at "the arch that saved the fort" from destruction when the bridge was built. Under the original engineering drawing for the bridge, the substructure ran right through this area, without the arch; the fort was to be demolished.

Then inspect the wayside exhibit on the stand in front of you. It has a fine illustration of the 1853 harbor defense plan, signed by Jefferson Davis, then Secretary of War, a cross-section diagram of the fort, and a photo taken before the 1900s when the fort stood alone in splendor on its point.

Walk, usually against a stiff headwind, toward the bridge and take the trail that zigzags downhill toward Fort Point. As one descends a view of the East Bay widens, first including the ribbon that is the Golden Gate Promenade threading along the shore, then the towers of San Francisco.

By some trick of light, from this distance when the day is fair San Francisco's buildings seem chalky white, with pale blue and purple shadows.

Pause a moment when you reach the unexpected fire hydrant. Installed before the bridge was built, it once served the two lightkeepers' houses that stood here when it was the Fort Point Light Station. Go over to the area nearest the fort to see where a bridge once crossed to the roof to give the keepers easier access to the rooftop lighthouse. The footbridge was later dismantled.

Then walk back to find the ramp downward on the south side of this little plateau. At the foot of the ramp and steps, turn left across the lawn to find a monument placed in 1966 by the Fort Point Museum Association after it had saved Fort Point from destruction-by-neglect. The monument stands on the site of Chief Lightkeeper James Rankin's house. Like the upper light-station houses, it was hauled away by Coast Guard helicopter in the 1960s and unceremoniously dumped near Lands End to be churned up in the pounding surf.

As you walk toward the fort, try to imagine rebel soldiers storming its seven-foot-thick walls. The fort was built according to the precepts of General Tolten's "Third System for Coastal Defense" rather than the plan used for Fort Sumter, where the volley occurred that launched the war between the states.

"We are coming, Father Abraham, 300,000 strong," wrote Quaker abolitionist James Gibbon when Fort Sumter fell to the forces of the South. San Franciscans, hearing the sound of distant drums, shuddered and wondered if Fort Point could protect them from the rebel onslaught they felt would surely come. They had reason to be fearful—after all, President of the Confederacy Jefferson Davis knew well the plans for defending the harbor.

Fortunately, the planned attack came too late. When the Civil War ended, the *Shenandoah*, under command of Captain James Waddell—last of the South's sea raiders—lay offshore, waiting for a favorable opportunity to send a landing party to extract ransom for not bombarding the cliff behind the fort.

Before you enter the big sally port into the fort, look to the right to locate that sunny east bastion wall where the benches are located. The counterscarp facing land moved out a few inches in the quake of 1906, was pulled back by Army Engineers in 1915, and moved slightly again in 1989. Enter through the beautiful studded door and look underfoot to your right to locate one of the fort's five underground cisterns. They held forty thousand gallons of water to supply defenders in the event of a siege.

Turn left and you are facing a model of El Castillo de San Joaquin and a life-size model of a 1776 soldier of Spain. This museum room also has the note Lieutenant Washington A. Bartlett wrote, changing the name of El Paraje de Yerba Buena to San Francisco.

Another unusual early exhibit shows the payroll for Fort Point during construction. Master bricklayer Lucky Baldwin got $200 a month, while a common laborer received only $28.50 for the same time, after his room, board, and payroll tax were deducted.

After noting the tribute to the late Sergeant Charles Hawkins, site manager of Fort Point until his death in 1989, for his efforts in restoring the fort, go out into the parade. Guided tours, announced by a bugle call, assemble by the biggest gun.

Since the fort came into the GGNRA in 1972, rangers have been dressed in Civil War uniform of the Union Army. It is fun to tag along with a ranger and participate in the gunnery drill. One can also wander through the fort unescorted. On the second tier, near the center, look for the photo of an eleven-year-old Civil War drummer boy. Can you read the thoughts behind his eyes?

Of interest to amateur chefs and dietitians will be the Officers' Mess on an upper floor, where a Sunday breakfast menu of the 1860s included beef stew. Boiled mush and syrup were served for supper. Ranger Dave Rice always asks kids, "What's missing from this diet?" An injunction from an 1862 Army cookbook posted here warns, "Remember that beans, badly boiled, kill more than bullets, and fat is more fatal than powder."

The quarters are fascinating for their sturdy simplicity. Youngsters of all ages enjoy the restored guns in their casemates. Visitors marvel at the precision of the cut-stone spiral stairs. Don't leave the fort without climbing to the barbette level to see the penthouses and to drink in the superb view that stunned Fray Font.

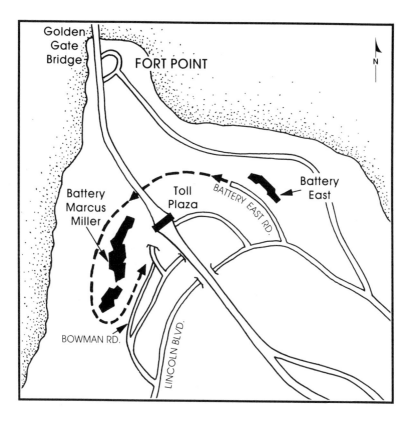

UNDER THE BRIDGE

WALKING TIME: Two hours.

DISTANCE: Two miles.

PUBLIC TRANSPORTATION: Muni bus 28 or Golden Gate Transit 84 to Golden Gate Bridge toll plaza.

PARKING: Great at Battery East Road and the Presidio's Lincoln Boulevard.

CLOTHES: Flat shoes and a wind shirt.

Although seldom discovered by tourists, the spectacular trail under the south end of the Golden Gate Bridge along the face of the southern anchorage is open to walkers. It meanders along the cliff once known as Cantil Blanco, revealing beautiful panoramas of the Bay that vary with every turn.

Pick a day that is California blue and gold to make this walk. Begin alongside the statue of Joseph B. Strauss, chief engineer of the bridge, usually surrounded by tourists, cameras at the ready. The reassuring plaque on the statue says, "Here at the Golden Gate is the eternal rainbow that he conceived and set to form a promise indeed that the race of man shall endure into the ages."

Nuclear fission, a more recent scientific achievement, has dated the eulogy but not the bridge. Neither did the 7.1 quake of 1989.

Climb the wooden steps up out of Battery Lancaster, immediately north of the statue. One of the great close-up views of the bridge awaits photographers at the top of the steps.

After you have marveled at this first complete view of the bridge, turn left and climb the few steps to the grassy plot surrounding the flagpole. Here you will find four things of interest: a plaque honoring the bridge placed by an historical civil engineering organization; the walker's entrance to the bridge itself; a close-at-hand look at bridge traffic; and a fiftieth anniversary garden, the gift of the Bank of Canton.

Save that noisy three-and-a-half-mile round-trip across the bridge for a time when traffic is light. For this walk, go back down the steps, turn left, and then turn right through the chain link fence. Immediately outside the fence you are in the freer world of the Golden Gate National Recreation Area.

You emerge alongside five wind-shorn cypress trees above Fort Point. In 1933, when bridge construction began on what was left of old Cantil Blanco, the white cliff foreshortened by Colonel René de Russy to accommodate Fort Point, this area became inaccessible to walkers. Opened by the GGNRA in 1980, it is now a link in the Coastal Trail connecting the Marin Headlands, via the bridge, with those lovely ocean margins on Baker Beach, Lands End, Ocean Beach, and, farther south, Fort Funston and Sweeney Ridge.

Indeed, since Sweeney Ridge has been added to the GGNRA, it is possible to begin walking north at Santa Cruz and go on connecting trails in county, state, city-park, or open-space land all the way to Tomales Point, an excursion about the distance of the west coast of Wales. Two remarkable San Mateo County women, Olga Ostrander and Olive Mayer, have done it, walking successive lengths of the trail. The complete route took them about two months of weekends.

Turn left, hugging the fenceline. As you walk, look down at the water. Two hundred feet below you is the place where the swift-flowing water of the Sacramento River meets the Pacific Ocean.

Notice the little lighthouse on the roof of Fort Point. The chief light-keepers's house once stood on the cut-down cliff, level with the roofline, and a small bridge crossed the space between to give the lightkeeper quicker access to the light. Across the water is the Lime Point Light, with Point Cavallo east of it.

When the foghorns are in play here, their different sounds define the north and south towers of the bridge and nearby points so seafarers can find safe passage.

The sheltered lagoon east of the bridge is the U.S. Army's exclusive yacht harbor at Fort Baker, an ideal place within the GGNRA for a ferry landing, as recommended by at least one study.

Walk a few steps to the west and you are under the bridge itself. The massive underpinnings will absorb all your attention for a few minutes. During construction of the bridge, while building the fender that surrounds the south pier pylon, deep-sea divers could work only four twenty-minute periods over twenty-four hours because of the velocity of the tide—four to seven and a half knots.

Even the trestle from Fort Point, used by the workmen, was an engineering achievement. It was barely in place when a freighter crashed into it in a November fog, carrying away a three-hundred-foot section. When the trestle had been replaced, a storm carried off another eight-hundred-foot section. Engineer "Strauss, like Robert the Bruce, had learned the patience of a spider and came back a third time with a better plan that worked."

Dangerous as the tide is here, until World War I, annual competitive swims were held between Fort Point and Lime Point. At Roberts at the Beach Inn, a photo of the proprietor and his horse, who both made the swim, used to be on display. Now surfers often brave the white water around Fort Point in wet suits.

Follow the asphalt, observing the yellow line if a cyclist comes your way, until you reach the lookout fence. Pause here for a look across the strait at Diablo Point Light, the little white structure near the water, at the well-hidden fortifications at sea level on Kirby Cove, and at Hill 129, also known as "Hawk Hill," the long flat batteries on the high point of the Marin cliff face.

When the asphalt runs upward (to admit only bicyclists to the west side of the bridge), bear right on the footpath, climbing the slight rise. Mile Rock, Lands End, China Beach, and a tree-framed glimpse of the Palace of the Legion of Honor are visible.

Go through the gate, which is supposed to be open at all times, and into the grove of wattle and cypress trees. You emerge into low coastal chaparral, with tidepools and Bareass Beach barely visible around the cliff below.

Cross the little bridge and go up some steps. Risers for these and other steps along the trail were built from ties of the Belt Line Railroad, thriftily reclaimed along the Marina Green.

Each twist of the trail reveals more of the Marin Headlands, with Point Bonita Light and its bridge making a landmark. Point Lobos looks more like Disney's Pluto nose in the water than a wolf.

Soon after you climb the longest flight of steps, the trail turns inland to emerge alongside Battery Boutelle. If you were going to Baker Beach, the route would be westerly. Instead, turn left on Bowman Road, the old red-rock connecter for the fortifications on either hand, Battery Marcus Miller and Battery Cranston. When you reach the Golden Gate Bridge District's ever-expanding corporation yard, go up the steps to the parking lot.

As you follow the stripes on the paving across the parking lot, remember that "The Peter Principle" cites the increase in the number of men required to paint this bridge after mechanization as a classic example of "work expanding to meet the time available." It could be applied to land use as well, since more and more of the space available to the bridge district has been pre-empted for vehicle storage.

When you reach the steps, go down. If you came by bus, there is a glass-shielded shelter in which to await your return bus about two hundred feet south. If you brought your own gas-guzzler, go through the tunnel under the toll plaza, arriving once again at the statue of Strauss, genie of the bridge.

GOLDEN GATE BRIDGE

WALKING TIME: Half hour to forty-five minutes each way.

DISTANCE: Three and a half miles round-trip.

PUBLIC TRANSPORTATION: Muni bus 28. Marin Transit buses bound for Marin may be boarded at Terminal and stops on Van Ness Avenue or at Fillmore and Lombard streets.

PARKING: Free at Battery East lot, off Lincoln Boulevard.

CLOTHES: Coat, hat, and gloves.

The Golden Gate Bridge has been called a poem in steel, an Aeolian harp, an eternal rainbow, and a floodgate for an avalanche of picnickers, but no one has ever called it ugly.

For artists it is as good a model as any of the bridges on the Seine. Photographers have made it the most shutter-bugged bridge in the world. Four-hundred-odd suicides have used it for a dramatic third-act curtain. Semanticists claim it is a statement.

For walkers, it is a gala walk, done for fun, eye-feasting, exercise, or romance. Almost no one walks the bridge of necessity, except an occasional migrant fruitpicker. On May 27, 1937, when it was opened to pedestrians for the first time, 202,000 people walked across it. Eighteen thousand were waiting on the bridge ramps when it opened. The next day, the bridge opened and twenty-five thousand cars crossed over it.

Orr Kelly, recalling the event for the *San Francisco Chronicle* in 1957, wrote: "Strangely, there were twice as many pedestrians on the bridge the first day as had been expected, but far fewer cars the following day. Apparently we knew we'd only be able to walk down the center of the bridge once," he speculated. "But we knew we didn't have to hurry to drive across it."

The long, long time brought the picnickers that foes of the bridge feared would flood Marin glades. They brought not only their baskets but their barbecues and bedrooms. As commuters—whom one wag has described as "weekend gardeners with sex privileges"—increase in numbers, so do rumbles about "second spans."

Most of the commuters, and every San Francisco walker, intend to cross the Golden Gate Bridge on foot. Every month about fifteen hundred of them are lured by the incomparable vistas of sea, sky, bay, mountains, city, villages, islands, and forts. In March of 1960 there were 993 pedestrians. In March of 1962, the number almost doubled to 1,878. This is not an accurate count, however, since children often sneaked under the turnstiles at the San Francisco side and many walkers who began at Vista Point, on the Marin side, returned without going through the stiles. Since the Golden Gate National Recreation Area became the landlord, there is no fee for walkers. The greatest number of walkers came on the fiftieth anniversary of the bridge, when the pedestrian gridlock lasted nine hours.

The walkers en route across the bridge on any fair day include families, sweethearts, serious hikers, bikers, and tourists. They seem good-natured, if noisy. The roar of passing cars, rather than wind singing in the cables, is what forces them to shout.

To add your presence to the one-million pedestrian count since the bridge opened, begin this walk at the toll plaza on the San Francisco side. Just below it, at the Presidio view area, is a statue of Joseph B. Strauss, who "built the bridge." It does not reveal that Strauss, like so many men of grandiose plans, was Napoleon-sized. The plaque reads, "Here at the Golden Gate is the eternal rainbow that he conceived and set to form a promise indeed that the race of man shall endure into the ages."

Stairs lead to the bridge north of the Roundhouse (last rest room stop for an hour and a half). As you cross the bridge, look away from the stunning panorama and glance over the side rail. The single track is for traveling workmen's scaffolding, not, unfortunately, for a monorail.

The hole in Fort Point's roof below the fencing is where a suicide went through. Bridge officials say suicides usually come by car, not on foot. South tower's famous moat, Lime Point Coast Guard Station, Fort Baker, and the unbelievable swift tide are all dramatically visible below. About midpoint on the bridge, if a ship has passed, look west. From this vantage, a ship, no matter how sleek, when quartering looks like a basset hound leaving home.

The little huts on the sidewalks house weather-recording machines. Only twice has weather forced cars off the bridge. It is not true that "small car warnings on the bridge" are issued when the weather is stormy, nor that you can spot the treasure ship *Rio* lying on her side. Like the legend of the ghostly hitchhiker (supposed to flag a ride at the bridge approach and disappear from your car before the span is crossed), weather and treasure are part of the mystique of the splendid span.

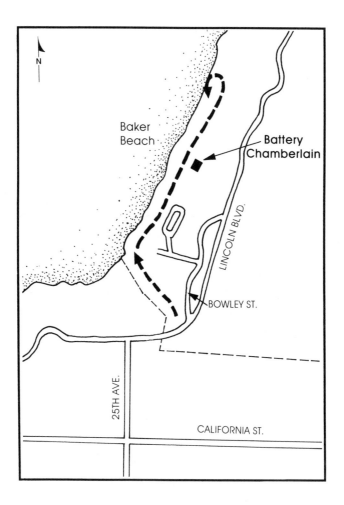

BAKER BEACH

WALKING TIME: Allow an hour.

DISTANCE: Three-fourths of a mile along the beach.

PUBLIC TRANSPORTATION: Muni bus 29.

PARKING: Good on all but the warmest of days.

CLOTHES: Casual. Sandals or sneakers are good for sand-walking and you will probably want a sweater.

The Golden Gate Bridge from Baker Beach.

"These have I loved," wrote Rupert Brooke, the poetic lister, "blue massing clouds . . . firm sands, / the little dulling edge of foam that browns and dwindles as the wave goes home; / and washen stones, gay for an hour . . ."

In San Francisco, the place he describes could be Baker Beach, an idyllic, pristine pocket of shore that lies between Seacliff and the serpentine outcropping of Fort Point. Baker Beach is a dreamer's oasis of simple sand. Old pines and cypress shelter it beyond the dunes. Rocky cliffs define its boundaries. The soft blue hills of Point Bonita frame the front-and-center horizon. While off at stage right, that unparalleled scene-stealer the Golden Gate Bridge soars dramatically up and over.

Meanwhile in the foreground, what Swinburne called "the great sweet mother and lover of men, the sea" constantly renews and refreshes the firm sand, sometimes dropping treasures like driftwood, sometimes retrieving trash, like beer cans. The sea makes a good maintenance man. No grassy park could absorb the use and abuse perpetrated on this and other city beaches. Sunbathers, sand-walkers, rock hounds, bass fishermen, shouting children, dogs, gulls, and, rarely, a cormorant, all are accommodated here without crowding. The friendly dunes also hide the Spring Valley Pumping Station near the terminus of Lobos Creek, which once served the city but now supplies only the Presidio.

Gibson Road gives the public access to Baker Beach. It begins at the center of Old Lincoln Boulevard, or as it is called on some maps, Bowley Street. There is one road that leads down. Walk from a parking lot that abuts the old red-brick pumping station through the corridor between the dune grass plantings. Just inside are signs welcoming the public to Baker Beach, now part of the Golden Gate National Recreation Area, advising fishermen to have permits and warning swimmers to beware the undertow and sharks. It was here, long ago, that a young man lost his life to a killer shark, despite heroic efforts of his teenage companion to rescue him.

Colonel Edward Dickinson Baker, the pioneer lawyer and senator for whom Baker Beach is named, once lived nearby in what is now Seacliff. He lies not far away in the National Cemetery, grave 488, row 124. Lawyers gave him a commemorative headstone on Memorial Day, 1962, because his speech at Union Square on May 11, 1861, celebrated California's entry into the Union.

Baker lost his best-known case to the Vigilantes, who hanged his client, gambler Charles Cora, murderer of an early San Francisco resident, William Richardson. They were afraid the persuasive "Gray Eagle" would talk him out of a conviction.

A great friend of Abraham Lincoln, Colonel Baker lost his life at the Battle of Ball's Bluff. As the walker watches the waves go home on Baker Beach, it may seem anomalous that Baker should have died for the same cause that kept the South in a stew so long—the rights of man as modified by the color of his skin.

Fifty years ago, in the right season, a walker would have seen clouds of blue butterflies, indigenous to these dunes, hovering over the sand verbena, beach primrose, and lupine. One, Pheres Blue, is now extinct. Dr. C. Don MacNeill, lepidopterist of the Academy of Science, says the other, Xerxes Blue, has not been seen since the 1940s, but someone, conceivably, could spot one in an obscure lupine patch.

Explore the beach as you wish, but don't miss the mini-museum or the disappearing six-inch rifle in batteries just east of the upper parking lot.

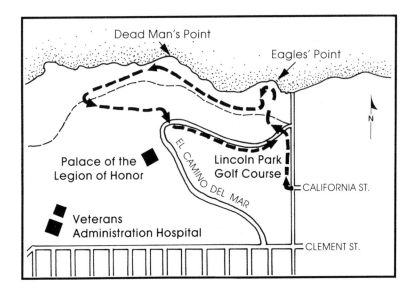

Dead Man's Point

Eagles' Point

N

Palace of the
Legion of Honor

EL CAMINO DEL MAR

Lincoln Park
Golf Course

CALIFORNIA ST.

Veterans
Administration Hospital

CLEMENT ST.

EAGLES' POINT

WALKING TIME: One-half day.

DISTANCE: Two miles.

PUBLIC TRANSPORTATION: Muni bus 1.

PARKING: So-so.

CLOTHES: Warm.

Eagles' Point in San Francisco is an aerie that people with their feet on the ground can enjoy. "A superb marine view in a frame of bold hills," Frank Morton Todd called it in his 1914 *Handbook for San Francisco*. In the days when the Sutro Ferries and Cliff House Railroad chugged along 33rd Avenue, rounding the curve at what is now El Camino del Mar, it was the first breathtaking glimpse passengers in the open-air cars had of the Golden Gate Strait, a panorama of blue water and sky, distant hills, and rocky cliffs. In its time, it was a counterpart of the Hyde Street cable car plunge downhill just past Lombard Street, or the great widening of landscape northbound on Panoramic Highway on the third curve above Stinson Beach when all of Bolinas Lagoon is revealed.

Hidden for years by Monterey pine and cypress planted by John McLaren in 1924, the lookout emerged from the woods when twenty-eight trees came down in a storm. Now part of the Golden Gate

National Recreation Area, it has been enhanced with sturdy retaining walls, footpaths, stairways, erosion-control plantings, benches, and safety railings. Thanks to the work of the dedicated youngsters of the Youth Conservation Corps and Young Adult Conservation Corps, the renewed view is as spectacular as ever it was.

To make this walk, wait for one of those scintillating autumn days when the air is like wine, then transport yourself to the northwest corner of the city, at the end of California Street near 32nd Avenue. Mount those imposing steps at the end of California Street. Bear right at the top of them. You will then be on the old roadbed of Adolph Sutro's Ferries and Cliff House Railroad, built in 1888.

About parallel to what is now Miss Burke's tennis courts, the sixty-passenger open excursion cars would begin their swing toward Eagles' Point. Cross El Camino del Mar in the crosswalk designated for golfers; then look for a gap in the trees, and a sign. This is the start to the Eagles' Point Trail to Lands End, a length of the longer Pacific Coast Trail.

Follow the trail about one hundred feet along the border of the seventeenth hole of Lincoln Park Municipal Golf Course. Just about the time you spy a stately pine and a lofty bench, you will become aware of the familiar brown and white GGNRA signs cautioning against the dangers of cliff and surf for those who leave the designated paths. Go up the tie-steps, made of recycled material like all the other reclamation work along this treacherous headland. Soon you are standing on a cobbled circle, with Seacliff and Phelan Beach immediately apparent on the right and the Golden Gate Bridge soaring like a harp of the winds in the distance. If you don't suffer from fear of heights, go down to the lowest barrier to glimpse the beach below the dangerous cliff. Steep as the cliff is, native rabbit-tail grass, lupine, lizardtail, and seaside daisies cling tenaciously to it.

When you have feasted your eyes long enough on this lovely sight, return to the trail and bear right. On an average day, this is sweat city, as runners, racewalkers, and joggers pass along on the soft sandy surface. (When was the last time you saw a jogger smiling?) Tracks were removed during World War II to make guns. Below the greens, vegetation is little disturbed, but beware the hooker—the golfer, that is, who misdrives a hooked ball.

When you emerge from the tunnel of greenery, you are approaching Dead Man's Point, named by the Coast Guardsmen who have fished many a body out of the surf below. Tempting as it seems, don't go out on the point. Instead, follow the path to the left and when Veterans Hospital looms overhead like a monster, bear left again on the asphalt road. It will bring you past the fourth hole of the golf course back to El Camino del Mar across from the Palace of the Legion of Honor.

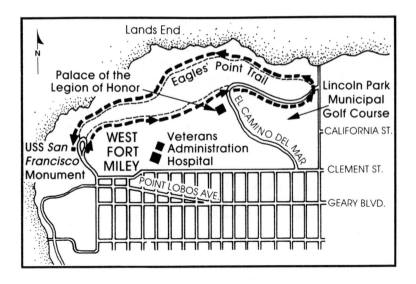

Lands End

Palace of the
Legion of Honor

Eagles' Point Trail

Lincoln Park
Municipal
Golf Course

CALIFORNIA ST.

USS *San*
Francisco
Monument

WEST
FORT
MILEY

Veterans
Administration
Hospital

EL CAMINO DEL MAR

CLEMENT ST.

POINT LOBOS AVE.

GEARY BLVD.

N

LANDS END

WALKING TIME: Two hours.

DISTANCE: Two and a quarter miles.

PUBLIC TRANSPORTATION: Muni buses 18 and 38A-X.

PARKING: Good on Seal Rock Drive and on Merrie Way.

CLOTHES: Take a windbreaker.

We call it Veterans Day now. In Canada they call it Remembrance Day. But if November 11 is still Armistice Day to you, made special by a moment of silence at 11 A.M. to honor soldiers who died in battle, consider a walk on that day around Lands End.

It is here that a monument has been made of the battered navigation bridge of the cruiser USS *San Francisco* to honor the 107 men killed when she was hit forty-five times at the Battle of Savo Island, August 9, 1942. It is mounted in concrete on a line with the Great Circle Course to the Far East.

To make this walk, transport yourself to El Camino del Mar slightly north of Seal Rock Drive, where a big parking lot surrounds the memorial.

Once at the big parking area, walk west toward the flagpole overlooking the Golden Gate Strait. (The other pole sticking out of an octagonal roof in the pines is a semaphore on the Marine Lookout

Station, built long ago to let merchants know which ships were entering the Bay.)

Names of the heroes who died aboard the USS *San Francisco* are listed on the plaque, but like the Tomb of the Unknowns, it really honors every citizen who served this country and paid with dear life. What the plaque doesn't tell you is that the cruiser survived Pearl Harbor and any number of other battles before she was irrevocably disabled in combat. Even at that, she managed to limp home to San Francisco, where she received our highest honor for a ship and crew, the Presidential Unit Citation.

Look underfoot to find that the long arrow on the compass doesn't point north, but at Guadalcanal, the primary route of our war with Japan.

When you have read the tribute on the plaque, walk to the edge of the bridge for a look at the view. Point Bonita and the leonine hills of

The USS *San Francisco* monument at Lands End.

Marin seem so serene from this vantage, it is hard to believe that the waters below are the most treacherous in the Bay.

The *City of Rio de Janeiro*, the *Coos Bay*, the *Lyman Stewart*, the *Frank Buck*, and the *Ohioan* are just a few of the ships that have cracked up on the hazardous rocks and cliffs lining Golden Gate Strait. The superstructures of some of them can still be seen at low tide. So can the remains of "Pelton's Folly."

Alexander Pelton, sometimes known as Ralph Starr, once built a tremendous contraption on a rock between the shore and Mile Rock Light for Adolph Sutro, who intended to harness the tides to develop electric power. He was ahead of his time. Sutro backed the inventor to the tune of $25,000, possibly more.

Three times the experimental "tide machine" was swept out to sea. On the day of the unveiling, it didn't work either; while a dedication party stood around on the cliff awaiting him, the inventor, his wife, and son disappeared. Callers at his house later found only clothes, furniture, and dirty breakfast dishes in the sink.

Walk north to the first bench. In 1880 the square outlined by the sidewalk in the foreground below contained the little Point Lobos Station of the Sutro Ferries and Cliff House Railroad, whose roadbed, also visible, is now a trail in the Golden Gate National Recreation Area. Railroad tracks were removed to make gun barrels in World War II.

For an interesting look at the erosion caused by winter storms on this headland, go down the steps and walk around that station platform.

When you have enjoyed this scenic overlook, return to the parking lot and look toward the pines on the opposite side, a favorite haunt of mushroom hunters. This is West Fort Miley, named for Lieutenant Colonel John D. Miley, who died at Manila in 1899. Now twelve acres of the fort are part of the Golden Gate National Recreation Area.

To find the entrance, look for the white-grid crosswalk painted on the asphalt. Then walk across it and up into the forest to enjoy another fine panorama. Odd structures on the right are part of an obstacle course used by the Urban Outdoor Adventure Center.

Bear right at the Y after you emerge from the trees to reach a grassy knoll. This eminence may well have been the spot where Fray Francisco Palou posted a cross in about 1774, the first in San Francisco.

From the vantage point high above Sutro Heights, one can see all of Ocean Beach, Great Highway, the Richmond neighborhood, Golden Gate Park, the Sunset, Fort Funston, and, on a clear day, Point Montara and Mussel Rocks.

Other parts of Fort Miley, except the Veterans Hospital complex, are also open for exploration, but for this walk, return to the big semicircular parking lot and look for the automotive barrier blocking El Camino del Mar. Closed to traffic for more than thirty years because of road rupturing landslides, El Camino del Mar now offers the walker an adventure through a little wilderness.

Start out along the broad avenue, lined with trees on one side and cliffs on the other. Soon you reach the slide area, where the road has repeatedly buckled. Look for the path that goes through tall fennel stalks (you'll recognize them by the pungent smell of licorice) and follow it across a little footbridge.

The path traverses about two hundred yards of slide area to arrive at steps that climb back up to another unspoiled section of El Camino del Mar, now used as a parking lot between the Palace of the Legion of Honor and part of Lincoln Park Municipal Golf Course.

Follow the path that skirts the roadway on the downhill side to reach a monument presented in 1960 by our sister city Osaka. It commemorates the arrival in San Francisco a hundred years earlier of the *Kanrin Moru*, the first Japanese naval ship to enter the Bay. The stones around it seem like islands in a swirling sea.

Across the road is another monument, George Segal's sculpture *The Holocaust*, recalling the World War II European horror. Standing a little uphill are equestrian statues by Anna Hyatt Huntington, *El Cid* and *Jeanne d'Arc*.

Keep walking along the edge of El Camino del Mar and you will find a second Japanese memorial, presented in April 1984 "in recognition of the continued quest for world peace by all people."

If all this symbolism seems to be getting a little heavy, you can always leave it to Rodin's *The Thinker* in the court of the Legion.

To return by a different route, walk almost to 32nd Street, where the Eagles' Point Trail will take you back to the USS *San Francisco* through slightly wilder terrain.

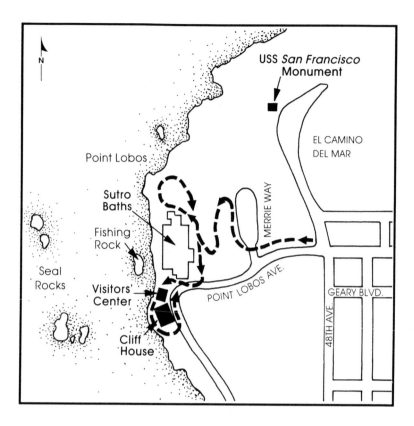

SUTRO BATHS

WALKING TIME: Allow a morning.

DISTANCE: A mile or two.

PUBLIC TRANSPORTATION: Muni bus 18 or 38.

PARKING: Excellent on Merrie Way.

CLOTHES: Hiking boots or Nikes and a warm jacket.

Near the end of its seventy years' existence, the grandiose anachronism known as Sutro Baths was the kookiest, the flukiest, and, for a while, the spookiest walk in San Francisco.

The contents of the gaudy relic made it kooky—like the juxtaposition of elegant oddities and cheap paint-pail trash cans. Or Tom Thumb's bed next to a 3-D *Last Supper*.

The fluke was that the huge glass building—opened in 1896 and seemingly the most fragile of philanthropist Adolph Sutro's self-constructed monuments—was still standing in 1966.

The spook, who inhabited the nether regions of the building, was known as the "Giggling Ghost of Sutro Baths." Many were sure it was the incarnation of some unfortunate who drowned in that once-fashionable watering place.

Visiting the rococo and moldy old pleasure dome out at 1000 Point Lobos Avenue was like calling on a dear, slightly dotty, antiquated aunt who, as she might say in an excess of delicacy, "had seen better days."

Today, the walk around the ruins that were Sutro Baths and Museum is equally strange. At the most dramatic meeting place of land and sea in San Francisco, against background music of crashing waves and yelping sea lions, one sees puzzling, cell-like concrete ruins, tunnels to nowhere, odd stairs, landings, and pathways, unexpected canyons, arches, tidepools, marshes, ponds, troughs, natural bridges, and sea stacks. Like the ancient ruins of Greek and Roman civilizations, it has a splendor all its own.

To enjoy this walk, transport yourself to the corner of Point Lobos Avenue and El Camino del Mar. Geary Boulevard at 48th Avenue is one block south.

Using your own wheels, park, if there is room, on Merrie Way, a platform of land about a third of the way downhill toward Cliff House.

This ledge was known as Ocean Terrace when it served as the terminus for the Sutro-owned Ferries and Cliff House Railroad. As one stepped off the train, an entrepreneur known as Bertie the Birdman would greet the crowd with his trained canaries. For a buck his canary would fire a cannon. For five it would light on your lady's bonnet.

In the heyday of the big, glass-domed Sutro Baths, just before World War I, as many as thirty thousand fun seekers would come here every weekend; taken over by the Golden Gate National Recreation Area, it has become almost as popular. On clear days, the ocean view from Merrie Way is so spectacular, it is more popular with sunset watchers than is Ocean Beach.

From Merrie Way, walk along the path that fronts the western edge of the parking lot and sit a moment if there is an empty bench. Once you have absorbed the ocean view and the dramatic wave action of the Pacific, look down at the tideline.

Fishing Rock will be in your middle view, with North Seal Rock to the right of it and Repose and Arch rocks to the left. Hermit Rock and Cone Rock are out of sight from this spot. These and the smaller Seal Rocks are a wildlife sanctuary.

Sutro Baths occupied the site of the largest water-filled pond below. It contained six Olympic-sized swimming pools, five filled with saltwater and one with fresh. The saltwater pools were heated to different degrees and went through a continuous cleaning process in a succession of settling ponds, still visible at the base of the cliff on your right. One of the settling ponds also served as an aquarium.

The blocky ruins were part of the dressing rooms. The laundry equipment for the baths could handle twenty thousand bathing suits and forty thousand towels per day. Off to the left stands Cliff House, the fifth structure on this site to bear that name.

If you had been here thirty years ago, a Sky Tram car might have come swinging along on cables from what is now the GGNRA Visitors' Center, to land at the platform of land on your right. Openings in the cliff wall admitted the tram and allowed a two-level waterfall to splash down the cliffside from above, near the tunnel visible in the cliff.

The tunnel sheltered a locomotive, pumps, pipes, and equipment. Sutro, who made his money building tunnels in the Comstock Lode, had five tunnels dug into the cliff.

After you get the lay of the land, walk to the north end of Merrie Way and descend the wooden staircase. About midway down the trail, the wooden steps change to a "sand ladder" of broad wood stringers, threaded on two wire cables.

Tempting as it is to follow the fenceline on the right, forgo it. The monster storms of 1983 badly eroded the section of trail that descends from the clifftop to the cinderblock-walled view area below it.

Instead, continue down the steps to the asphalt road, once the roadbed to a spur of Sutro's railroad. Follow it around to the right. At the middle curvature of the hill, bear right again at the fork. Soon you come abreast of the tawny cinderblock wall.

Stroll to the right to the place where the wall continues on the north side of the observation platform, and look over the side at the canyon below. Follow the wall to enjoy a changing panorama that includes the hills of Marin, Mile Rock, and, on clear days, Point Bonita, Bolinas Point, Duxbury Reef, and Bodega Head.

Artificial tidepools immediately below the wall were used as a model for a larger "tide machine" that Ralph Starr, who was also known as Alexander Pelton, inventor of the Pelton Wheel, was commissioned to build for Sutro. After at least $25,000 had been spent trying to harness the tides of the Golden Gate Strait, on the day of the unveiling of the tide machine, with an eager crowd awaiting a demonstration, Starr failed to appear. The dirty breakfast dishes were still in the sink at his home, but Starr and his family were gone.

Shards of the machine, often confused with wreckage from one of the many ships that perished in the treacherous water of the strait, are sometimes visible at low tide.

Descend a few steps on the southwest side of the view platform to enjoy two mini-viewing areas offering a more intimate look at the tidepools, then follow the main staircase down to the lower level for a closer look at the tunnels and footbridges. The larger tunnel is more inviting, now that several loads of pea gravel have paved it. Go in. At two points in the tunnel, both railed for safety, one crosses sea caves carved in recent storms.

Retrace your steps to the tunnel mouth, cross the bridge, and follow the road around toward Louis's Restaurant. As you pass the foundation of the old baths, you are near the point where the "Giggling Ghost," a derelict, lived, until my son Rick, then twelve, discovered his secret defense, a tape player and a network of tripwires.

When you reach the ramp on the south wall of the cove, go up to Point Lobos Avenue. At the street, turn right for another perspective on the ruins.

In a few steps you are abreast of the place where staircases went down to the ticket booths for both Sutro Baths and the museum. Cases full of old buggies, shays, phaetons, and moth-eaten stuffed birds surrounded the stairwell.

At the foot of the stairs, you paid your quarter to the Whitney family, who also operated Playland-at-the-Beach nearby. What you saw thereafter was called a museum.

In the catchpenny tradition of seaside spas, the museum was a hilarious and motley amalgam of trash and treasure. The treasures included Mayor Sutro's own collection of Egyptian mummies and *ushabtis*, gathered in 1884.

The Egyptian collection, restored by students of Egyptology at San Francisco State University, is divided, part at the university, part in the Rosicrucian Museum in San Jose. Many of the other artifacts were sold at auction, long before Sutro Baths and Museum burned. They were part of the clutter that included rickshas, cigar-store Indians and circus wagons, old photos of San Francisco, a sideshow of freak cows, and the marvels of the Musée Mécanique, one of the wayside exhibits that now stand by the wall in front of Seal Rock. Its row of old coin-operated machines has slots yawning greedily for your change.

Continue downhill past the Pronto Pup and descend the stair alongside the totem pole to find the GGNRA Visitors' Center.

Out on the deck, behind Cliff House, is another survivor from earlier times—the Camera Obscura, with its incredible 360-degree view and holograph display.

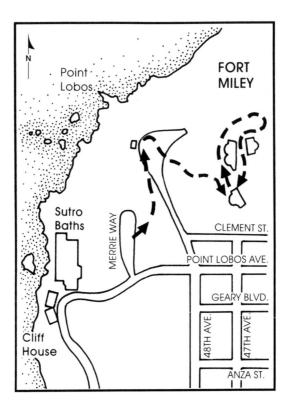

FORT MILEY

WALKING TIME: Allow a morning.

DISTANCE: An easy mile.

PUBLIC TRANSPORTATION: Muni bus 18 or 38.

PARKING: Easy and free on Merrie Way.

CLOTHES: Warm duds, whatever the weather.

The least-known section of the Golden Gate National Recreation Area is a spectacular twelve-acre knoll that has been known for the past eighty years as Fort Miley. Sometimes it has been called San Francisco's forgotten garrison.

First named the Military Reservation at Point Lobos, Fort Miley offers a dramatic view south toward Sutro Heights, the Great Highway, Ocean Beach, Mussel Rocks, Point San Pedro, and Montara Mountain.

It also has a fine view, rampant tree-growth permitting, north over Golden Gate Strait to the Marin Headlands and, surprisingly, of the Golden Gate Bridge.

View collectors who have never walked around Fort Miley should pick a clear day. Then, to make this walk, go to the northwest corner of San Francisco, at Point Lobos Avenue.

At the outset, you'll be attracted, as thousands of visitors to San Francisco have been, by the splendor of the Pacific Ocean crashing on the Seal Rocks, visible beyond the ruin of Sutro Baths immediately below Merrie Way.

When you can take your eyes from this mesmerizing scene, cross the parking lot and look for a single footpath through a little meadow. Follow it through the trees and turn on the fine broad trail on your left. In 1888 this was the roadbed for the Sutro Ferries and Cliff House Railroad, built by Mayor Adolph Sutro and his cousin Gustave. It was famous for its five-cent fare and scenic ride.

The trail winds through low trees, mostly wattle and acacia. When you reach a clearing overlooking Golden Gate Strait, pause at the little fence for a look at Mile Rock, which once had a house and lighthouse on it. Now the light is automated and the top is a helipad.

Nearer at hand, the foundation beyond the fence once held the Lands End Station for the railroad. Cliff-eroding storms of 1982 and '83 washed out several of the trails below. Don't be tempted to go beyond the fence. More than one overeager walker or fisherman has had to be rescued from these crumbling cliffs by rangers, ropes, and helicopters.

Do an about-face and climb up the simple stairway across the trail immediately inshore of the little fence. The steps are cut into the cliff and reinforced with six-by-six-inch timbers. It will bring you up onto a big half-moon of parking on El Camino del Mar.

Pause a moment when you reach the top of the steps to look over the pines just east of the parking lot to locate the semaphore and octagonal roof of an historic lookout, created by the Marine Exchange to report the approach of sailing ships. As ships were sighted from this octagonal building, the information was transmitted six miles to Telegraph Hill, first by the semaphore and later by the first telegraph in California.

Perhaps the greatest signal of jubilation was October 29, 1850, when the steamer *Oregon* sailed through Golden Gate, bringing the news that California had been admitted to the Union of States.

Enticing as it may be to follow the scimitar of walkway to the north, for this walk, turn right instead. Soon you will be at the memorial for the cruiser USS *San Francisco*.

The bronze tablets commemorate the 107 men killed at the Battle of Savo Island on August 9, 1942. The ripped metal surrounding the flagpole is intentional. It is the riddled navigation bridge of the cruiser, facing eternity and Guadalcanal forever.

After reading this valiant story, continue south. In about one hundred yards, look beyond the hedge for the white lines of a painted crosswalk. Use it to cross El Camino del Mar toward the tall Monterey cypress and pine trees. A friendly brown-and-white GGNRA sign welcomes walkers, but not cars, into this little forest.

As you walk up the slight incline, look off to your right to discern what seems to be a floor leaning against two trees. It is part of the skill-building Fort Miley 4-H Ropes Course, created for the Urban Outdoor Adventure Center. Chief ranger Steve Gazzano told me, "Women rangers are better at it than the men. They walk those high ropes and boughs like ballerinas."

Ignore the road that goes off to the left and continue on the main trail. In a few minutes you will reach a small rectangle of concrete on your left. This once supported the sentry post for Fort Miley. Sometimes little girls play the ancient childhood game of jack-and-ball on the foundation.

In another few steps you will be between an inviting green lawn and the massive concrete bunker named for Civil War veteran Major James Chester. Leave the path and climb up on the lawn for the vast southern view over Golden Gate Park and Ocean Beach.

This great sun trap of lawn has replaced a gravel road and a pair of Quonset huts that stood here during the time Fort Miley served as a Navy Pacific Coast harbor defense base and later as an Air Force Reserve center.

Be careful of the drop-off into the concrete gun mount inside Battery Chester, which once held twelve-inch mortars and twelve-inch rifles. Later it had six-inch guns that startled half of San Francisco when they were first fired in 1941. Notice at the north border of the bunker a fine wayside exhibit placed by the Golden Gate National Recreation Area.

Who was Miley? A visitor here must inevitably wonder. If you know, compliment yourself as a sharp military historian. During the Spanish-American War Lieutenant Colonel John D. Miley of the Second U.S. Artillery, senior aide to General William R. Shafter, wrote a classic campaign text, *In Cuba with Shafter*, and was also the negotiator of the Spanish surrender. He had the honor to be one of three men who hoisted Old Glory at Santiago when Admiral Dewey destroyed Spain's naval fleet. Miley died a hero in Manila—of fever, not battle wounds.

To see more of the fort, return to the main trail and look north. Instead of taking the low road into the next bunker, go uphill on the paved pathway that skirts the bunker and the trees. Soon you will be peering down on the Marine Exchange lookout on the left and into a bunker on your right. Artful graffiti enlivens the walls surrounding the old gun mount circle.

Walk to the end of this short trail to find another hidden place for sighting approaching ships. The compass underfoot on its roof was part of the two-acre naval communications system installation. When you have enjoyed the vignette framed by trees, go under the branches to your right and in a few steps you will be overlooking the Golden Gate Strait toward the Golden Gate Bridge.

Turn back and follow the path to the bunkers. At the first circular foundation, look for a path through the trees on the south side. It will lead to a stairway. When you reach these concrete steps, go right, downhill. The descent is into the center of a bunker. Turn left in the bunker to return to that attractive overlook lawn. Picnic or linger here as you like.

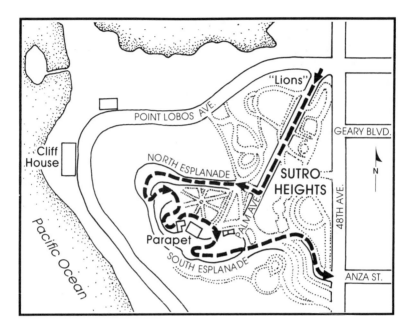

SUTRO HEIGHTS

WALKING TIME: Allow a half day.

DISTANCE: A mile or two.

PUBLIC TRANSPORTATION: An 18 or 38-L Muni bus to the end of the line.

PARKING: Good on Merrie Way.

CLOTHES: Take a windbreaker.

> *In a coign of the cliff between*
> *lowland and highland*
> *At the sea-down's edge between*
> *windward and lee*
> *Walled 'round with rocks as an*
> *inland island*
> *The ghost of a garden fronts*
> *the sea.*

Poet Algernon Charles Swinburne, a contemporary of Mayor Adolph Sutro, wrote those lines, and both the description and Swinburne's fashionable melancholy anapests fit Sutro Heights like a silk glove.

Sutro Heights.

Once the elaborate, overadorned home of San Francisco's philanthropic mayor, Sutro Heights has celebrated its centennial. Mayor Sutro opened his ornate grounds to the public in his lifetime, and Sutro Heights has been a park ever after. For many of the intervening hundred years, it was a place where a few plaster statues disintegrated among fine old trees. Battalions of rabbit-tail grass climbed the granite parapet in which Sutro's ashes were hidden.

A devoted corps of walkers also climbs the parapet to see the panorama from Sutro's commanding cliff—a view including the Cliff House, Seal Rocks, the Farallon Islands, Point Reyes, Ocean Beach, the Great Highway, Montara Mountain, and what the Costanoan Indians native to San Francisco called the Sundown Sea.

After six decades as a San Francisco city park, Sutro Heights became part of the Golden Gate National Recreation Area, where to make the park more inviting, the GGNRA has restored several of the statues. Turn right and bear seaward. Soon you will be abreast of the restored Well House, a gazebolike building that is the only structure remaining from Sutro's residence. It was left when the mansion, conservatory, stables, water tank, and watchtower were razed in 1939, after the death of Sutro's daughter, Dr. Emma Merritt. Merritt, who had accompanied Sutro in 1881 when he acquired the property for $15,000, later left Sutro Heights to the city as a public park. The grounds have been manicured, one of the colorful "carpet beds" of the mayor's flower garden has been replaced, and a new picnic grove has been established in the hillside woodland.

Mayor Sutro would have loved everything but the picnic grove. In his time, visitors were required to leave their picnic baskets and peanuts with the gatekeeper.

Walkers were always admitted to Sutro Heights for free, but there was a time when Sutro charged twenty-five cents each to those who rode a Southern Pacific–owned railroad out to the park. It was a rival to his own Ferries and Cliff House Railroad.

Golden Gate Park Association, which assists in the maintenance of the GGNRA, sometimes provides chamber music suitable to Sutro's era, ranger-guided walks, and refreshments.

When Sutro first opened the big ornate gate of his estate to the public, visitors walked through the dunes or came by horse-and-carriage on the Point Lobos Toll Road.

From the eastern border of the park, along 48th Avenue between Point Lobos and Geary Boulevard, look south toward Anza Street and try to imagine a tower with a glowing eye.

According to Walter J. Fitzpatrick, of Tottering-on-the-Brink, Denman Island, British Columbia, "In no place have I ever seen mention of the 'Victorian Gothic' stables belonging to the [Sutro] estate. This building stood on the south side of Anza Street, just outside the present area of Sutro Heights. . . . To me as a boy, the building was 'creepy,' especially at sunset time when the tower windows caught the reddish glow of the setting sun. We kids used to think that it was the evil eye."

Walk north to the corner of Point Lobos and 48th Avenue to find the formal entrance to Sutro Heights, marked by two recumbent lions. Once past the lions, you are on Palm Avenue. Along this same route for Sunday brunch, a tradition at the mayor's salon, came President Benjamin Harrison, poet Oscar Wilde, William Jennings Bryan, and Andrew Carnegie.

As you walk along Palm, you will pass the area known as "Old Grove" on the east. Farther along, near the statue of Diana, goddess of the hunt, was a classical maze of hedges. Visitors at the time of the full moon often leave flowers by the statue of Diana. Rangers constantly find fresh flowers and incense there. She is not only Diana the Huntress, but Diana of the Moon. Perhaps a group of moon worshipers leave her the blooms.

Keep walking and you will reach the view area. From the lower parapet, walk to the north side of the foundation and climb up steps past the mayor's wine cellar to reach the uppermost lookout. Each crenellation was once topped by a statue or urn.

When you have enjoyed the broad vistas, go down the opposite steps. Cross the lawn toward the southern pathway. It leads to Dolce far Niente balcony, where beautiful Beatrice Lewis plunged to her death just a month after performing a midnight pastorale on the same spot.

Walk east, noting the wayside exhibit depicting the building, then continue toward the mound near 48th Avenue where Sutro's conservatory once stood.

You will recognize the area by the carpet bed of flowers and the tall palm, which once grew inside the glass house, overlooking the path. Immediately across the broad walkway is a picnic grove.

Ten gardeners created a floral wonderland here in the 1880s when Sutro was in residence. The GGNRA has only three gardeners to spare on a part-time basis for Sutro Heights, but they are hopeful that the time will come when the gardens seem forsaken and ghostly no longer.

FORT FUNSTON

WALKING TIME: A half a day.

DISTANCE: Four miles.

PUBLIC TRANSPORTATION: Nearest is Muni bus 70.

PARKING: Great.

CLOTHES: Warm.

"Now the great winds shorewards blow," wrote Matthew Arnold, entranced by the ocean in winter. "Now the salt tides seawards flow; / Now the wild white horses play, / Champ and chafe and toss in the spray."

The Pacific Ocean makes a great show, and never better than at the time of full moons and new moons. Walking along the waterside is also the ideal place for making resolutions for the new year, whether you intend to keep them or not. Footprints on the sands of time, intimations of mortality and all that.

Fortunately, San Franciscans are blessed with plenty of shoreline to walk. Nowhere is it more interesting than at Fort Funston, the cliffy dunescape that lies within the Golden Gate National Recreation Area at the southwest corner of the city. There are several choices for walking here. For the beachcomber, at low tide there is a broad strand that is often bestrewn with fossils after a storm. For the cross-country strider, there are loony moonscape dunes, a natural amphitheater, an old military battery, a one-time gun club, and any number of native plants to discover. For the whale watcher, there is a high overlook. For the handicapped, the lame, and the elderly, there is a well-paved, short, and completely level trail suitable for wheelchairs.

Given the right winds, when you walk on the beach, hang gliders soar overhead. Climb up the cliff and they are at eye level. Climb even higher to the top of Battery Davis and you may be above them. At any level, it adds an interesting dimension to walking, and one, like the presence of mounted rangers, that increases the safety of the walker.

My favorite of the Fort Funston possibilities is a walk that combines all the options. To make it, put on your lugsoled hiking boots and down jacket. Then transport yourself south toward the city's charter line via the Great Highway and Skyline Boulevard. Slightly past the zoo, watch on the west side for parking.

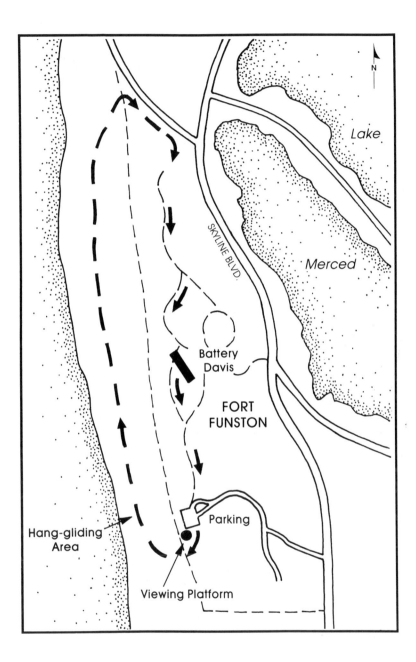

Lake

Merced

SKYLINE BLVD.

Battery
Davis

FORT
FUNSTON

Parking

Hang-gliding
Area

Viewing Platform

N

One long ramp goes from road to beach. Near the foot of it, a broad path leads upward through the dunes. Take the latter, and follow it up through a draw until you are parallel to the Fort Funston sign, then bear right on the old military road, a legacy from a time when this was Lake Merced Military Reservation, renamed following the earthquake of 1906 in gratitude to General Frederick Funston for his helpfulness to the city.

Follow the road up to Battery Davis, with Lake Merced, all the Sunset district, and the San Miguel Hills visible on your left as you walk. (For an even better view, the spry can climb to the top of Battery Davis from its northern end.) At the southern entrance, go through the massive battery and follow the trail for the handicapped as it rambles along the cliff. Natural windbreaks in the chaparral have been pressed into service by the park to shelter picnic tables and benches.

Bearing consistently south on the paved trail, you will soon arrive at the hang-gliding overlook. To make a reconnaissance of the beach, and scan the distance for any passing pod of gray whales, walk toward the fenced overlook above the glider launching pad. On a clear day you can see the Farallon Islands.

Once you have scoped out the beach, walk back to that low wooden bridge on the overlook approach and look south to discern beyond the hang-glider launching place a narrow single-file path through the sea fig. Skirt the hang-glider pad to reach it. It rambles southerly, then makes a sharp L-shaped turn and drops steeply a hundred feet to the beach. Once down on the strand, look back to see from where you descended, then south to locate Pedro Point, parallel to Sweeney Ridge, the last addition to the Golden Gate National Recreation Area.

As you walk, keep your eye out for a smooth round gray wave-worn stone, the ideal flat shape best for "skipping the waves," one of childhood's oldest games. This is *Anorthoscutum interlineatum* Stimpson, an extinct sand dollar, which washes out of the Merced formation from a V-shaped fossil bed that lies offshore. If you find one, take it to the Fort Funston Environmental Education Center at the south meadow of Fort Funston. Such trophies belong to the park.

When you become aware that the cliffs have sloped down to the level of the Great Highway, you are parallel to the San Francisco Zoo. If this widely varied terrain, a sample of what San Francisco was like before the city was built, was so distracting you forgot to make a resolution, here's one for our energy-hungry times—Resolved: To walk as often as possible.

PHILLIP BURTON BEACH

WALKING TIME: Two hours.

DISTANCE: Two miles each way.

PUBLIC TRANSPORTATION: Nearest is Muni bus 70.

PARKING: Three ocean overlook areas border Great Highway south of
Sloat Boulevard.

CLOTHES: Dress warm.

Phillip Burton Beach, which lies within the Golden Gate National
Recreation Area below the steep Fort Funston cliff, is named for the
late, much loved congressman who did more for preserving America's
parklands than anyone since Teddy Roosevelt. To walk along it, with
nothing but the blue Pacific to the west, is one of San Francisco's finest
strolls, especially after a winter storm. Old-timers remember this sandy
strand as "Sand Dollar Beach."

"Well, I'll tell you what happened to me at Fleischhacker Zoo the
other day," vocalist Bob Helm used to sing in an old Turk Murphy
comic number called "Evolution Mama."

In the song, someone makes a monkey out of the storyteller by
shaking his family tree. At Fleischhacker, Murphy was closer than he
dreamed to a true evolutionary revelation. Some two hundred yards
west, across the Great Highway, one can find prehistoric relics in the
form of smooth round stones.

For this is where *Anorthoscutum interlineatum* Stimpson, an extinct
sand dollar, washes out of the Merced formation from a V-shaped fossil
bed of the Pliocene epoch, which lies just offshore. Like flotsam on
beaches everywhere, this sea treasure is most easily found by the
person on foot. Piltdown man, Cro-Magnon man, and Neanderthal
man might have found *Anorthoscutum* on Phillip Burton Beach if
he had walked there, just as the stroller may today, for this fossil
sand dollar had been around from one to eight million years before
humans made it out of the primordial ooze onto the beaches of Planet
Earth.

Certainly, the Indians who loved the Sundown Sea must have marveled at the rock patterned like petals. Quite possibly Jose Antonio
Galindo, Francisco de Haro, and Francisco Guerrero y Palomares, all of
whom owned Rancho Laguna de la Merced at one time or another,

77

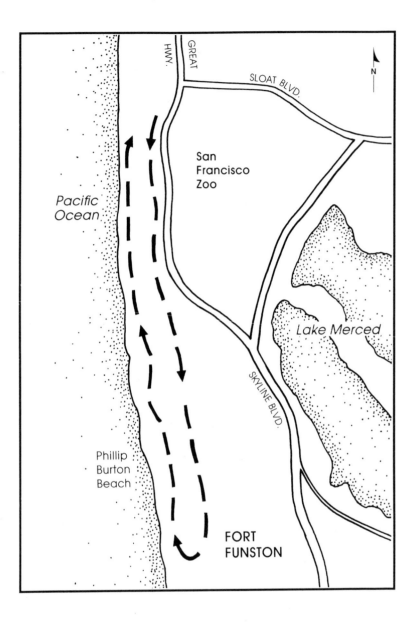

puzzled over it. But it was not until 1856 that the fossil was scientifically described and identified.

Most of us today would pass this unique sea loot with barely a glance; not the young students from the Fort Funston Environmental Education Center, however, who regard it as a prize for their museum. The fossil sand dollars are abundant, but erosion leaves few that are pristine. The walker who finds a perfect specimen should consider himself or herself very lucky. If you come upon one of the fossil sand dollars, look and marvel, but toss it back again or give it to the Fort Funston Environmental Center, because this is part of the GGNRA and even the stones belong to the park.

There is so much else to see at Phillip Burton Beach, you won't feel deprived. After you walk south down the easy ramp that descends to the beach, across from the San Francisco Zoo, continue south. A seventy-two-foot blue whale that washed up on the beach in 1988 is buried just below the first overlook. In a moment or two, you will be at the point where the Great Highway swings inland. The little gully on your left, which also has a path from higher up along the north border of Fort Funston, was the place where nearby Lake Merced once reached the sea. The 116 acres of Fort Funston itself are actually the dike, thirteen-hundred-feet wide, which holds back the Pacific Ocean and prevents it from resalting brackish Lake Merced.

When troops of the Spanish-American War camped on this land in 1898, it was called Laguna Merced Military Reservation. The records don't show whether anyone thought it droll in 1917 that a fort situated on a seismologically tender ledge should be renamed for General Frederick Funston, whose troops policed San Francisco after the 1906 quake. Until 1961, Fort Funston was used for "war games" landings and was inaccessible to the public. Walkers on the beach still find odd bits and pieces of military matériel from that period.

If it is a fair day with the right winds as you walk the beach, the shadow of a man with wings is sure to come gliding along the beach. Although several enthusiasts have lost their lives here, hang gliders still regard this as the primo gliding place this side of Peru or Chile.

Fort Funston's most unusual airborne accident remains a mystery. It occurred during the 1940s before the invention of the hang glider when a dirigible from Treasure Island, making a search for submarines along this shore, crashed in Daly City. Police searched the disabled blimp and found the pilot's hat, the parachutes, and the life rafts, but not a soul on board. Nor were any ever found.

Looking south as you walk, you will see Castle Rocks, from which old pier pilings jut into the sea. Rockaway Beach is the next point of land, identifiable by its rocky sea stack. Mori Point is the projecting land immediately south of it, with Pedro Point beyond.

Look toward the cliffs, eroded in some places into a Mount Rushmore of anonymous faces. Different times of day give the Fort Funston cliff different expressions. In certain lights, it seems to be full of hieroglyphic or runic Hobbit writing. Fifty-three different kinds of marine fossils, mostly mollusks, have been eroded out of the marine clays, shales, sandstones, conglomerates, and shell layers between here and Mussel Rock.

Like many beaches, Phillip Burton Beach has its regulars. Two of them are Jerry Werthimer, professor of journalism at San Francisco State University, and his wife, Pat, who like to make the walk along the beach to watch the sunset. "We use the clump of three cypress trees as a landmark," Jerry told me, "and climb up the cliff on a sand ladder, as the hang-glider pilots do." Don't be tempted to try this unless you have the agility of a mountain goat.

When you have walked far enough to feel the exhilaration that waterside walking bestows, turn back. You may not have spotted *Anorthoscutum*, but the exuberant sea offers a consolation prize, *Dendraster excentricus* Escholtz, also a sand dollar, but neither extinct nor fossilized.

In this trigger-tender atomic age, the fossil and the contemporary sand dollars are a classic example of the continuity of evolution. Holding the two in my hands, and comparing them to our own troubled world, I find I can't get that refrain out of my head: "Oh, Evolution Mama, don't you make a monkey out of me."

UNION SQUARE

NOTE: *For maps, see Maiden Lane, page 84, and Mason Street, page 86.*

WALKING TIME: Six minutes.

DISTANCE: One square block.

PUBLIC TRANSPORTATION: All roads lead to Union Square.

PARKING: Down the rabbit hole.

CLOTHES: Your everyday mink.

No one has recorded whether there were any pigeons watching, but some one hundred years ago, the placards in the public square on lower Geary Street quoted Dan'l Webster: "The Union, the Whole Union and Nothing but the Union" and "Liberty and Union, Now and Forever, One and Inseparable." These were read on May 11, 1861, during the biggest public-park powwow the city had seen. The message came across. San Francisco voted not to secede and Union Square got a name that stuck.

These days the placards in Union Square are more apt to urge "Get out of Central America" or "Stop Air Pollution Now," but the purpose is the same. For Union Square, in addition to being a garage roof, pigeon sanctuary, gerontological congress, floral showplace, stage prop for chic shops and hotels, breathing space, and promenade is also where the voice of the people is heard on the land.

No walk in town is so cosmopolitan as a stroll around and across the 2.6 acres of land bounded by Post, Geary, Powell, and Stockton streets. Its perimeter is Vanity Fair. Its center is Victory aloft. Its stable population includes chess players, smokers, idlers, urchins, tourists taking pictures, foot-weary shoppers, homeless sleepers, newspaper readers, religious exhorters, sun worshipers, trysting lovers, crones, cronies, chronic crumb spreaders, and a hazard of pigeons.

"Repent!" shouts a man hopping along the border of an elegant bed of violas. "You have nothing to lose but your soul." The Yuppie in the designer suit, shortcutting from Saks to Magnin's, accepts the tract that is tendered, murmurs a polite, "Thank you," glances at "Warning, you are in great danger!" and never misses a step. As she passes, two male street people sprawled on a bench turn their heads simultaneously in an appreciative swivel. Idlers watch all the pigeons. A clerk, out of his office for a stolen smoke, looks around furtively. An old man using a

Union Square.

magnifying glass reads aloud to himself. Another man in a wheelchair moves an ornately carved white queen on a chessboard, says, "Check!" and waits.

"Tucka-to-coo. Look at the fool," say the pigeons, looking at you. "Look at the few! Look at the view!"

The ranter intends to say "condemnation," but his harangue comes out with an unintentional fillip—"You gotta get rid of the godamnation against your soul!" Sly smiles along the benches indicate listeners.

A young pigeon-feeder makes a sudden grab, launching a holocaust of flap, calms his catch, stuffs it into a pasteboard box, and says to his friend, "Watch me get the brown one next time."

Across the plaza, he has been overheard. A pigeon-shaped man brushes a pigeon off his pigeon-splattered shoulder and bobbles, pigeonlike, toward the boy. "I heard-a you!" he scolds. "You leave-a da brownie alone!" In a sudden movement he unlids the box, freeing four pigeons triumphantly.

"I suppose they all have psittacosis," one gray-suited, gray-haired professional man comments to his gray-suited, gray-templed companion as they walk, fending off flapping wings.

"Ornithosis."

"Too bad. So we can't say psittacines of San Francisco, unite! You have nothing to lose but your square." With one hand he shields his face. He holds out the other, palm up. His friend reaches into a side pocket, puts a quarter in the hand, and asks, "Ever been in St. Peter's in Rome?"

"Hellfire awaits you!" interjects the religious exhorter.

"Mate!" says the crippled chess player.

Two old people move to a sunnier bench.

A girl in sandals arrives with a placard: "AIDS Threatens Us All." A crowd begins to gather.

This is Union Square. Just a short walk from corner to corner, but it measures the distance between Beijing and Washington. In an age overwhelmed with communication, it is still the only *vox* always open to all the *populi* of a democracy. Los Angeles and Chicago may refer to their areas of public assembly as "Bughouse Square" but they sell them short. The tradition is an old one, urbane and proud. It came to us from Hyde Park in London. By Forum. Out of Agora. Complete with pigeons.

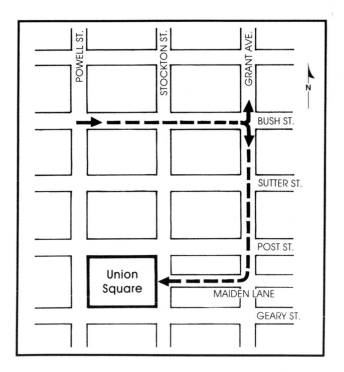

POWELL ST.

STOCKTON ST.

GRANT AVE.

N

BUSH ST.

SUTTER ST.

POST ST.

Union
Square

MAIDEN LANE

GEARY ST.

MAIDEN LANE

WALKING TIME: Negligible.

DISTANCE: Two blocks.

PUBLIC TRANSPORTATION: Legion.

PARKING: Sub-sub basement of Union Square.

CLOTHES: Chic. Add a hat if you're lunching at the St. Francis.

Maiden Lane, a chic two-block streak from Union Square to Kearny
Street, is a promenade of the comfortably buttered feminine upper-
crustacean, which one disgruntled bill-paying paterfamilias has described as the "shortest distance between affluence and bankruptcy."

He may be right. This is a world of gifts from Chanel, shifts from
Lanz, fabrics from Britex, pets from Ansel Robinson, jet reservations
from Swissair, cameras from Brooks, and chimeras from more than
one well-known portrait photographer.

Start this walk at either end between the elaborate candelabra one
wag has described as belonging to the "nouveau richelieu period."

Look down the little lane at the handsome plane trees set into the undulating curb, framed in red brick and matted with white dolomite chips. Don Clever and Welton Becket remodeled the street in 1958 to give it a saucy ambiance.

A sally down this elegant alley reveals that a more appropriate name might be Matron Lane. The citywatcher who avails himself of one of the thoughtfully placed benches on a shopping day will observe matrons archaic and matrons nubile and matrons of resolute mien, each upholding San Francisco's reputation as a city of well-dressed women. Sporty country types sidle by on the bias. Prim high priestesses from the Junior League world of good works march, conspicuously white-gloved, into the furriers'. Models, overdressed and underfed, prance by like high-schooled horses. Stately clubwomen, boned and buttressed like ambulant churches, parade to the inaudible organ swell of "Pomp and Circumstance." Coveys of secretaries break cover for coffee. Clerks flit by hastily. Buyers stroll in pairs. The men are few.

A hundred years ago the men were many, for this was once notorious Morton Street, the bargain basement of the Barbary Coast. Until that sweeping house-cleaner the fire of '06 wiped out the Morton Street cribs, prostitutes sat here in open windows, nude to the waist, and solicited passersby. A man could fondle one breast for a dime, or two for fifteen cents. More intimate services cost a quarter.

Iodoform Kate was the most infamous of Morton Street madams. She employed only redheads and bragged that her girls took on a hundred customers a night. The street must have been as crowded in an evening then as it is during the annual daffodil festival today. Old records fail to reveal whether the one-murder-per-week average could be chalked up to impatient miners tired of waiting in line.

Sin gave in around 1909. Merchants tried two new names, Union Square Avenue and later Manila Avenue, to wipe out the lurid past. Neither stuck and finally they borrowed the name of Maiden Lane from New York's former diamond market.

As you walk, notice number 140, architecturally, Maiden Lane's outstanding building. It was designed by Frank Lloyd Wright in 1949 and anticipated the controversial Guggenheim Museum of New York in its circular ramp.

Culturally, the most unusual shop is Junipero Serra Bookstore, at number 50. Gastronomically, the choice includes Mecca and Charcuterie. On fair days, tables are set up in the street at lunchtime. Historically, the oldest business establishment is the pet store at number 135, founded in 1849. Owner Ansel Robinson has a picture hanging in the shop to prove that it stood on Washington Street, not on Morton in the gashy-flashy days.

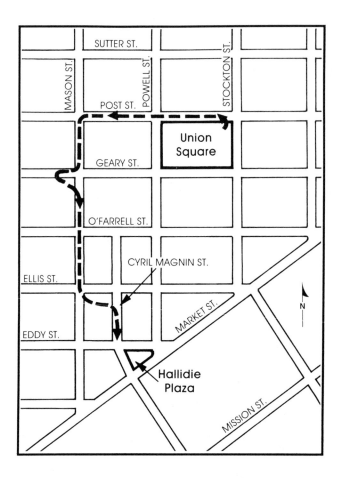

MASON STREET

WALKING TIME: Elastic.

DISTANCE: Seven blocks.

PUBLIC TRANSPORTATION: Hyde or Powell cable cars.

PARKING: Under Union Square, or forget it.

CLOTHES: Urbane.

"There's a small hotel . . ." A romantic old swing number from the big band era kept lilting through my mind as I crossed Union Square one evening not long ago. Graduates in long evening gowns and tuxedos were clustered outside both the Hyatt and the Westin St. Francis on Union Square.

With more than a thousand rooms between them, neither of these hostelries could be called "small," but within easy walking distance of Union Square there are many that do fit that description. Hotels, both large and small, have been changing the face of the city in this area during the past few years. Mason Street, one block west of the square, has turned into a "Hotel Row" and is a good place to see how this part of tomorrow's city is evolving.

For historical perspective, the place to start this walk is Union Square, the focal point for shopping, tourism, antiques, galleries, and all the civilized pleasures that attend our urban culture. A gift to the city in 1850 from its first mayor, John Geary, Union Square got its name eleven years later when Abraham Lincoln's friend Colonel Edward "Gray Eagle" Dickinson Baker made the speech that brought California into the Union of States.

Old photos show churches and family homes on the west side of the square. Saloons, bars, and notorious Morton Street, renamed Maiden Lane after prostitutes were banished from it, were on the east side of the square.

The garage under the sunny park, the first of its kind in the world, was designed in 1942 by architect Timothy Pflueger. Inspired by Union Square Garage, Switzerland has dug even deeper and put a garage under Lake Geneva.

Lively during the workweek with sunbathers, brown-baggers, political demonstrators, and street performers, Union Square is a welcome sun trap.

Cross Powell Street, but first wait for any cable car loaded with tourists to pass. At Post Street, walk west under the two St. Francis Hotel marquees that announce the English Grill and the Dutch Kitchen. The shell of the St. Francis survived the earthquake and fire of 1906 that leveled much of this part of the city. To serve meals, a temporary "Little St. Francis" was erected across Powell Street in Union Square.

Look across Post Street to see the thirty-room Inn at Union Square, which lists itself as a "B&B," or bed-and-breakfast inn. A phenomenon that came to the Bay Area with the opening of the Magnolia Hotel at Yountville, B&B's are now so popular that there are more than 126 of them between Monterey and Eureka. At last count, San Francisco had twenty bed-and-breakfast hostelries. One—the Kensington Hotel across the street—has Theater on the Square upstairs.

Pause when you reach Mason Street, named for Richard B. Mason, colonel of the First U. S. Dragoons and military governor of California during the Gold Rush, from May 31, 1847, to April 13, 1849.

The newest landmarks at Post and Mason are the elegant Portman and Donatello hotels. The comfort of their lobbies compares easily to the private clubs—the Bohemian, Press, and Olympic clubs—farther west on "Club Row," as Post Street is also known. Look west to locate another newcomer on the horizon, the Post Street Towers, a complex of mini-condos especially designed for corporate pieds-à-terre.

The Marines' Memorial Theater is uphill, but turn left, downhill, on Mason. Soon you are abreast of a genuine outdoor shoeshine parlor, operated since 1975 by Nevig Ato Osilio.

On the sidelines, the austere San Francisco Water Department building and the Native Sons building seem to be looking down their gray noses at the little One Act Theater, the Regency III movie house, and the Improv comedy club.

Derby Alley, next to the Improv, was named for Lieutenant John Derby, whose humorous writing under the nom de plume of John Phoenix includes a satire on governmentality: *Of a Military Survey and Reconnaissance of the Route from San Francisco to the Mission of Dolores, Made with a View to Ascertain the Practicability of Connecting These Points by a Railroad.*

At Geary Street, make a slight digression to the west to note, among other things, the handprints of Leontyne Price and Chita Rivera in the sidewalk outside the glitzy Hotel Diva.

In the same block, across from both the Curran and Geary theaters, David's Deli has been a favorite with showfolks for thirty-five years. Some smart theatergoers have also discovered that David's small hotel, recently refurbished in art deco style, has an entire nonsmoking floor.

Retrace your steps back to Mason Street to pass, en route, the San Francisco Art Exchange, which features prints of the "Vargas girls," favored as pinups by G.I.'s during World War II.

Turn downhill on Mason to find Washington's Newsland, which offers out-of-town papers, even if your hometown is London. Farther on, Lori's Diner stays open twenty-four hours a day, and at the Piano Bar, there is jazz reminiscent of the big-band era. The visual scene-stealer, however, is the handsome King George Hotel, which has traditional English tea service daily on the mezzanine. Across the way, the Downtown Center Garage has an indoor mall lined with small shops and a ticket brokerage, much like a hotel lobby.

At O'Farrell Street, named for San Francisco's visionary early surveyor, Jasper O'Farrell, you have reached a length of Mason once known as "The White Way" for its cafes, saloons, and sporting houses.

Until 1917, it was a border of the Uptown Tenderloin area (the others were Market, Larkin, and Mason streets). The lights of Kelly's

Place, Jimmy Stack's Cabaret, the second Poodle Dog Restaurant, and Billy Lyon's infamous saloon The Bucket of Blood all went out in January 1917, when the city enforced a red-light abatement act. Before that dramatic climax to a rip-roaring age, Mrs. M.R. "Reggie" Gamble, who operated a parlor house on Mason, rounded up three hundred prostitutes in their best finery and paraded them up Mason Street to call upon the Reverend Paul Smith, pastor of the Central Methodist Church and central figure in the "cleanup."

They went to ask what he planned to do to feed, clothe, and house them. When he suggested that they go to work at decent jobs—the average wage then was $10 per week for women—they laughed in his face.

"Statistics show," said Smith, "that families all over the country receive less."

"That's why there's prostitution," replied Gamble. "C'mon girls, let's go."

What Smith began, Prohibition completed: "The White Way" turned into a dim and shabby fringe of the theater district—the Tenderloin of bookies, gambling lofts, and secret fleshpots.

The area is a slum no longer. The new hotels on Mason Street are so impressive that the few remaining pawn, porn, or strip joints stick out like a pimple on a debutante's nose. Part of yesterday's history, they are almost picturesque.

The new Hotel Nikko, on O'Farrell toward Powell Street, has its marble lobbies up one level. In contrast, the Hilton, which occupies an entire block across the street, called Hilton Square, offers a street-level approach from O'Farrell. Go in the Hilton and you are in an indoor mall. When you reach the wider main lobby, take the escalator down and you will emerge at Ellis Street.

Cross both Ellis and Mason streets and enter the new Ramada Renaissance Hotel. Walk east, parallel to Ellis, then turn within the hotel to walk south, parallel to Cyril Magnin Street. When you descend, you will be at Eddy Street, across from that sunny sunken garden Hallidie Plaza, a transportation crossroads as elaborate as a three-dimensional chess game.

Other small hotels—and an increasing number of fine restaurants, art galleries, and entertainment depots—are springing up almost monthly in this area. You're sure to discover some I have missed, especially if you walk back to Union Square on the tourist-trinket trail along Powell Street.

Better still, cross Market and continue this walk in the new San Francisco Centre. It, too, has given San Francisco's throbbing heart another beat.

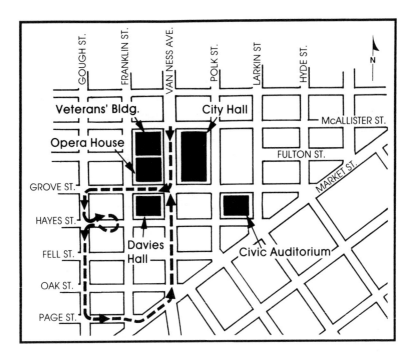

CIVIC CENTER

WALKING TIME: Half a day.

DISTANCE: Three blocks.

PUBLIC TRANSPORTATION: BART and Muni buses 5, 19, 42, 47, and 49.

PARKING: In Brooks Hall.

CLOTHES: Dress for stress.

San Francisco's City Hall calls to mind the old romance of Beauty and the Beast.

Whatever else it may be—symbol of local government, headquarters of the city's housekeeper, stronghold of the myth that says "you can't buck," and home of the nine-copy memo "buck-sheet"—City Hall is a beautiful statement. In the words civic leader Tom Magee used in 1909, far-seeing San Franciscans intended Civic Center's statement to be: "This is the modern city beautiful and the modern city useful."

Two international authorities, Christopher Tunnard and Henry Hope Reed, have called it "the grandest Civic Center in the country."

Another author, Mel Scott, described it as a physical demonstration "that a city is its people; that community character and love of place and faith in the future can transcend the greatest calamity; that the spirit is unquenchable . . ." These are heady words. If they seem too sweet compared to the way three national magazines have described San Francisco as "a myth," "narcissistic," and "on the skids," come with open eyes and the following scorecard to take a walk around Civic Center.

Begin at Fulton and Market, the focal point from which the City Hall's elegant French Renaissance splendor (high score of 10 points on the plus side of the card) was designed to be viewed. Walk west on Fulton, which the first Civic Center plan of 1911 intended as a grassy tree-lined mall. (Mark the card +7 for the United Nations Plaza.) Now you know how to play this walking game so, as civic values always are, the points are up to you.

CIVIC CENTER SCOREBOARD

Visual Feature	*Minus*	*Plus*
City Hall		
United Nations Plaza		
Handsome old Federal Building		
Lick Monument		
Three-fourths of a library		
Brooks hole		
Temporary 100 Larkin Building		
Flagpoles		
Powerhouse smogstack		
Tall dull Federal Building		
State Office Building		
Old Faceful fountain		
Civic Auditorium		
Gas station where office building should be		
Louise M. Davies Symphony Hall		
Rotunda, staircase, and colonnade of City Hall		
Opera House		
Veterans' Memorial Building		

The handsome old Federal Building, placing national close to local government, was designed in 1936 by John Bakewell and Arthur Brown, Jr., the architects of City Hall. On the south side of the street the theater mimics the concave Federal Building setback in clever, high-flown contrast to the flyblown flytraps raveling out of Market.

Fulton widens pleasantly at Hyde. It takes a sharp eye to discern that the stately Main Public Library, designed by George W. Kelham in 1915, has a bite missing out of the northeast corner. Budget was the biter, as it was on Brooks Hall, under the plaza.

Windy Civic Center Plaza has two "leaky" corners, to use a phrase planners invented to describe a breakdown in design continuity. Ugliest is the contemporary hay bin at McAllister and Polk. In more gracious days stables and smithies hid on back alleys. This corner belongs to the city and, according to Civic Center plans of 1911 and 1957, should be the site of an office building to house the fire, water, and civic service departments overflowing City Hall.

Oppressing the plaza as you walk west (dodging Old Faceful, the fountain that looks like a sewage aeration pond) is another monolithic monument to monumental government, the dull too-tall block of the Federal Building. In contrast, the State Office Building seems refreshing, but it isn't as handsome as the Civic Auditorium, the work of John Galen Howard, Fred H. Meyer, and John Reid, Jr., and built in 1913, contemporary with City Hall.

At City Hall the dome, rotunda, staircase, colonnade, and other details are a joy forever. Once out the other door at the tragedy that is Van Ness, the walker meets a barricade, not a promenade. One must detour to cross and inspect Louise M. Davies Symphony Hall, the Opera House and Veterans' Building, mall, and pretty golden picket wicket.

Tote up your own score to find out whether San Francisco is "on the skids." Seattle and Philadelphia (the governmental homes of which excel) notwithstanding, Civic Center may be unfinished, but it is still a beauty. The beast, politics, could turn out to be a handsome prince after all. The scenery is appropriate to romance.

SYMPHONY HALL

NOTE: *For map, see Civic Center, page 90.*

WALKING TIME: An hour.

DISTANCE: About a mile.

PUBLIC TRANSPORTATION: Muni bus 47 is known as "the opera bus."
Also handy: Muni buses 5, 21, 42, and 49.

PARKING: So-so.

CLOTHES: Swank for the performances.

The gallant madness that is San Francisco has had a great new cultural infusion. It is the Louise M. Davies Symphony Hall, the impact of which, better than any redevelopment agency, has manifested itself in neighborhood renewal for blocks around.

The walker who goes to hear *The Bartered Bride* or "Scheherazade"—or to admire the monumental auditorium with its tremendous people-roundabout facade—will discover there are good places nearby to dine, galleries to explore, shops, courtyards, and parking lots to discover.

Pick a scintillating winter afternoon when the air is as fresh as bugle notes. Then transport yourself to the Civic Center. At McAllister Street take a good look at San Francisco's "city beautiful" City Hall, often described as the outstanding example of Beaux Arts French Renaissance architecture in the United States. Arthur Brown, Jr., and John Bakewell, Jr., were the architects, winners in a 1912 design competition.

Stop in the Veterans' Building on the west side of Van Ness to see the redesigned Herbst Theater, if it is open; a little reprise on the melody that swells at the Opera House next door, four murals by Frank Brangwyn interpreting earth, air, fire, and water grace the side walls.

If the gate is open on the Thomas Church–designed Opera Court, between the Veterans' Building and the Opera House, a formal little green oasis behind a handsome picket wicket, step inside to see how adroitly a $5 million addition containing rehearsal, storage, and library space has been tagged onto the back of the Opera House. It is almost indistinguishable from Arthur Brown's original design.

When you reach Grove Street, stop on the north side for a breathtaking perspective on Symphony Hall. Filled with concertgoers, the great three-story expanse of curved glass looks like it was dreamed up by F. Scott Fitzgerald. Actually, Charles Basset of the hometown firm of Skidmore, Owings, & Merrill, with an assist from Pietro Belluschi of Portland, was the hand behind the plan. The great reclining figure on the corner is by Henry Moore.

Bear west on Grove Street to see Zellerbach Rehearsal Hall. First hint of the neighborhood "gentrification" comes at Franklin Street, where Kimballs' Restaurant and Bar re-uses a handsome old brick building, enlivened by a new skylight. Cross both Franklin and Grove to discover "All About Music," a bookshop whose name tells the tale.

At Vorpal Gallery, 393 Grove, the vorpal blade may not be going snicker-snack when you pass, but the nicely revealed redwood beams of the resurrected warehouse, the whirligig fire escape slide, the shrine, a conversation pit–cum–casting couch, and the textile gallery make it worth a visit, whatever artists are being featured. When you reach the freeway, notice how the eucalypti have softened the stark lines. Bear left on Gough. At Ivy and Gough, window boxes spill red geraniums from the Barrister's Chambers, one of several such Victorians imaginatively re-used in this long-neglected corner of the city. Another is the Gough-Hayes Hotel. Mark Pendragon Bakery, which also serves meals, Martha's Mexican Food, and David's House west on Hayes are for future reference, but bear left at Ivy Court. Ivy's Restaurant, its neighbor, City Picnic, Hardcastle's, and Ed Brown's Gallery all open into the garden courtyard as well as into the street. The Hayes Street Grill and Mandarin Opera Restaurant are cheek by jowl a little farther along.

Double back on the south side of Hayes to Gough to find both an historic marker—acclaiming the San Francisco Laundry and Dry Cleaning Union, which started here in 1901—and to discover Dorothy Starr, whose Music Stand has been supplying opera scores here for twenty-one years.

Keep walking toward Market and at Fell you will discover the Toyo Pottery Workshop and Christian's Golden Bowl, washbasins imported from Mexico. Supersub takeout sandwiches and Our Kitchen reveal the distance the ripples have spread from the Music Center. When you reach the Bessie L. Smith Children's Center, bear left on Market and left again on Van Ness to pass the old Masonic Temple, a delightful Bliss and Faville building just crying to be turned into a music school or rehearsal studio. The Federal Greek Revival building next door, which old-timers recall as Godeaux Funeral Home, now houses a credit union.

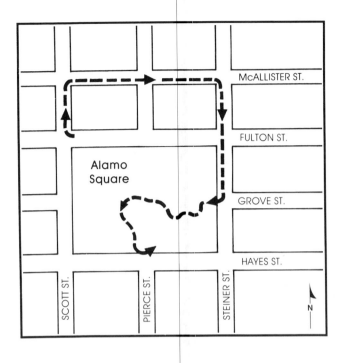

MCALLISTER ST.

FULTON ST.

Alamo
Square

GROVE ST.

HAYES ST.

SCOTT ST.

PIERCE ST.

STEINER ST.

N

ALAMO SQUARE

WALKING TIME: An hour.

DISTANCE: A square city block.

PUBLIC TRANSPORTATION: Muni buses 5 McAllister, 21 Hayes, 22 Fillmore, and 24 Divisadero.

PARKING: So-so.

CLOTHES: Not your best.

"Postcard Row" is famous internationally, although many a San Franciscan would be hard-pressed to tell you where it is located.

That handsome line of Victorian homes, so often photographed with the contemporary skyline as a contrasting backdrop, is on the 700 and 800 blocks of Steiner Street, the eastern periphery of Alamo Square. Next to the celebrated picture of the cable car struggling up Russian Hill with the Golden Gate Bridge in the background, or the Transamerica spire, it may well be the best-known worldwide image of San Francisco.

95

Happily for the neighborhood, and indeed for all of us, it is now safely incorporated within the Alamo Square Historical District and is assured of community design review lest any developer drop a heavy hand on it.

In becoming an historic district, the community has done itself another surprising favor. The "ripple effect," as planners describe improvements adjacent to an upgraded neighborhood, is making Alamo Square a center of distinguished bed-and-breakfast inns.

This is one of the most accessible places in the city. Proximity to City Hall first gave Alamo Square good public transportation in 1860, when County Clerk Thomas Hayes built an extension of his Market Street Railway up Alamo Square's south boundary. He named the street for himself. Since development inevitably follows transportation, the boundaries of the park soon had their share of attractive houses overlooking the gracious green lawns.

Alamo is Spanish for poplar tree. A single cottonwood gave the 225-foot-high Alamo Hill its Spanish name when it was a midpoint resting place and watering hole on the narrow footpath between the Presidio and Mission Dolores. The name survives in the 12.7-acre park bounded by Fulton, Hayes, Steiner, and Scott streets.

A planning legacy from the earliest colonizers of San Francisco, Alamo Square is one of the "breathing holes of the city" described in *The Annals of San Francisco*, by Soulé, Gihon, and Nisbet. Shown as a public plaza in the 1853 Britton and Ray city map, it wasn't until 1868, when one of San Francisco's most tenacious squatters—"Dutch Charlie" Duane—was finally ousted that it was formally declared public land by the city fathers.

Begin this walk at 1198 Fulton Street, across from Alamo Square. Described by the Victorian Alliance as "grandly impressive," this Stick-Eastlake building constructed in 1889 is now an official San Francisco landmark—number 135. It is also a bed-and-breakfast inn called the Warner Embassy. In the 1930s, White Russians used the building as a social center and informal "embassy." In the basement ballroom during that period was a restaurant called Dark Eyes.

Guglielmo Marconi, inventor of the wireless and friend of an early owner, once broadcast from the building's tower. Some years later, a magician who lived in the tower room kept five hundred candles constantly burning, for some obscure occult reason.

Go north on Scott Street, away from the park for the moment, to see the attractive "workingman's Victorian" at 812 Scott, whose garage entrance has been imaginatively designed like a classic lych-gate.

Turn right on McAllister Street to pass a nice row of board-and-batten Victorians. Notice the banana trees across the street, an indicator of the mild weather in this neighborhood.

The Third Baptist Church at Pierce and McAllister streets had one of the first black congregations in San Francisco. Originally it stood on Russian Hill. Norman and Queen Anne towers and Frenchified townhouses stand farther along the street.

At Steiner Street, turn right, but look north first to locate the historic district boundary and, beyond it, the redevelopment area, which stopped short of Alamo Square. Fortune also smiled on the square in 1906 when the winds of fate blew the big fire of April 19 northward away from the square.

Turn right on Fulton Street and you are abreast of a spacious mansard-roof manor house built in 1904 for the Roman Catholic archbishop of San Francisco. It, too, has received official landmark status from the Landmarks Preservation Advisory Board. After a long history that included years as a home for working boys, it is now a bed-and-breakfast hostelry called, accurately enough, the Archbishop's Mansion. The three archbishops who succeeded Joseph Sadoc Alemany ruled their sees from here, and the cardinal who became Pope Pius XII was once a guest.

When you have admired the grace of the building, cross to Alamo Square's precious park and walk uphill on the Steiner Street periphery. One of the seven natural springs in the park still seeps along the sidewalk below the square.

Go into the park, and by working your way along the formal concrete steps and walkways ever upward, you reach a planted circle of Lombardy poplar trees. They surround the center of what once contained "Dutch Charlie" Duane's home.

As incredible as it seems, Duane was not only a convicted ballot-box stuffer, known killer, and member of the Muggins Gang, but also a top man in the city's fire department. To quote Theodore H. Hittel in his *History of California*, "On December 5, 1853, Charles P. Duane, an individual of lower instincts but of great activity, who was afterwards sent out of the country by the Vigilance Committee of 1856, was elected chief engineer, and the moral character of the fire department soon showed signs of deterioration."

Duane drove off other squatters from Alamo Square with his bare fists. During his exile in 1858, by no coincidence, the Legislature confirmed the square as a public park. Two years later he was back in the city, trying to regain the land. He might have succeeded in this outrageous claim if he hadn't imprudently shot Colonel William G. Ross on the City Hall steps one day.

Climb to the apex of the slope and walk east from the trees to see the best view of the famous houses of "Postcard Row." Annually the Victorian Alliance holds a house tour in which many homes are opened to the public.

The historic district extends in an irregular shape around the park, in some cases only half a block deep; in others, as much as two blocks. Explore as you wish.

To find other bed-and-breakfast spots nearby, look for Alamo Square Inn at 719 Scott, the Fay Mansion at 834 Grove, and Albion House at 135 Gough Street. Each has Victorian charms of its own.

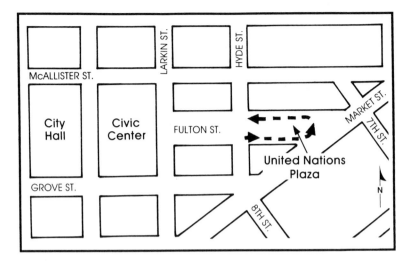

VEGGIES IN THE CITY

WALKING TIME: Allow an hour.

DISTANCE: One long block.

PUBLIC TRANSPORTATION: Muni buses 5, 6, 7, 9, 21, and 71. BART and Muni Metro lines have an exit on the Plaza.

PARKING: Best on Sundays.

CLOTHES: Casual. Bring a market basket.

TIMES: Wednesdays and Sundays 10 A.M.–6 P.M.

Cities change, for better or for worse. One of San Francisco's changes for the better in the past few years is the Heart of the City Farmers' Market, which blossoms occasionally in the United Nations Plaza. Like many European, South American, East Indian, and Oriental markets, it appears only at certain times, popping up as miraculously as a mushroom, vanishing without leaving a bean behind. An ever-varying cast of merchants populates this remarkable market.

To enjoy this colorful and walkable street scene, bring your market basket to the corner of Hyde and Fulton streets. United Nations Plaza is the point from which its original planners, John Galen Howard, Frederick H. Meyer, and John Reid, Jr., intended City Hall to be viewed.

Off at stage north, appropriately near the Main Public Library, Ashurbanipal, godfather of libraries, stands ready to set his pet cat on tardy book-borrowers. George W. Kelham was the architect of our Italian-

Renaissance treasure house of books. Now considered too small, one of the library's choice legacies is the vast Schmulowitz Collection of Wit and Humor.

Andrew Carnegie helped with the library's financing. Andrew Hallidie, inventor of the cable car, and Henry George, author of *Progress and Poverty* (New York: Robert Schalkenbach Foundation, 1979), served on its first board. George would have been appalled to see President Reagan's lasting legacy—the homeless—warming themselves like shabby, discarded books on the sunny south shelf of the library's splendid terrace.

Across Fulton Street, the ramp descends into Brooks Hall, Civic Center's underground garage–cum–exhibition hall, a place so nondescript that guidebooks seldom mention it. Marshall Square, beyond it, has been reduced to a parking lot.

The great South American liberator Simón Bolívar sits in bronze, booted and spurred, astride his steed at Fulton Street, about to cross Hyde Street on his way to City Hall. On his pediment on market day, overloaded shoppers surrounded by clumps of overflowing bags often rest to watch a street puppeteer artfully manipulate Charlie Chaplin's strings into a graceful pirouette.

Pause a moment to take in the whole happy scene. At first glance the panorama—the festive blue-and-gold umbrellas and awnings, cleverly placed between the handsome square columns of plaza street lamps, all backed by street trees, lawn, and well-designed buildings—looks like a party in progress.

In front of every booth facing the brick paving, clusters of Vietnamese, Cambodians, Thais, Taiwanese, Koreans, Chinese, East Indians, urban Native Americans, Hispanics, and Filipinos, sometimes dwarfed by Samoans or Tongans, are indicative of our city's changing population mix.

Women in Asian high-necked, padded jackets stand beside natives of Bengal in saris from India. Here and there among the many toddlers is a Hmong child in the bright red headdress traditional to these mountain people.

Smartly dressed African-American mothers from the nearby Western Addition stand beside Yuppies "into haute California cuisine" or jostle joggers in running shoes and sweats. A gray-suited, gray-faced professional man buys a pear for lunch alongside a portly woman buying a bushel of tomatoes to can.

Sometimes a gaggle of glowering punks of indeterminate gender is interspersed with the families, the tots in strollers, and the oldsters in outdated clothes pulling two-wheeled wire grocery toters.

The occasional disheveled street person passes almost unnoticed in the cosmopolitan crowd, but tourists stand out instantly as they stop to stare or focus cameras.

Work your way up to one of the stall fronts and you may not recognize one vegetable. Unusual among the stalls are the vendors of leaves. On one counter you may find okra leaves, chayote leaves, sweet pepper leaves, yam leaves, bitter-melon leaves, chrysanthemum leaves, and several kinds the salesladies know only by names in other languages. "Stir fry," one clerk told me. "Use in soup," added the other. "Cook small time. Like spinach."

Ten kinds of squash, along with squash blossoms, may await at another stall. I spotted turban, banana, white, Danish, acorn, butternut, pattypan, crookneck, Hubbard, Uto, and two kinds of zucchini.

On any given market day, an average of thirty farmers will be selling their produce in the plaza. This rural United Nations may come from any of forty California counties, for out-of-state produce is not allowed. Fresh flowers, dried tomatoes, newly harvested nuts, yams roasted on the spot, green olives, honey, locally caught fish, and shellfish all appear. Farmers may sell only what they raise themselves.

Halfway along the row of stalls, a group of round, white tables interjects a Continental touch into the scene. They are part of the little coffeehouse in the charming art deco building on the south side of the plaza. Pause for coffee and croissants if a table is empty and watch the market for a while.

There is something unifying about food and hunger. It is a jovial crowd that passes, happy at finding the foods of their homeland or the rare bargain of a bountiful harvest realistically priced. This is protein politics at its best.

When you have rested, continue down the double aisle of stalls toward Market Street. The water in the plaza fountain usually makes a splashing backdrop for the fishmongers. Many fish offered here have little or no market value elsewhere. The skate, shark, octopus, squid, kingfish, and live crayfish are easy to recognize. Some of the other small fish would be thrown out as "trash fish" by the average weekend fisherman and used only for bait by professionals. At the Heart of the City Farmers' Market, they are snapped up quickly.

Plant growers often have the booths nearest Market Street. Among their goods are fine collections of cactus, citrus trees, rose bushes, and, at Trini Escovedo's booth, ripe nopals and cactus pads, gourds suitable for drinking flasks, quinces, and lemons.

When you reach Market Street, reverse direction and take in the long view toward City Hall. The benevolent dome of City Hall, looming 308 feet aboveground in all its French Renaissance splendor, defines the western horizon. Dedicated in 1915 by Mayor James Rolph, Jr., it was designed by architects John Bakewell, Jr., and Arthur Brown, Jr., and cost $3.5 million to build.

When you have drunk in the beauty of our Beaux Arts governmental complex, stroll back toward Hyde Street passing stalls on the north side, where you will discover that the obelisk beside the United Nations Fountain disappears into the crowd. Look near it to find the longitude and latitude of San Francisco inscribed underfoot.

Under the first Civic Center plan of 1911, this approach to Civic Center was to be a grassy, tree-lined mall, a goal finally achieved in the late seventies by the Market Street Redevelopment Project. Handsome as it is when it is empty of people, it is much more fun on market days. Now what else was it I needed? Oh yes, dates. Halfway back toward Hyde Street, in a northside booth near Weber's oranges . . .

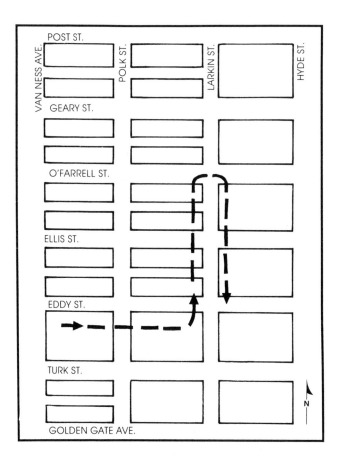

NEW TENDERLOIN

WALKING TIME: An hour.

DISTANCE: One mile.

PUBLIC TRANSPORTATION: Muni buses 19 Polk, 42, and 47.

PARKING: Tight.

CLOTHES: Whatever.

Like wildflower seeds that have found homes in cement cracks, resettled refugees of Cambodia, Laos, and Vietnam are putting down their roots in downtown San Francisco.

Within the rapidly changing fifty-block area centered along O'Far-

rell, Ellis, and Eddy streets between Market and Larkin, at least half the
population is now Southeast Asian. Larkin Street may have little re-
semblance to Phnom Penh or the Mekong River, but it has become the
main drag for these primarily rural people. Popping up throughout
the area are new restaurants where food has the delicate spices of
the tropical Indochinese peninsula, grocery stores where exotic foods
stand side by side with dishes and toys, and a few Oriental gift shops.

Brothels in the red-light district, long known as the Tenderloin, were
ordered closed in 1917, leaving what one writer described in 1963 as
"a pallid version indeed of the hoodlum districts of some cities." What
was left in the Tenderloin was "a number of perfectly respectable
hotels—along with others not so respectable . . ." Since that time,
oldsters and alcoholics have found they could afford the rents. So did
the social agencies resettling Southeast Asian refugees.

Call it gentrification if you like the word. For the walker and the
connoisseur of food, indeed for the Tenderloin itself, the changes bode
well. Tourists are already seeking out this section of the city as they do
Japantown, Chinatown, and the Latin barrio.

Smaller than their neighbors to the north, the people of the Indochinese peninsula are a forty-five-hundred-year-old blend. Cambodian legend says that the first of them popped out of pumpkins on a
vine that had grown from the nose of a chieftain's dead water buf-
falo. Some, the darker Malay type, came out of a spot burned on
the pumpkins. Others, the lighter Lao people, slipped through knife
slashes the chieftain made to let the men come forth.

Conquest from north of the peninsula brought the Thai—"the free."
Other waves of migration included the Funan, the Han, the Shan, and
Kublai Khan. According to Scott C. S. Stone and John E. McGowan, in
their book *Wrapped in the Wind's Shawl* (Presidio Press, 1980), "The
migration and the wars, the conquests and the exchanges of concepts,
the mistrust and skirmishes between highlander and lowlander—all
brought a kind of surface similarity to the face of Indochina. Beneath it
the ethnic differences continued to keep old animosities alive and
volatile . . ."

Begin the walk at the corner of Van Ness and Eddy streets. Walk east
two blocks on Eddy. En route, aficionados of the detective story may
want to glance at 620 Eddy, where Dashiell Hammett lived for several
years. At Larkin Street, the Caravan Lodge and Old Europe Restaurant,
long established in the area, give little hint of change.

Walk north on the west side of Larkin. Immediately you see the
Hung Wan Cafe, where the menu, posted in the window, reveals it as
Vietnamese.

Next door at Massis' Flowers, newspaper clippings of interest to
Southeast Asians are posted in the windows. If the Armenian owner,

Massis Bedayan, is out, there will be a Southeast Asian behind the counter. Bedayan is delighted with his new neighbors, commenting on their honesty and industriousness. "Ninety-nine percent of the people now living in this area are honest," Massis said. "It's better than most other peoples." While we talked, a tour bus pulled up next door to let its Chinese visitors lunch at the King Palace Restaurant.

Next door to the King Palace is another restaurant. "Why did you name it First Restaurant?" I asked Mrs. Van Botran, who owns the establishment with her husband. She replied simply, "We wanted it to be best." Refugees from Saigon, they opened the First Restaurant in 1982.

Beside the restaurant, just crying for venture capital, the big hole in the ground held the Marlow Hotel until it burned five years ago. Street people use the cavern under the sidewalks as a hotel, here in the shadow of the Federal Building.

Cross Willow Street to find the first Cambodian restaurant in San Francisco, the Phnom Penh, light and airy, with historic prewar photos of Cambodia on the walls. One of its owners, Ty Keav, was formerly a chef at the Big Four Restaurant on Nob Hill. Cambodian dancers sometimes perform here on a small stage.

"There are twenty-five hundred Cambodians in San Francisco," Ty's brother-in-law, Sari Karet, told me, "and there are twenty-five thousand in the Bay Area." California's Cambodian leadership has its offices over the restaurant.

Red bananas, lemon grass, Fuzu persimmons, three kinds of taro, tamarind, Japanese eggplant, and any number of unfamiliar spices are on sale next door at the Nhu Produce Market, the Vietnamese proprietor of which is proud to have been in the location for thirteen years. Calligraphic characters on the signs of Fairwind Travel, W & K Realty, and the Lucky Cafe down the block are another indication of the presence of an important new population.

Cross Ellis Street to find, at the southwest corner, Da La Thien, which specializes in seafood and has a tank of live lobsters in one window. Farther along Larkin, Treu Phong grocery stocks such Vietnamese specialties as gourami fish and silvernuts.

Cross Olive Street to pass Totie's, a long-established neighborhood bar that opens early in the day, a reminder of the old Tenderloin. J & E Delicatessen gives a cosmopolitan touch to the street, with grape leaves, feta cheeses, olives, and fried meat pies.

Elderly residents sitting on the many benches in the sun at the mini-park named for Sergeant John McCarthy at O'Farrell and Larkin are a blend of the old and new populations. Some wear the fur hats and long coats of the mountain people of Southeast Asia.

Cross to the east side of Larkin alongside another neighborhood bar, the Vagabond, and turn south to return on the opposite side of Larkin Street. As you cross, look east to locate the Cordon Bleu Vietnamese Restaurant and Yoko's Oriental Massage. An auricaria tree farther east on the street must be a welcome spot of green to expatriates from rural Southeast Asia.

Long lists of Cambodian, Laotian, Thai, Vietnamese, and Hmong names on apartment buzzer panels, as well as Oriental newspapers on doorsteps, are other indicators of the new population. Unused to the commodious living spaces available in this country, several families share many of the apartments.

At 730 Larkin Street is the Mekong Restaurant, which restaurant critic Patricia Unterman has given two stars for its food. Next to it, Dong Khanh grocery sells pickled banana flowers and a dozen kinds of rice sticks. Sanviet Dao's Rainbow Haircuts has one price for either men's or women's haircuts, as is the practice in Asia.

Look in at the southeast corner of Larkin and Ellis to find Ahmed Dajani, one of San Francisco's Palestinian grocers. Down the block is the Danh Mi Cafe, an ice-cream parlor that opened, owner Nancy Nguyen told me, just four years ago.

Nguyen's next-door neighbor, owner of yet another Vietnamese grocery, spoke so little English when I came this way that she had to fetch a friend from down the street to tell me she had been in this country four years. It is the lack of language that brings home the indomitable courage of the war-torn people of the Tenderloin. Starting a shop in a strange land in a language one barely comprehends has its challenges, but they must be as nothing to people who have weathered years in Khao I Dang camp or escaped out of Can Tho in a boat set upon by pirates.

Explore as you will in the nearby block. There is much else to discover, including Newman's Gym, a Filipino establishment called the Manila Beer Garden, Rent-a-Wreck Garage, the Bay Area Women's Resource Center, and Nancy's Antiques on Ellis, which has a window full of Black Mammy dolls. Keep your eyes and ears open and you may bring back, as I did, the poignant impression of a group of brown-eyed little boys hunkered on a sidewalk, creating from a tin of water a miniature river with many branches like the Mekong. They were floating straws on the stream, possibly the only toys available to them.

And they were laughing, quietly, happily . . .

PORTSMOUTH SQUARE

NOTE: *For map, see Chinatown, page 128.*

WALKING TIME: Allow an hour to relax.

DISTANCE: Four city blocks.

PUBLIC TRANSPORTATION: Muni buses 9-X and 15.

PARKING: Down under.

CLOTHES: Casual.

Among American cities, San Francisco is that rarity, an exciting town to walk. Indeed, as more people are discovering now that walking as noncompetitive sport is fashionable, it is the only way to truly know her. The hasty motorist may taste, between his home and office, a tantalizing sample of her charms, but it is the man on foot who feasts on this rich and saucy city.

The fare could vary daily all his life. The city offers infinite choices: great walks and good walks, lusty walks and sad, hiker's walks, children's walks, sea walks, secret silent walks known only to the aficionado, and the noisy promenades of the gaudy, the greedy, the cheap, the gauche, and the rest of us. Or if he chooses, a walker can go quietly through dell and highwater with the birdwatchers and still never leave the city.

As an opening excursion in San Francisco's manifold diversions, the novice walker might, for the sake of his calves, avoid both sand and peaks and begin his explorations where the city itself began, in Old Town.

"San Francisco has always been a city!" native sons sometimes boast, and by their definition, they are undeniably right. Before it became a city, however, San Francisco was for some eleven years the *pueblo* (village) of Yerba Buena (from the old place name El Paraje Yerba Buena—The Place of the Good Herb). It nestled between Broadway, Pine, and Stockton streets and the Bay. Its waterfront has since become Montgomery Street and its heart was the plaza we now call Portsmouth Square.

Around Portsmouth Square on January 30, 1847, clustered twenty buildings. Four of them were shops, one was a hide warehouse, one a mule-powered gristmill, one a washhouse, two doubled as hotels and taprooms, and one was an out-and-out saloon. The rest were homes.

On the plaza itself was the most important building in the village, the Customs House, which was the local seat of two governments in its time. It stood in the Walter U. Lum Place and Washington Street corner of the square (about opposite the site currently occupied by the excellent Sun Hung Hueng Restaurant) and was built in 1844 on order of the Mexican governor, José Figueroa. Typical of the municipal structures, it cost $2,800, instead of the $800 allotted for it. This was a substantial price for an adobe building fifty-six-feet long, twenty-two-and-one-half-feet wide, containing only four rooms. Outside were two long verandas and a tile roof. Many San Franciscans feel that the Customs House, our most significant historic taproot, should be reconstructed.

In 1962 Portsmouth Square, after many dowdy years, emerged from a face-lifting that included installing a garage in its depths. Now the garage is leaking and a renovation is also planned for the park perched on its roof. On the surface, it is one of the most usable small metropolitan parks in the world, notable especially for its children's play area, complete with a contemporary toy dragon to climb, and an outdoor game room for adults, removed from the children by the simple device of elevation.

The walking in this neighborhood is enjoyable indeed. For historical appreciation, begin at the corner of Kearny and Clay streets. When William Heath Davis stood here in 1833, this area was a potato patch, planted by Candelario Miramontes, who lived near the Presidio. Two years later, on June 25, Captain Don William Antonio Richardson built Yerba Buena's first residence uphill on what is now Grant Avenue and the village was started. The following year, neighbors arrived to build nearby. By the time Captain John B. Montgomery, commander of the American sloop of war the *Portsmouth*, marched his marines up Clay Street to fly the American flag on the plaza in 1864, there was a fair crowd to watch.

The marines landed at a propitious time. Sam Brannan and two hundred or so Mormon followers arrived just twenty-two days later, looking for a place to settle.

One report has it that when Brannan saw the flag he grumbled and swore, but he stayed. A year later, there were one hundred fifty-seven buildings around the plaza including a printing press and a school. It was Washington A. Bartlett, *alcalde*, as the mayors were then called, of the village, who renamed it San Francisco. He did it to get the jump on another ambitious village now called Benicia at a time when settlers felt the town that bore the same name as the Bay would be the one to prosper.

The Gold Rush and the forty-niners did the rest to make a city of San Francisco. Almost as soon as the words "Gold! Gold from the American River!'' were shouted by Sam Brannan on the plaza, the transformation was under way. Soon there were saloons, gambling houses, shops, and hotels surrounding the square. Edward Bosqui, famous for his printing house, recorded in his memoirs that he once climbed a ladder to the attic of the old Customs House and found the forgotten effects of officers killed at the 1846 Battle of San Pasqual.

It was in the Customs House, about 2 A.M. on the morning of June 1, 1851, that Bosqui awakened to see the vigilantes hang thief John Jenkins from a beam at the south end of the building. Bosqui records that Sam Brannan honored the last request of Jenkins for a cigar by giving him his own to smoke. Brannan, in charge, then called for a mighty heave of the rope and Jenkins's cigar and life went out in the same puff. Legend says Brannan retrieved the cigar.

By 1879–1880, when poet Robert Louis Stevenson arrived in San Francisco, the city had already expanded beyond Larkin Street, and there were Chinese children playing in Portsmouth Square as they do today. The marker given by Stevenson's friends and the tablet commemorating the square's historic flag raising are both there for the walker to discover. On the Washington Street perimeter, look also for Buddha's Universal Church, built by hand by its parishioners. Park renovation may delete the ''Bridge over the River Kearny,'' but if it is still there, cross it to reach the Holiday Inn, which resembles a shogun's palace and has the Chinese Cultural Center on its third floor. In its side alley, Merchant Street, the famous Blue Fox Restaurant continues to flourish, just across from what was once the old city morgue. Watch for historical markers throughout Old Town.

MONTGOMERY STREET

WALKING TIME: Thirty minutes.

DISTANCE: Seven blocks.

PUBLIC TRANSPORTATION: Muni bus 15 or 30.

PARKING: Ghastly.

CLOTHES: Yuppified.

If the legion of unquiet dead hover in the hectic air of late October, seeking out on All Hallow's Eve the ways they frequented in life, then surely the place to find them in San Francisco is on lower Montgomery Street, counting house of the West and, without doubt, the grandest canyon in our jungle.

From a distance, the bastions of the San Francisco financial district that cluster about the meshwork of city lanes abutting Montgomery near California soar as part of that romantic skyline that has been called, among other things, "an architectural zoo" and the "most beautiful in North America."

The scale was closer to human dimensions in 1850 when the mail steamer *Oregon* landed, bringing official news that California had been admitted to the Union. Every banker, broker, and merchant on the street closed shop to watch or march in celebration. The reviewing stand was at California and Montgomery and the favorite tune of the day was "Yankee Doodle."

Parades rarely march along Montgomery today, but the street from Columbus to Market is an interesting walk at any time. On weekdays Montgomery awakens before daybreak, when trading starts on the "big Board" in New York, and becomes a world with its own language, laws, traditions, and superstitions. By 9 A.M. the "catastrophe of sky-scrapers," as world-famous architect Le Corbusier called them, absorbs enough brokers, bankers, insurance and clerical workers to populate Stockton. On Sundays, it is an empty echoing unroofed vault.

Compactness, always a fine feature of the financial district, makes it possible to see the big new buildings without seven-league boots. San Francisco's first significant office building, commonly known as the "Monkey Block," stood for a hundred years on Montgomery at Washington. It was built in 1853 by "Old Brains," General Henry W. Halleck, on a foundation of redwood logs. The Transamerica Pyramid, a spire in scale with the city's new tall skyline, now sits on the site, complete with mini-redwood grove.

In the next block, the Bank of Canton has neatly wrapped itself around the 1854 Subtreasury Building and given it new life as the Pacific Heritage Museum, with shows from all the Asian countries. Other significant buildings are farther along the street. The walker will enjoy visiting 420 Montgomery, where the Wells Fargo Bank has its history room. Here, as nowhere else in the city, the drama, humor, dignity, and sometimes all-too-human scale of man's pursuit of money, is revealed. A stunning 1877 photographic panorama of San Francisco lines the walls of Wells Fargo's fourteenth-floor executive suite. The photographer was Eadweard Muybridge, famous today as the father of the motion pictures. It was he who photographed horses trotting so Leland Stanford could win a bet. In his own time Muybridge was infamous for killing his wife's lover. A jury acquitted him with the comment from its foreman, "Hell, we'd of done the same thing!"

Some financial-district buildings are visually exciting from the street. Look at the Bank of America Building, the Crown Zellerbach, with its small and witty carousel outbuilding, the Industrial Indemnity Building, whose arches roof the sidewalk to the delight of rainy-day shoppers, San Francisco Federal Savings, which has an air curtain, and the Bethlehem and International buildings. All of these have architectural concern for the eyeline as well as the skyline, a wonderfully human consideration common in great European cities but, in the past of wall-to-wall canyons, much lacking in ours. Such architectural enrichment could be a factor in saving cities as cultural centers.

The walker will encounter many other trends quickening. One is that industry has discovered the best employees, especially those whose work is dull, go to the firms that have the most pleasant surroundings. This has made it good business to provide generous space, imaginative color, good lighting, comfortable furnishings, and elegant lounges unto the least of these. Calendar art and institutional blah are out. Gardens in the sky and fountains are in. Original art is now not only de rigueur in top-brass bailiwicks but also in corridors, cafeterias, waiting rooms, and public lobbies. At one point there is a fountain below the street, inviting the walker down to it. To hundreds of San Franciscans, reflecting the city's tradition of merry irreverence, the Mascharini bronze sculpture in the Crown Zellerbach lobby is fondly known as "Olive Oyl," the great stone lump at the Bank of America mall as the "Banker's Heart."

Montgomery Street had its share of stony hearts, among them financiers Charles Crocker, Collis Huntington, Mark Hopkins, James G. Fair, James C. Flood, Lucky Baldwin, Darius O. Mills, and Senator

William Sharon. The stoniest that ever showed up on Montgomery was that of the city's first suicide, William Glen Rae, one-time factor of a Hudson Bay Company trading post at Montgomery and Commercial. When workmen were putting the first gas line through this corner, they found Rae in a glass-covered coffin. His face was eerily identifiable through the oval glass. Some bystander admitted, "Alas, poor Willie, I knew him, Horatio," or words to that effect.

Another Montgomery ghost one might encounter is banker Billy Ralston, who swam to his death at Aquatic Park in the days of rough-tough speculation in Comstock mining stocks. Black Friday and Asbury Harpending's great diamond hoax are both fantastic chapters in the city's business life.

History continues to walk the street. The new Standard Oil Building, at 555 Market, is another museum that is free to the public. Until other Pacific ports can match it, anecdote for episode, and inch for thousand-dollar-running inch of front footage, San Francisco will continue to be The City, and the West Coast stronghold of a freedom sometimes called Capitalism.

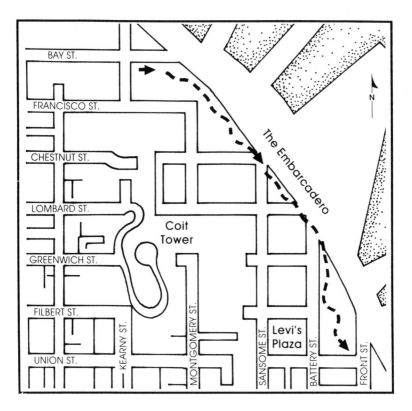

THE EMBARCADERO

WALKING TIME: Allow an hour.

DISTANCE: About a mile.

PUBLIC TRANSPORTATION: Muni buses 32 and 42.

PARKING: Metered.

CLOTHES: Jogging sweats will do.

That broad airy fringe of piers we call The Embarcadero swings around the city's northeast corner and along its east side like a smile.

It was here that the great ships came and went, bringing passengers and cargo from faraway places with romantic names like Karachi, Caracas, Kowloon, and Callao. There was nothing in the city that could quite compare with a walk along it.

The waterfront presented a kaleidoscopic panorama, full of compelling vitality and contrasts. Cavernous pier sheds, mysterious when shut, revealed imports from all over the world when their doors were open. Tubs of soy, tins of tea, barrels of porcelain, ranks of autos, or bales of hay stood beside great sacks of coffee beans or boxes of Scotch, sometimes spilling their wares out into the street.

Sleek hulls loomed between the sheds—sometimes brown and rusty, bringing a whiff of the South Seas, sometimes elegant and white, pennants flying, awaiting the passengers that would board for Honolulu, Yokohama, Manila, or Bangkok. The encircling Bay lapped cold and deep in easy drowning distance on one side. On the other, freight locomotives shunted cars along the "Front," as maritime men called it, sometimes stopping at the old Eagle Cafe while their crews ran inside for coffee. It was a colorful place.

Slowly, subtly, The Embarcadero has been changing from industrial to recreational. Vigilant members of the Telegraph Hill Neighborhood Association have fought to keep new construction at the four-story height limit of the old "godowns," or warehouses, so the skyline hasn't been altered for the worse. The big change that has happened in this transition is the addition of bits and pieces of parkland. Studded with lawns, berms, trees, and meandering walkways, it makes the waterfront increasingly urbane, as well it might be, for when it was built, the Belt Line Railroad consumed a twenty-nine-acre waterfront park. Thanks to the good offices of the Bay Conservation and Development Commission and the San Francisco Planning Department, some of that land has been returned to public park use.

To make this walk, begin at the corner of Kearny and Bay streets. At the outset, look west through one of the city's most beautiful double lines of street trees. When the *Noordam* or *Pacific Princess* is in port, Bay Street makes a welcome avenue for cruise passengers, who often throng the street en route to Cost Plus Imports and Fisherman's Wharf.

The great art deco buildings set about with lawns on either side of Bay Street are part of the Northpoint Sewage Treatment Plant. For a pigeon's eye view of the plant, take a one-block digression up Kearny Street via the wooden steps to the dead end of Francisco Street.

Then walk east on Bay Street until you reach a new red-brick office building near The Embarcadero. Pause beside it when Bay Street terminates to look north toward the 5.2-acre park that fronts Pier 39 and, south of that, the big masts of Hornblower Yachts.

Turn right and pass the Rusty Scupper Restaurant, whose clientele gets a suitably salty view of the Bay, while walkers draw pleasure from the shrubbery around it. Continue along the serpentine walkway that meanders among groups of trees. Pause when the pathway descends near a building to see how the berms of earth and thick foliage diminish street noise in this welcome green space.

At Montgomery and Chestnut streets, you reach the home of KNBR, the local NBC radio outlet. Beyond it is Physis, a trendy health club. Downtown office workers often jog along the other side of The Embarcadero. On weekdays around noon, there are so many joggers and runners coming along the sidewalk fronting the piers that a walker can be bowled over.

Zig and zag with the sidewalk, crossing the streets that terminate at The Embarcadero, but don't be tempted to cross that busy road except at a stoplight.

When you reach the little triangular plaza that was the apron of the old Belt Line quarter-round house, notice how cleverly cobbles have been laid around the tracks that led into the building. A new bench outlines the portion that faces Sansome Street. Look up at the face of the building, now remodeled, where five huge doors once admitted locomotives to the five bays for servicing. Walk over toward the tracks and go south to discover that the old water spout, where steam engines were tanked up, now has become an imaginative little fountain. The Sandhouse, the office building next to it, contained sand for cooling engines. After you have explored the well-planted little atrium, go alongside the Sandhouse to exit near Battery Street, and head toward the shiny Fog City Diner.

Long ago, there really was an artillery battery on Battery Street. Telegraph Hill was rounded at the time and the battery stood on the slope of the hill, two hundred feet higher than today's street level.

Turn left on the first path you reach after passing the Fog City Diner. Within a few steps you enter Levi's Plaza, with a park that is undoubtedly the most ambitious and sophisticated of the additions to the waterfront. Almost immediately, you will begin to perceive Levi's Plaza's most elaborate conceit, a little mountain stream that pretends to find its way to the Bay, passing through a mountain meadow and creating a miniature lagoon en route.

When you reach the footbridge, pause a moment to look bayward to see how cleverly the mini-watercourse seems to run under The Embarcadero. Then continue south, rambling along with the pathway until you reach a "Sierra waterfall" over the huge granite slabs, where the stream seems to originate. Actually, the water is recycled back from the terminus near The Embarcadero to start its melodic journey again and again. Lawrence Halprin was the park's designer.

When you reach Filbert Street, three great choices await. One is Grace Marchant Garden, uphill beside the Filbert Street steps. Another is the eastern and more citified block of Levi's Plaza, which also has a remarkable fountain of many waterfalls. The third choice is to turn east instead, just past the "Sierra waterfall." Within steps you are back at the Belt Line tracks again. The choice is yours.

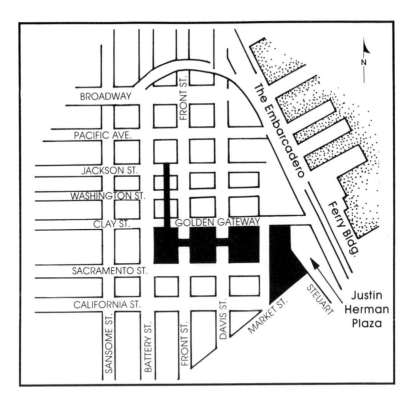

EMBARCADERO CENTER

WALKING TIME: One-half day if you linger.

DISTANCE: Almost a mile.

PUBLIC TRANSPORTATION: BART, the Marin Ferry, fifteen bus lines, and any Market Street streetcar.

PARKING: Underground and expensive.

CLOTHES: Urbane.

San Francisco has a convenient trail-system-in-the-sky. With the completion of John Portman's Four Embarcadero Center, it became possible to walk from Ferry Park at Steuart and Market streets to Sidney Walton Park at Pacific and Front streets, safely removed from traffic all the way. This remarkable walk, fourteen years a-building, connects three parks by means of a festive upper-level promenade designed to be

Embarcadero Center and lily (symbol for the center).

strolled. The amenities must be seen to be believed. Monumental works of public art, fountains, sidewalk tables for brown-bagging it or just lingering in the sun, greenery, comfortable benches, open courts, ramps, bridges, streetside restaurants and watering holes, galleries, bookshops, trendy boutiques, and entrancing vistas of San Francisco Bay make the mile-long walk unique.

There are several good times to make this walk. For art lovers and architecture buffs, it is Sundays, when the crowds are diminished. For shoppers, Saturdays or the midweek hours before and after lunchtime. For romantics, it is twilight. On a clear day, when the sun sinks slowly into the west as in an old travelogue, there is nothing to compare with sitting at Lily's or Scott's or La Fuente, watching the pink afterglow deepen while twinkling lights around the Bay wink on one by one.

To make this walk, transport yourself to Ferry Park. Early franchises granted originally to serve the Ferry Building have created better public transportation here than anywhere else in the city.

Walk into Ferry Park and bear southeast to examine the berms, benches, street furniture, tall trees, and sculpture. The equestrian is Juan Bautista de Anza. The bus turnaround is another legacy from a time when San Francisco had perfect public transportation. The first turnaround was below street level on The Embarcadero, where it was possible to walk into the Ferry Building via a ramp, or from this level, via bridge. Go through the Justin Herman Plaza to experience the celebration of rushing water in the Vaillancourt Fountain, designed so that the walker can go under the falls without getting wet by walking on big concrete stepping stones.

As you emerge, look up at the big tulip-in-outline, the architect-designed sculpture known as "lily," which has become a symbol for this group of office buildings, hotels, and skybridges. Walk across the Plaza toward it. An outdoor theater is part of this wide expanse of brick.

Go up the broad steps toward the sidewalk tables and the double line of zelkova trees. When you reach the handsome staircase that spirals upward, you are at Commercial Street. Like Market Street, it has always had an open view to the Ferry Building clock tower and the booklike slabs of office buildings were designed to keep that openness clear.

Tempting as it is to go up the stairway immediately, look around this level first for such winners as Huckleberry's Ice Cream Parlour, the Expresso Experience coffeehouse, Mrs. Field's Chocolate Chippery, and the San Francisco Boulangerie. Some other surprises worth seeking on street level are the Nature Company, where everything for sale delights the nature lover without exploiting the natural world; Chris-

tian Bernard, a French jeweler where jeweled gold-handled tooth-
brushes and razors are an ultimate status treasure; the World of Cut-
lery, which has samurai swords; Waldenbooks; and Richter's, where
one can choose a song for your music box from a library of three
hundred.

Walk up the spiral ramp when you have discovered these and other
unusual shops to reach the lobby level, where almost all of the clothing
shops feature designer clothes. Two of the important pieces in Embarcadero Center's remarkable fiberworks collection hang through this
level. They are big soft sculptures by Sheilah Hicks. Go past the escalator to find them. After you enjoy their depth of color and texture, look
for the hundred-year-old wooden Indian at Somerset General Store,
then go in to discover that the store lives up to its name, selling
shoestrings and nails, among other unlikely things. Also worth seeking
out on this level is Peck & Peck's, which has antique French pressed-tin
wall panels.

The bridge leading west over Drumm Street promises more entice-
ments, but for the moment return to the big spiral ramp around the
tulip, which, incidentally, is lighted in rich pink at night, to reach the
podium level of Four Embarcadero Center. Unusual on this level are
Applause, where the desk embellishments would suit a czarina; Games
Women Play, where everything is designed by women for women's
comfort; and Pastabella, which makes its own pasta and offers a choice
of sauces.

Walk toward Lily's Restaurant, a branch of the famous Philadelphia
establishment, to find another skybridge, which leads into the lobby
level of the Hyatt Regency Hotel. Go in and bear left through the lobby
for one of this new mini-city's great visual experiences, the Eclipse
Fountain and the soaring atrium. Then go down the steps at the eastern
end to find you have made a little loop bringing you back to Justin
Herman Plaza.

If you are game for more walking, go back to the circular staircase at
the end of Commercial Street, climb to the lobby level, and explore all
those other enticing shops. Or, to see twenty or more additional public
sculptures, cross Drumm Street via the skybridge. Following the upper
level along the line of Commercial Street across Davis and Front streets
will reveal the other three Embarcadero Center buildings, each of
which has its own collection of unusual restaurants and shops to
explore. Turn north in One Embarcadero Center to cross skybridges
over Sacramento, Clay, Washington, and Jackson streets. En route you
will pass through Maritime Plaza surrounding the Alcoa Building, and
Golden Gateway, to reach Sidney Walton Park. The return trip is just as
much fun.

GOLDEN GATEWAY AND EMBARCADERO CENTER

NOTE: *For map, see Embarcadero Center, page 116.*

WALKING TIME: Allow an hour.

DISTANCE: About one mile.

PUBLIC TRANSPORTATION: Union Street bus 41.

PARKING: Ouch!

CLOTHES: Sophisticated.

James Morris of *The Guardian*, in his excellent book *Cities*, called San Francisco "the most lyrical city of the New World, one of the half dozen loveliest on earth . . . She is unique. . . . She represents the civilization of North America at its most subtle and imaginative. She proves how gracefully Western man might have learnt to live, were it not for the preoccupations of war and power."

These are delicious words. But he also said: "I think we are watching the last years of San Francisco's prime." His reason was that the city is becoming too much like other places, especially too much like other parts of the United States. "She is a little more tawdry than she used to be as the conformity of capitalism begins to swamp her . . ." As in other places "we live in a rookery, and phoenixes are out of date."

This is a consideration the walker can take along in his mind while inspecting the redeveloped forty-four acres now known as the Golden Gateway and Embarcadero Center. Well planned with buildings tall and short, much contemporary art, lively fountains, malls, and open spaces, it lies between Market Street and Broadway, close to the water but separated visually from it by the barrio of traffic. Native sons recall the area as the old produce district of their grandparents, as Yerba Buena Cove where hundreds of sailing ships were abandoned in the Gold Rush of 1849.

A likely place to begin this walk is Sidney Walton Square, at Pacific and Front streets, a contemporary Gramercy Park. The lowrise Golden Gateway Commons defines the square on the north and west sides. As you enter the park under the old brick arch that was once a part of Colombo Market, try to imagine the excitement that bubbled like champagne in the spring of 1960 when a design competition described

Vaillancourt Fountain (Justin Herman Plaza).

as "San Francisco's Hundred-Million-Dollar Contest" was judged by an international architectural panel. The experts chose a plan submitted by the Perini Corporation, the joint efforts of Wurster, Bernardi and Emmons, Demars and Reay, and Pietro Belluschi.

The sculpture in the park, François Stahly's *Fountain of the Four Seasons*, is also a clock on which one can tell time by the rise and fall of water within an hour cycle. Climb the footbridge that leads to Buckalew House and to Whale Ship Plaza, a square surrounded by

The Eclipse Fountain in the Hyatt Regency at The Embarcadero.

eleven small two-story townhouses that give Golden Gateway airiness and perspective. The Richard Henry Dana Building is the great stack of cookies that fronts on Battery Street, Macondray House, the blue tower. All have contemporary art worth seeking out. From Whale Ship Plaza, take the footbridge across Washington Street to the Alcoa Building, designed by Skidmore, Owings, and Merrill. Only die-hards insist that it looks like the box the Crown Zellerbach Building came in. The charming *Dandelion Fountain* of Robert Woodward is one of the delights of the second-floor public park, which has an eastern staircase that leads down through trees between the freeway off ramps toward the big blocky Vaillancourt Fountain, a symphony of water at play. From some vantages it looks like the front yard of the great ziggurat that is the Hyatt Regency Hotel.

Another footbridge crosses Sacramento Street to reach One Embarcadero Center, the southernmost book in that tall row of books sans bookends. John Portman Associates were the architects of these buildings, and the late M. Justin Herman was the farsighted man who would not let them block off Commercial Street's view to the Ferry Building. The phallic three-story stainless steel sculpture that pierces two levels of the plaza is not a smokestack. Willi Gutmann designed it.

Two blocks northeast is the misleadingly numbered Hyatt Regency, located at Market and Drumm streets, but called Five Embarcadero Center. Elsewhere in San Francisco, with easy-to-remember logic, street numbering begins at the water or at Market Street. The high hanging ball in the Hyatt's vast interior central court is *Eclipse* by Charles Perry. Steps at the far end lead directly to Justin Herman Plaza and its lively scene. Linger here a while to reflect on poet Phillip Whalen's complaint that the United States really exports nothing but "downtown," and that it is possible to travel the world and never lose or escape it. And yet, viewing these towers from this mellow spot, one wonders perhaps if there is a fashionable phoenix after all.

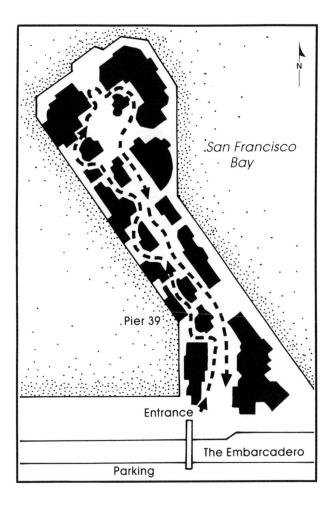

San Francisco
Bay

Pier 39

Entrance

The Embarcadero

Parking

PIER 39

WALKING TIME: Half hour, or all day.

DISTANCE: Two city blocks.

PUBLIC TRANSPORTATION: Muni bus 32 Embarcadero.

PARKING: Great at Pier 39 garage (approach from Stockton and Beach streets).

CLOTHES: Take a sweater. Bring money.

If revels and jollity are what you seek, why then the world's thine oyster. At San Francisco's tourist mecca, the posh pseudo-wharf called Pier 39, you don't even need a sword to open it.

The recycled industrial wharf, our trendy latter-day Playland, is a stage set for pleasure. San Francisco children voted it the place where they have the most fun. Credit for this appeal must be given to its carousel, calliope, talented street performers, roving food vendors, and to Funtasia. A 1980s version of the old penny arcade, The San Francisco Experience re-creates the 1906 Earthquake. There are also electronic games, bumper cars, and Music Tracks where you can record your own hit song, and there's the new Mindscraper, a thrilling simulated ride on the imaginary Colossus, billed as the tallest, fastest roller coaster in America. A terrifying two-minute ride, its simulated trip is so realistic that even the most daring viewers are strapped to their seats. Kids love it.

Colored lights outline Pier 39's vaguely Victorian roofline, tracing the deliberately frivolous architecture. Little white lights twinkle in festoons, hanging baskets, and a menagerie of topiary animals add a sweet sense of nostalgia to the romantic scene. For counterpoint, there are the salty flap of halyards from sailboats on one side of the pier and the friendly hum of busy tour boats on the other.

Over, around, between, and beyond Pier 39's nearly one hundred shops and dozen restaurants, there is a million-dollar view. In three directions, all of San Francisco Bay is the backdrop, with its bridges, boats, highlands, islands, changing moods, fleeting clouds, dappled sunlight, frothy whitecaps, and occasional probing finger of fog. Look inland, and the city's sophisticated downtown skyline peeks over the three nearest hills.

Whatever the season, it is a festive scene. Banners from tall flagpoles at the north end of Powell Street to the west flutter in the breeze. Nicely kept lawns, set off by floral borders, are punctuated by shrubs, sculpture, and cobble-surrounded benches. Sycamore trees parade two abreast along the walkway, shielding Pier 39 from the traffic noises of The Embarcadero. A long observation pier defines the far border of the western basin, where tour boats of the Blue and Gold fleet purr in and out.

Look east, where the three-hundred-fifty-berth marina is fronted by a pier for large visiting yachts. Facing it is a children's playground and, on the broad lawn, sculptor Roger Barr's keyhole for cloud-viewing, the twenty-six-foot-high ribbon of stainless steel called *Skygate*. Located beyond will stand Underwater World, a seven-foot-tall seamless transparent acrylic tunnel, four hundred feet long and shaped like a figure eight. Twin to one in Auckland, New Zealand, this aquarium lets visitors stay dry while getting a diver's view of the sea life indigenous to the Bay.

The forty-five-acre Pier 39 complex is connected at every watery border by a public trail. Thanks to the foresight of the San Francisco Planning Commission and the Bay Conservation and Development Commission, the public shoreline was built into the boot-shaped pier ten years ago, anticipating the Bay Rim Trail being planned by the Association of Bay Area Governments to encircle San Francisco Bay.

First-time visitors should follow Pier 39's own walking tour. It begins at the entrance plaza, upstairs on the west balcony alongside the Eagle Cafe. (If you are in a wheelchair, take an elevator behind Funtasia on the east side to reach the upper level.)

For eighty years, the Eagle Cafe stood on the Powell Street intersection of the Belt Line Railroad tracks, a favorite hangout for longshoremen when ours was an active working port. Unchanged since it was lifted—clock, stock, and berry pies—to this aerie, the Eagle has a flavor of yesteryear, with its homestyle cooking and collection of historical photos.

Start walking along the broad balcony into the depths of the pier and you soon reach a footbridge. Go to its center for an overview of the jumping commercial heart of the pier. (The San Francisco Experience multimedia movie may entice you further.) From the bridge, one can see that the street below has changing elevations, cleverly varied by short side lanes and little byways. Unless there is a performance under way at the stage below, raise your eyes to the roofline. Reminiscent of an earlier time, the roofline appears to define cut-stone buildings. Actually, the gray-and-white facing of these lighthearted structures is distressed wood, much of it salvaged from the old working pier that preceded Pier 39 on this site.

Architects John C. "Sandy" Walker and Bruce Moody intended their design to be "postmodern or ad-hoc populistic." To say it another way, "the buildings are, in the vernacular, intended for mass consumption merchandising."

Although detractors were many when the pier opened in 1978, the visiting public has loved it from the outset. If there are performers entertaining at Stage One below you, linger for a while and watch the show. Then return to the west side and continue north, visiting the shops that interest you, admiring the views, reading the plant labels on the many big containers of seasonal plants, or watching the boats below—whichever suits your fancy.

There are at least nine toy stores to visit or avoid, depending on your pleasure. Gift shoppers can find gems, clothing, posters, yo-yos, T-shirts, music boxes, magic tricks, and dozens of collectibles, including specialized items for left-handers, gardeners, and needlecrafters as well as for music, baseball, film, and auto buffs. A second stage is located in the next court. You'll know if a juggler, a puppeteer, or a mime is performing by the crowd that begins to form whenever it's near the time posted on an old vaudeville apron board. The third atrium has the double-deck carousel, handcrafted in Reggio, Italy, as its centerpiece. Calliope music spills from the carousel when the ponies and gondolas are rocking.

Go all the way to the end of the pier for a stunning Bay view and a good look at the colony of sea lions that recently have taken up residence here. Then loop around to the east balcony, descend when it ends, and make your way back through the interior at its lower level. Last time I wended my way through this kaleidoscope, laughter and music filled the air. A young man thrust out his chest to display a T-shirt he had just bought. Nearby, three girls dropped hot popcorn onto a fluff of pink cotton candy to give it a smiling face. A little troupe of Spanish-speaking strollers went by, carrying hot *churros*, laughing and chattering as they passed. An older couple emerged from the San Francisco Music Box Company with a snow globe playing "Send in the Clowns."

It may not have "Laughing Sal," the papier-mâché frump who once welcomed the crowds to Playland-at-the-Beach, but Pier 39 has that playful ambiance that lets us all be kids again. After all, as Fred Thompson, one of the entrepreneurs who built Coney Island, insisted, all adults are just boys and girls grown tall. Especially near Christmastime.

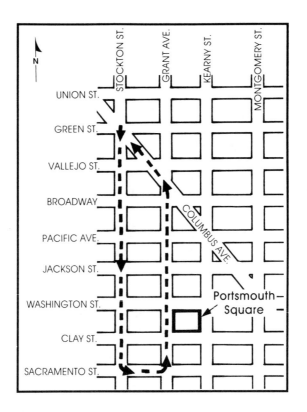

CHINATOWN

WALKING TIME: Two to four hours.

DISTANCE: Two miles.

PUBLIC TRANSPORTATION: Muni bus 15 or 30, known as the "Orient Express."

PARKING: Under Portsmouth Square.

CLOTHES: Casual.

In old Chinese calligraphy, the character "to walk" originally resembled a crossroad. Now it looks more like two road signs, according to Gordon Lew, publisher of the bilingual weekly *East-West*, who thinks, "The slanted one was probably damaged by a nearsighted motorist who wanted to read the sign but was a little slow on the brakes."

Logically enough, the character for pedestrian is "walking person"; for a planet, "walking star"; and a priest, "walking feet," referring to the traveling monks of old China. "Walk," however, also means a business firm, possibly because such firms were destination for a walk. So a bank is a "money walk," and of course every Chinese hopes the bank won't. Because the thunder god is walking around, in Chinese the word is actually "walking thunder." The folklore is that you can tell from the loudness whether the thunder god is walking toward or away from you.

Gordon Lew also tells a great walking story: "Once someone asked a wise man, 'If a man comes up and says there is a pot of gold somewhere, should I ignore him or should I hurry there to find out if he's right?'

" 'If you ignore him, you may miss something valuable,' said the wise man. 'If you rush over, you may be disappointed.' " To find the wise man's answer, see the end of this walk.

Meantime, to begin it, start at Green Street and Stockton. Make your way along Stockton Street, bearing south. Within two blocks you reach "Little Hong Kong," as Chinatown's busiest crossroads, Broadway and

Chinatown Gate (Grant Avenue at Bush Street).

Stockton, has been nicknamed. Often it teems with shoppers six abreast.

At the outset, notice Acme Center, whose frozen specialties are visible through the window, so you needn't enter if they don't have what you seek. As with many Hong Kong shops, it is half the size of an ordinary shop. Head south on the east side of Stockton for this first block, to get a distant perspective on the fish, fruit, pastry, vegetables, and meat shops. The fronts of many open to the street and their wares spill out; these shops are usually aswarm with people of both genders, carefully selecting each kingfish, bitter melon, water chestnut, or long bean. From this aspect, the ubiquitous shopping bags sometimes seem to be pulling the people, rather than the opposite.

At Pacific, cross to the west side of the street and join the throng just for the fun of it. "Color was everywhere. A thousand little notes of green and yellow, of vermillion and sky blue assaulted the eye," Frank Norris wrote of Chinatown in *Blix*. "Here it was a doorway, there a vivid glint of cloth or hanging, here a huge scarlet sign lettered with gold, and there a kaleidoscopic effect in garments of the passersby." The mélange is still the same. At Chinese New Year, piles of oranges, pomelos, and tangerines; red and gold paper streamers; flowering tree branches; kumquat and azalea plants on sale intensify an already lively area. New shops, such as Kay Wah Pastry, the Bon Vivant, Lun Wah, and Sun Sang markets, interspersed with older ones such as On Ning Tong Herb Shop, Wing Fat, or Fong Creamery tell the story of the resurgence that followed the passage of the Immigration and Nationality Act amendments in 1965. Chinatown, almost bursting at the seams with new energy, has some of the ambiance of a boom town. Big, green potted plants with congratulatory red streamers traditionally indicate a new business.

As you reach Mandarin Towers, Chinatown's first highrise apartment building, you are nearing the portion of Stockton that publicist Charlie Leong called "The Street of Celestial Wisdom" because of its schools, churches, civic groups, and Chinese institutions. The Presbyterian Church in Chinatown, which dates from 1907 at this site, has the largest tree on the street. St. Mary's Catholic Center across the street is also an old-timer.

At Clay Street you reach the Kong Chow Building, which houses the new post office. Between 1 and 4 P.M., go into the discreet foyer and take the elevator to the Taoist Kong Chow Temple on the fourth floor, where seventeen gods sit on the altar. Chief among them is Kwan Ti, god of war and peace. Re-created after more than a hundred years on Pine Street, the temple, designed by architect Ed Sue, also has a fascinating view of the cityscape. Inspect the altar and its offerings including the toy motorcycle that stands alongside the god's horse and other pets. Note the ancestors' room behind the main altar and observe the fireplace for sending prayer papers to heaven, then go out on the Stockton Street balcony. Unexpectedly, both Angel and Yerba Buena islands are visible. So are both levels of the Stockton Street tunnel. Next door, the Chinese Six Companies is informally known as the city hall of Chinatown. Central Chinese High School and Kuoming Tong are other institutions in the block visible from the balcony.

If you are game for more walking, Grant Avenue, Chinatown's main street and the tourist trinket trail, is one block downhill. Loop back on it to your point of origin for this walk.

The wise man's answer, incidentally, is, " 'If there is no gold, you may enjoy your walk, which will always bring you good health, for good health is better than gold.' "

JAPANTOWN/DOWNTOWN

WALKING TIME: Allow an hour.

DISTANCE: Six blocks.

PUBLIC TRANSPORTATION: Powell Street cable cars.

PARKING: None.

CLOTHES: Executive posh.

Little by little, without fanfare and almost unnoticed, an outpost of Japantown has been emerging downtown like a cluster of mussels on the rock that is Chinatown. It is linked to the waves of tourists that ebb and flow through the city.

Perceptive lunchtime gourmets who try a different restaurant daily may be aware of it. Japan Air Lines skippers and crews who fly in and out of the city know about it. So do thousands of Japanese visitors who have poured into San Francisco since the yen outstripped the dollar. But so subtle is the change you could stop an average downtown worker a block away to ask for directions and draw a puzzled look.

The Japanese cluster of hotels, restaurants, and specialty shops lies near Chinatown's great gate along Bush Street in the 400–600 blocks between Monroe Place and Mark Lane. Begin at Powell and Bush and walk east. The cosmopolitan ubiety becomes apparent on the north side of Bush Street at Monroe Place, with La Coquille French Restaurant in the Colonial Hotel, and nice French fanlights in the windows of the apartment building at number 636. Since 1930, Chelsea, the first of two dead-end lanes on the south side, has been the secret sneaky entrance to the one-thousand-car garage under the great Mayan monument to man's infirmity, 450 Sutter.

Continue strolling east and you soon pass Big Shot film, which specializes in color enlarged photos for posters, and gets foreign travelers for passport photos—Japanese, Chinese, Vietnamese, German, and French.

Pause at 608 Bush, once the site of a boardinghouse operated by Mary Carson, to read the historical marker to Robert Louis Stevenson, who lodged there between December 18, 1879, and March 1880. "And there wrote essays, poems, autobiography and fiction," according to the plaque placed by the California Historical Society and admirers of the writer. *The Wrecker*, in which the blind political boss Chris

132

Buckley is described, was one of the novels that came from his sojourn here. Stevenson, an adventuresome man, would probably have been delighted to find the ramen, beef teriyaki, or Korean spiced beef listed on the menu of Racer's Cafe, number 604.

At Stockton Street, you are up over Michael O'Shaughnessy's tunnel, constructed in 1914 for what now seems an unbelievably low sum of $656,000. Although it is 911 feet long, 36 feet wide, and 19 feet high, from here, it might go unnoticed if not for the name of the Tunnel Top Bar across the street.

Fong's Coffee Shop gives a clue to nearby Chinatown, but it is at the Food Fair that a visitor might first become aware of the Japanese ambiance. Japanese tourists sometimes buy out every piece of fruit and frozen orange juice from neighborhood groceries to take back home. Meat, especially steaks, are also big sellers to the traveler flying back to Japan.

Cross Stockton Street and you are at Hotel Victoria, where the clerks speak both Japanese and English. Bush Garden Restaurant features *jun Nihon fu*, authentic Japanese cuisine. *Nabeyake* and *moriawase* are among the delicacies on the menu that make the gustatory transition from East to West easier for the Nipponese tourist.

A few more steps bring one to a convent school operated by the Sisters of St. Joseph and the Marist fathers of Notre Dame des Victoires church next door. According to the church bulletin, French miners pitched their tents on this slope during the Gold Rush. The first Marist pastor, Father O. Renaudier, came to San Francisco in 1885. The 10:30 Mass is still said in French.

The alley next door is Chatham Place—look uphill to spot the Chatham Hotel. The garage that stands in front of it on Bush was once a livery stable, a sharp contrast to the Sutter-Stockton garage, its overweening descendant across the street. But the architectural scene-stealer on the next block is the airy Goethe Institute, the German cultural center, with its tremendous windows.

Notice Onna No Shiro Restaurant, then stick your head into C.&E. Grocery, often full of Japan Air Lines hostesses. A sign in the window touts the piroshki on its deli counter, but there is also One Cup Ozeki, sake on ice, in the cooler.

Grant is the nucleus of this little ray of the Rising Sun. "The pioneers were the Beverly Plaza Hotel, Midori Restaurant, and Fuko gift shop," Yoshiko Terajima, a partner in the Midori Restaurant told me. "My partner, Hisako Morford, and I opened Midori thirty-nine years ago to accommodate the JAL crews who stayed at the hotel and yearned for the breakfasts of their native land."

Standing beside the Chinatown Gate, within a half-block in any direction, are Michikusa Restaurant, Akasaka restaurant, Ramen Tei, a Japanese fast-food place specializing in *gyoza*, Kinokawa Restaurant, Roppongi Piano Bar and Restaurant, and Han II, a Korean restaurant. Counterpoint to the tempura, sashimi, and shabu shabu these offer are the dragonburgers of the hamburger shop on the corner, The Omelet, whose specialty is its name, the cassoulet at Le Central Restaurant and Brasserie, and the salad at Fred's Fruit Bowl.

If you want to make a quick transition from Japanese to Chinese, go through that elegant gate on Grant Avenue.

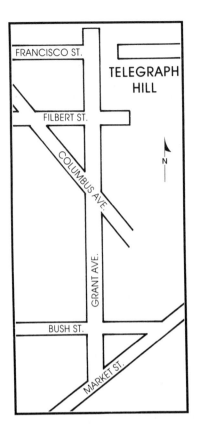

GRANT AVENUE

WALKING TIME: Two hours.

DISTANCE: 1.2 miles.

PUBLIC TRANSPORTATION: Cable cars, Muni bus 15 or 30, locally known as the "Orient Express."

PARKING: Union Square garage.

CLOTHES: Citified.

CAUTION: Bring money.

Grant Avenue, the oldest street in San Francisco, has six separate worlds skewered on its short 1.2-mile length. A man could stride from its nether end at Market Street to its northern end at Francisco in a leisurely eye-filling hour. If he walked Grant Avenue daily for a lifetime, he would never truly know them all.

One is *le haut monde*. The many branches of New York shops in the section between Market and Bush have led one local joker to nickname it Fifth Avenue West.

Two worlds are *le haut goût*. Sang Yee Gah, to use the Chinatown name, is a gaudy higgledy-piggledy quiddity transplant from Canton, the street-level tourist trinket trail. Gee Gah is the warm walkup world of flats, family associations, fish on wash lines, herbalists, rice, and cha, cha, cha. What is cha, cha, cha? The agile teens of Du Pon Gai, as the Chinese call Grant Avenue, say it means tea for three. Chinese New Year, when the dragon comes out to play, is nationally known.

World four, Upper Grant Avenue, begins at Columbus. Once Bohemian, once Beat, it is once again offbeat North Beach, a pastiche of people, paint, pasta pots, and bibelots. The tribal festival of Upper Grant is a street fair with mimes, rhymesters, folknicks, puppeteers, artists in nondress display, and dancing in the street.

Above Filbert, Grant turns into otherworldly Telegraph Hill, a latter-day Camelot that costs a lot.

The sixth world of Grant Avenue lives in history and in memory. This street began at a slightly more diagonal kilter as Calle de la Fundación, the first thoroughfare of the original Mexican pueblo. Captain Don William Antonio Richardson, the first inhabitant of Yerba Buena, laid it out in 1834. He chose it because Vancouver, Beechey, and Dana had commended it in print as an anchorage. Formerly, Spanish ships anchored inside Fort Point's cove.

At what is now 827 Grant, Richardson pitched a tent for his family on June 25, 1835. Three months later, after paying $25 for the first lot ever sold in what was to become the city of San Francisco, he built a house, lined it with the tent to better protect his wife, Doña María Antonía Martínez Richardson, and fenced it to protect his three small children from mountain lions and bears. The old one-hundred-*vara* lots were 275-feet square (a *vara* was the length of a man's walking stick). Today, $10,000 a running foot is a bargain for land on Grant Avenue.

David Brodie Torres, great-grandson of Richardson, who lived at 1251 Willard Avenue, owned the Mexican citizenship papers of his forebear. He could remember when his grandmother shrugged her shoulders because the gracious days had passed and said, "Let the gringo worry about that."

The gringos worried about trueing up the Calle de la Fundación, and when they did it, Lieutenant Washington A. Bartlett, then *alcalde*, named it for Captain Samuel F. Du Pont, a friend, in much the same way that mayors today dish out political plums.

Any site on Grant Avenue has a history of its own. The infamous Mammy Pleasant's boardinghouse, which offered interesting dishes, including blonds, once stood at Dupont (as it came to be misspelled) and Washington. Norton I, Emperor of San Francisco and a favorite town character, died on the southwest corner of Dupont and California in front of the old First Congregational Church. In time, commercial vice gave the street such a bawdy name that merchants pleaded for a new *nom de bourse*.

Grant was granted. It has been a long time since a tipsy miner spilled a poke of gold dust there, but Grant Avenue is as lively as any street in the city. It may be a shish kebab of truffles, bok choy, ravioli, baklava, cracked crab, and the good herb, but a line from Bob Hope's theme song fits it: It may sometimes have been a headache, but it's never been a bore.

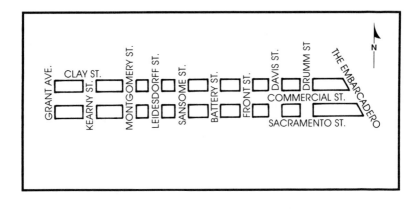

COMMERCIAL STREET

WALKING TIME: Allow half an hour.

DISTANCE: Nine city blocks.

PUBLIC TRANSPORTATION: California Street cable car, Muni buses 1 Sacramento to Grant Avenue and 32 Embarcadero, or choice of buses at Ferry Building at walk's end.

PARKING: Nearly impossible around Chinatown.

CLOTHES: Suitable for the city.

The cradle of San Francisco, the source from which all urban blessings flowed in the city's formative years, is a narrow, little-known nine-block byway called Commercial Street.

Raffish, smelly in places, vital and complicated with meaning for city walkers, it is a lithograph of nineteenth-century buildings scaled to the human dimensions of a six-foot pioneer. On it you may well meet a portly man of business with a Rolls-Royce, or a workman trundling an open barrow of salted fish. Both are part of the continuum of San Francisco's great banking, shipping, commodity, packing, produce, and printing industries, which began humbly on or near Commercial Street when its lower half was the city's first important wharf.

Early maps show it as Long or Central Wharf, extending from Montgomery Street some two thousand feet into the Bay. Sansome was once a plank walk leading to it. In 1989, the lower half of Commercial Street entered the present with an imposing stairway into the Embarcadero Center. Alongside the old Federal Reserve Bank, it now has two levels. Although change is happening slowly, the upper part still offers the walker a sense of historical perspective that is hard to come by this side of London.

The ideal time to begin this walk is late afternoon. The starting place is the Calle de la Fundación, which is what Francisco de Haro called Grant Avenue in 1834 when he was *alcalde* of Yerba Buena. Not surprisingly, a plaque at 823 Grant announces that this site was the home of Captain W. A. Richardson, first resident of the town. Commercial Street, however, had more to do with his next-door neighbor, Jacob P. Leese, resident number two. It began as a backdoor footpath from Leese's home at Grant and Clay to the clapboard store he built in 1837 at Commercial and Montgomery.

Backdoor it remains for some of the buildings that front on Clay or Sacramento streets. A notable example is the old U. S. Subtreasury Building at 608 Commercial, begun in 1877 and metamorphosed into the Pacific Heritage Museum in 1985, when the Bank of Canton tucked it into a side pocket of its new building.

Today Commercial slips unobtrusively out of Grant, across from the elegant Four Seas Restaurant. Just down Commercial a step or two, watch for the establishment of the second oldest business in Chinatown, Mow Lee and Co., Grocers, which opened nearby in 1856.

Grant is the highest point of Commercial and offers a pleasant view of the Ferry Building framed at the Bay below, the only street other than Market that does so. Pick any name out of early San Francisco history—Little Pete the tong dong, the Comstock kings, Miss Piggot the crimp, Sam Brannan, Theodore Durrant, the "Demon in the Belfry," General William Tecumseh Sherman, poet Bret Harte. All walked on Commercial and would feel at home on it today. The first block is nontourist Chinatown. Each successive block introduces knots of businesses, ending with Embarcadero Center.

Landmarks, plaques, quixotic signs, architectural oddities, and minutiae for the history buff are everywhere at hand and underfoot. Set into the concrete you may see names of brass, or old lavender-and-green glass, sun-discolored from original transparency.

The neglect that has preserved this old pickled onion of a street is at an end. There are still vestiges of the unreconstructed roots of the business legacy that has nourished San Francisco—but walk it soon.

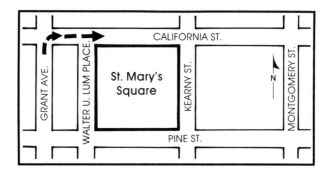

ST. MARY'S SQUARE

WALKING TIME: With a stop at Old St. Mary's, allow an hour.

DISTANCE: Two city blocks.

PUBLIC TRANSPORTATION: California Street cable car.

PARKING: St. Mary's Square garage.

CLOTHES: Chic.

Not every street that disappears from a city is a loss. A case in point is St. Mary's Alley, once the vile and squalid bailiwick of an international and mercenary stench of wenches. Thanks to the persistence of the Paulist fathers, whose injunction, "Son, observe the time and fly from evil," can still be seen under the clock across the street, this one-time slough of sin is now a public park. It is St. Mary's Square, acceptably landscaped and garage-roofed and one of downtown San Francisco's most-used breathing spaces.

A walk around it samples several of the city's unique flavors. For historical perspective, begin at the corner of California Street and Grant Avenue, one of our most admired, sketched, and photographed confluences. To the rest of the world, the pagoda roofs, "dragons' glow" street lamps, festoons of lanterns, cable cars, and outdoor telephone booths (whose calligraphy says "Electric Voice House") are unmistakably Chinatown. Dai Choong Low, or "Tower of the Big Bell," as the Chinese call Old St. Mary's Church, forms an agreeable architectural contrast, which is not surprising because the one-time cathedral was there first. Archbishop Joseph Sadoc Alemany dedicated it at midnight Mass, Christmas 1854. Parishioners complained it was too far from town.

Tourists, aficionados of church decor, and the faithful often find a quiet hour inside rewarding. The more secular can look south on Grant, imagining as they cross a time when brothels mocked the masses en route en masse to Mass. Protests to city officials moved the lewd women off the dirt floors of Grant (then Dupont) and finally to the parallel backstreets of Quincy and St. Mary's Alley, but it took a shimmy along San Andreas Fault to clean out the vixen warrens.

Turn east on California and walk downhill. On one side is the Hartford Building; on the other, the striking International Building, designed by Anshen & Allen for American President Lines, dominates the block with a foretaste of financial Montgomery Street beyond. It stands on Kearny where the Old Plank Road, San Francisco's first highway, began in 1850. Unlike freeways today, the Plank Road had a destination, and its route to Mission Dolores became Mission Street.

St. Mary's Square begins at Quincy, now renamed Walter U. Lum Place, and California. The casual observer might assume it is the front yard of the International Building. It is not. The Japanese have a word for this use of a neighboring garden in an architect's plan. They call it *shakkei*, ''borrowed scenery.''

On the south side it also borrowed the picturesque Kong Chow Temple, which stood here a hundred years until it moved to a roof at Stockton and Clay streets. Hou Wang, a monkey who made it to Heaven, and Kuan Kung, a general and patron of miners, are worshiped there.

The statue dominating St. Mary's Square, his back to Walter V. Lum Place, is Sun Yat Sen, as sculptor Beniamino Bufano conceived him, with a robe of stainless steel and head and hands of rose granite. In 1937, Lin Sên, then President of China, wrote the words at the base of the twelve-foot statue: ''Father of the Chinese Republic and First President . . . Champion of Democracy . . . Proponent of Peace and Friendship among nations.'' The statue looks toward a place where children play and old men dream in the sun.

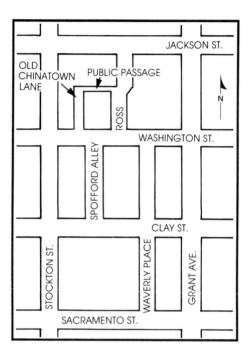

THE LITTLE LANES OF CHINATOWN

WALKING TIME: At least an hour.

DISTANCE: Fourteen city blocks.

PUBLIC TRANSPORTATION: California Street cable car or Muni bus 55 Sacramento.

PARKING: Under St. Mary's Square or Portsmouth Square.

CLOTHES: Don't wear white.

Eddying around busy Du Pon Gai, or Grant Avenue, San Francisco's oldest and possibly most famous street, is a chain of tributary lanes that visitors seldom see. Native San Franciscans, unless they grew up in Chinatown, rarely know them. The odds are that those who do made the discovery while jockeying for one of those pearls without price, a Chinatown parking place.

Compared to the lively inviting doors of Grant Avenue, the face these narrow streets present to the public is as reserved and noncommittal as rice. Yet most of the culturally sustaining facets of Dai Fow, the Chinese "big city" within the city of San Francisco, are to be found here and not in the brouhaha of the streets.

The walker who loves the byways will find a stroll around the lanes of Chinatown as exotic and mysterious as the smile of a girl behind a fan. The well-known restaurant of Johnny Kan on Grant, just off Sacramento, makes an excellent landmark from which to start. History buffs will find the story of the Chinese in America on Kan's third-floor banquet room walls.

Look downhill from Grant to 755 Sacramento at the Nom Kue Elementary School, which resembles a mandarin *yamen*, or courthouse. At 730 is the Chinese Chamber of Commerce, where the dragon dwells when he is not out parading.

Uphill, Sacramento leads to Waverly Place, best known of the Chinatown side streets. The YMCA and a church guard it. Its heart is the charming Chinese playground, which for many years contained a collection of fabulous kites, including a traditional rain kite made by Oliver Chang. The rain kite has eyes that whirl and a long tongue to tell the gods the people of earth are thirsty. No one has flown it recently.

Waverly has had several names in the past, among them Street of the Tin Hou Temple. Tin Hou, queen of Heaven, protects walkers, travelers, sailors, actors, and ladies of the evening and is still worshiped at 125 Waverly. Make sure the temple is open before you climb the four floors leading to it. Family associations and other temples on the lane are not open to the public.

At Clay Street go uphill to Spofford Alley, where a Masonic lodge is located. Masonry, in one form or another, was known to the Chinese before Christian times, and Chee Kung Tong predates, but is no relation to, the western lodge. Radio station Sinocast, which broadcasts in fifteen languages, is nearby. The walker who comes this way on a Saturday morning may also have his stroll livened by the music of the prize-winning girls' band from St. Mary's Catholic Chinese Center as they practice.

Cross Washington to Old Chinatown Lane. The moon-gated house at the end was known as the "International Market" in the bad old days of singsong girl slaves. Look overhead for a house-to-house bridge, one of the last architectural remnants of the tong wars. At the end of the lane, turn right. This narrow passage, guaranteed to raise the hackles, leads to Ross Alley. The only pawnshop in Chinatown is here. Ross ends at Jackson Street, where goldsmiths, bakers, and sweetmeat dealers can be seen at work.

Half a block below Grant, the walker may pick up another chain of lanes where workaday Chinatown keeps its accounts in calligraphy and ships dried fish, Mexican-canned abalone, fortune cookies, and dresses all over the world with very little fanfare, nourishing the stream of "Old Gold Mountain," as San Francisco is called along Grant Avenue.

The Chinese, who enjoy proverbs, have one that goes, "When you drink from the stream, remember the spring." In Chinatown, the little lanes are the spring.

WASHINGTON SQUARE

WALKING TIME: Allow a morning to explore.

DISTANCE: A steep city mile.

PUBLIC TRANSPORTATION: Muni buses 15, 30, 39, and 41.

PARKING: None.

CLOTHES: Inconspicuously urbane.

North Beach, a piece of verbal jetsam left by the tide that once lapped Chestnut between Stockton and Jones streets, is synonymous in San Francisco with informality, hospitality, and Little Italy. It is also a fairly well-defined city within the city, many of whose citizens remember the vineyards and olive trees in Tuscany, Sicily, Abruzzi, in Liguria, Apulia, Venezia, and Lucca.

They brought the flavor with them. A stroll around North Beach is no substitute for a trip to the Mediterranean, but it offers a delicious antipasto. In North Beach, Broadway is the Rialto, Fisherman's Wharf the Porto, Aquatic Park the Lido, and Columbus Avenue the Via Romano. But it is to the piazza, Washington Square, that you must go to try the tempo of the community.

With a droll Venetian wink, Washington Square laughs at the advocates of single-use zoning. Its periphery can supply most sensible human needs. Its center, many more. Around its church, Saints Peter and Paul, revolve the weddings, confirmations, saints' days, funerals, and *festas* for feeding the soul. Two of them—the blessing of the fishing fleet in the name of the Blessed Madonna del Lumé, on the first Sunday after October 1, and the Columbus Day parade and pageant—are among the most colorful festivals that San Francisco celebrates.

Like the plaza in Sonoma, or any charming little Continental city, the border of the square also has a post office, a theater, Malvina's coffeehouse, North East Medical Services clinic, a bakery that creates *focaccia*, two good cafes—Casa Constansa, a senior residence upstairs from the Fior de Italia Restaurant, the other the writer hangout called the Washington Square Bar & Grill, more familiarly known as "the Washbag"—and other blandishments.

Benjamin Franklin upon a post office box is the curious piece of bric-a-brac in the heart of the square and a trio of firemen at work decorate the northwest side. Perhaps no one has described the latter so well as

North Beach mural with Russian Hill highrises in the background.

poet Ron Loewinsohn, whose *The Mendacity of Sculpture* reads: ''. . . one holding a Stricken Lady in his arms, another holding a nozzle / a third with a horn, his right arm thrown up in a gesture, pointing: / Don't you see her! up there on the 4th floor, / garlanded in flames! the child in her arms is screaming terrified / —SHE'S GOING TO JUMP!

''That gesture for 23 years across Columbus Avenue, the bronze jacket / splattered with pigeonshit, out of whose sleeve a wrist & hand, also in bronze, / pointing / to a spot in the air 40 feet above the Pagoda Theater.''

Benjamin Franklin is the gift of an unloved eccentric, Dr. Henry D. Cogswell. The volunteer firemen statue is the bequest of an equally eccentric but much-loved donor, Lillie Hitchcock Coit. The United States Coast and Geodetic Survey also left a trail marker, the tablet dated 1869–1880, which established the latitude and longitude of San Francisco.

It is the sweet and simple life of the square that gives it character, however—the squadron of tai chi exercisers at dawn, the old men reminiscing about crab fishing, the *zias* and mommas gossiping while children play nearby, the shoppers who pause, the lovers who laugh, and the diners who stroll all share the informality.

Hospitality as a pattern was probably established long before the Italian community arrived. The genie of place who first occupied this site was a bountiful lady named Juana Briones y Miranda, whose adobe hut stood at Powell and Filbert streets before 1843. The diary of a seafarer, William Thomes, of the crew of the *Admittance*, records that Juana Briones was generous with milk, eggs, and vegetables from her farm in North Beach. "If the men had some of the energy of that buxom, dark-faced lady," Thomes wrote, "California would have been a prosperous state, even before it was annexed to this country, and we would have had to fight harder than we did to get possession."

Walk uphill half a block on Stockton Street to see an early Bernard Maybeck building at number 1736. This was formerly the Telegraph Hill Neighborhood Association, founded by Alice Griffith, a pioneer San Francisco social worker. Here's one of the classical anecdotes about her: A sedentary type looked out of the window of the Pacific Union Club one day and saw Miss Griffith surrounded by children of various ages and races. "Who was it that Miss Griffith married?" he asked the man in the next chair.

Uphill on Greenwich will take you quickly, via steps, to Coit Tower, sometimes past streetside conversational groups speaking animated Italian. The aria from an opera may come belting out of a bathroom window. Over all hovers a rich odor of garlic and oregano or basil, if you pass when dinner is cooking.

TELEGRAPH HILL / FILBERT STEPS

WALKING TIME: A morning.

DISTANCE: A steep mile and a half.

PUBLIC TRANSPORTATION: Muni buses 39 up the hill, 42 at the east base.

PARKING: Chancy.

CLOTHES: Casual.

"The counterpart of Telegraph Hill exists in no other large city in the United States," Frank Morton Todd wrote in his little *Handbook for San Francisco* in 1914. "No one can begin to know San Francisco until he has climbed it."

Todd was entranced with the view, as is everyone who climbs the Hill, but there is more to it. For Telegraph Hill also embodies all those qualities that make San Francisco unique: insouciance; leafy, lofty beauty; a sense of spaciousness, intimacy, and grandeur coupled with down-to-earth tolerance and everyday practicality. The walk that was good in Todd's time is even better today.

To make this walk, begin at Columbus and Greenwich streets. Walk uphill on Greenwich, toward the east. In Todd's time this route led "by rough ways through a thickly settled tenement district"; in ours, it passes the North Beach Library, used by several generations of poets, a swimming pool in which thousands of San Francisco youngsters have learned to swim, and the North Beach playground that spawned such athletes as Joe DiMaggio and Tony Lazzeri.

The area near the steep, cleated sidewalks after you pass Grant Avenue reminded Todd of the south of Europe. "The Italian pervades it, though Greek, Sicilian, Mexican, and Spaniard are also in evidence, and yet," he wrote, "it is distinctively San Franciscan, for San Francisco is a city of all nations; of and for all races of men." These days the western slope is increasingly Chinese.

When you reach Child Street, pause a moment to mourn the passing of "The Street of the Good Children," shortened almost beyond recognition to "Child" to fit the size of the available street sign.

Climb the steps and you emerge at Telegraph Hill Boulevard. Watch for traffic before crossing to take a second set of steps upward in this leafy bower below Coit Tower.

Bear right when you reach a broad footpath. It is the same width as

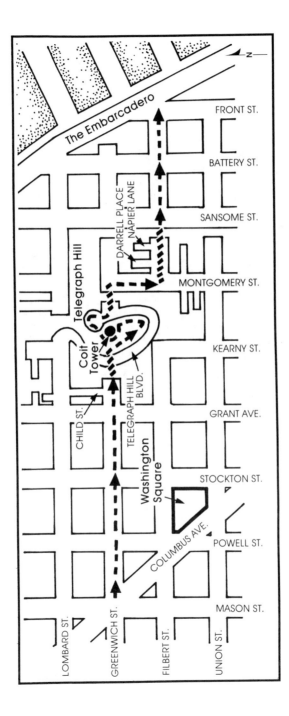

FRONT ST.

BATTERY ST.

SANSOME ST.

The Embarcadero

DARRELL PLACE

NAPIER LANE

Telegraph Hill

MONTGOMERY ST.

KEARNY ST.

Coit Tower

TELEGRAPH HILL BLVD.

CHILD ST.

GRANT AVE.

Washington Square

STOCKTON ST.

COLUMBUS AVE.

POWELL ST.

MASON ST.

LOMBARD ST.

GREENWICH ST.

FILBERT ST.

UNION ST.

Coit Tower tops Telegraph Hill.

the original road that led to Old Amusement Hall, a castlelike structure that once adorned the hilltop. The castle had fallen to ruin long before fire buff Lillie Hitchcock Coit's generous bequest replaced it in 1933 with Coit Tower, the fluted cylinder designed by Arthur Brown, Jr.

"Crazy owld daisy owld Telygraft Hill," poet-humorist Wallace Irwin called it early in this century, in the days when "th' goats and th' chicks and th' brickbats and shticks" were "joomoled all over the face av it." It was then a place of modest homes. Many had dimensions comparable to the tiny green "refugee" cottage visible across the boulevard as you near the street again. It was built in 1906 to house refugees who had lost their homes in the earthquake and subsequent fire.

Continue left uphill to arrive at the rear of Coit Tower. Before you go up on the tower parapet, head to the clearing just south of the building for an unusual view downtown. Then climb the steps and walk around on the west walkway for glimpses of Nob and Russian hills, immediately to the west, through the trees.

The zigzag pattern of Lombard Street makes a good landmark. It was formed in the days when horses tacked back and forth on the streets, an easier way to pull a heavy load than straight uphill. Gradually, the view widens out to encompass the Bay, Mount Tamalpais, and the lush hills of Marin.

When you reach the steps, go down and stroll around the walk encircling the parking lot. It was here that residents came in February 1849 to view the first steamship to arrive in San Francisco Bay, a side-wheel steamer. Helen Throop Purdy described the scene in *San Francisco As It Was, As It Is and How to See It* (Paul Elder, 1912): "War vessels lying in the bay greeted the newcomer with a display of bunting, salutes, music by the band and cheers by the crews. People flocked to Telegraph Hill and there was great rejoicing that San Francisco was connected by steam with the east."

As you circle, Columbus stands in bronze on your right. After the 1910 failure of the Greek community to erect a white marble reproduction of the Parthenon on the hill, Italian-American businessmen made a gift of this statue by Vittorio di Colbertaldo.

The telegraph, from which Telegraph Hill took its name, looked rather like the semaphore monument on the northwest side. As James Benet told it in his *Guide to San Francisco and the Bay Region* (New York: Random House, 1963): "In 1850 George Sweeny and Theodore E. Baugh, founders of the Merchants' Exchange, bought the two-story lookout and signal station erected a little earlier, and installed a semaphore to signal to Montgomery Street the arrival of ships. They built another lookout on Point Lobos and connected the two with the first telegraph line operated in California. On October 29, 1850, the station signaled the arrival of the steamer *Oregon* with the news that California had been admitted to the Union, and that night a huge bonfire was built on the hill."

Visit Coit Tower, if the waiting line isn't too long. The murals inside the rotunda, controversial at the time, were painted by twenty local artists employed by the Works Progress Administration in 1934, during the Depression. The view is spectacular from the top of the tower.

Then return to the eastern edge of the Telegraph Hill Boulevard circle and look for the Greenwich Street sign. Here, red-brick steps lead down into a hushed tunnel of mounded shrubs.

After a gentle curve, the steps pause at the villa built in the 1930s. The vista overlooks the cliff dynamited into the hill in the late 1800s by the brothers Harry N. and George F. Gray, two contractors who blasted once-rounded Telegraph Hill to provide the fill for The Embarcadero. Julius Castle Restaurant is just below.

Bear south on the lane to the Filbert Street steps, past half-hidden houses and gardens. Go down the concrete staircase, noting the European flavor of the gardens, sculpture, and nicely remodeled cottages. As you cross Montgomery Street north of the Shadows Restaurant, try to imagine the smell of wine on the air. Blankets and burlap bags soaked in wine that was made on the hill were draped on roofs during the great fire of 1906, saving the hill dwellings from destruction.

Bear left where Filbert Steps become wooden just beyond the marker acclaiming Grace Marchant, longtime resident on the hill face who converted this steep slope into a garden. Her daughter, Mrs. Desmond Heslett, has gardened Greenwich Street, a block north, much the same way.

Jog with the walkway to the left again for a look at Napier Lane and Darrell Place, two wooden sidewalks, one above the other flanked by sea-stained cottages, some among the oldest in San Francisco. For seventy years this has been a haven for cats and artists.

Then return to the steps. Nearing the bottom, the walker will be jolted by an abrupt transition to commerce in the pleasant new form of Levi's Plaza.

Filbert Street goes for two more blocks—for walkers but not cars—through the middle of Levi's Plaza, ending at the waterfront. Pause in this pleasant oasis. Then, unless you are among the Spartan and wish to climb back up, seek out the glass kiosk on Battery Street at Filbert for a bus to take you home.

GRACE MARCHANT GARDEN

NOTE: *For map, see Telegraph Hill/Filbert Steps, page 149.*

WALKING TIME: Half a day.

DISTANCE: A mile uphill and back.

PUBLIC TRANSPORTATION: Muni buses 15 and 32.

PARKING: Very little.

CLOTHES: Whatever.

The oldest, most historic, and least changed of San Francisco's neighborhoods lies on the steep eastern slope of Telegraph Hill. Difficult to reach on foot, impossible by car, its modest fisherman's cottages have been preserved in part by their very inaccessibility. Contemplating the logistical difficulties of hand-carrying building materials, furniture, or the mountains of groceries we all consume, one might ask, "Why would anyone want to live with such inconvenience?"

The answer: It is a magical place.

The Grace Marchant Garden along the Filbert Street steps accounts for some of the magic. So does the intimacy of the community itself, contrasted with the distant vistas all around it. More than a little of the enchantment comes from the human scale of the well-loved, brightly painted, little vine-covered cottages.

To see for yourself, consider walking up the Filbert Steps. Yes, UP . . . if you want to get the full flavor of life on Telegraph Hill. Filbert Street begins at The Embarcadero, about parallel to Pier 23. Begin this walk at the watery end of Union Street. Look for an asphalt walkway on your left which meanders through trees and well-kept lawns. Follow this walkway north. When the walkway meets the old Belt Line tracks that fringe The Embarcadero, turn left, go down a few steps, and you are in the Sierran section of Levi's Plaza. An eighty-foot-wide swath of the plaza is still Filbert Street.

Stroll through the park toward Battery Street. Cross in the crosswalk and continue on the second block of Filbert that transects Levi's Plaza. As you walk toward Telegraph Hill, notice how handsomely a green waterfall seems to sweep down the cliffside ahead. This is the Grace Marchant Garden.

The architectural firm of Hellmuth, Obata, and Kassabaum tried to approximate the zigzag skyline of Telegraph Hill cottages in the rooflines of the low red-brick buildings that house the Levi Strauss Company. Years of planning with the Telegraph Hill Neighborhood Association brought about this felicitous continuity of design.

As you cross Sansome Street, look at the white H. G. Walters warehouse and its roof garden on your right, a reminder that from 1854, when Flint's Warehouse was built handy to the Battery Street piers, this area was filled with industrial godowns.

Alongside Telegraph Landing, on the left, developer Gerson Bakar has rebuilt the lower forty feet of Filbert Steps, which were wooden and much less safe. His building, too, continues the roofline pattern, which allows greater breadth to the view.

Start up this staircase. In a few moments you are looking at sheer rock face on your left. Dynamited into the hill long ago by the brothers Harry N. and George F. Gray, who used the rock for fill on The Embarcadero, whole lots toppled because of six selfish years of blasting that left once-round Telegraph Hill craggy. Feelings ran so high among residents that two people were shot to death before the dynamiting was controlled. One of them was contractor George Gray.

In 1949, when Grace Marchant, newly retired, planted her first pot of the little creeping ground cover known as baby's tears on the land alongside Filbert Steps, the garden was not only as bare as the cliff face, it was also filled with old bedsprings, legless chairs, and broken glass. Grace hauled it all away herself, bringing in soil, shrubs, and trees during the thirty-three years she gardened here, at no cost to the city.

Pause when you reach each landing and look east toward Yerba Buena Island to see how the view widens as you climb.

When you reach the first of the homes along the steps, there is a significant change in the flora. The hillslope seems increasingly Mediterranean as you climb. Red bougainvillea festoons a red cottage, purple pleroma fronts a white one. Banana trees, flowering plums, palms, sequoias, camellias, and roses all thrive here.

As Grace worked in the garden, neighbors first improved their own frontages, then pitched in to help her. They also formed an organization called Friends of the Garden (FOG). One neighbor, Gary Dray, who has tended the garden during the years since Grace Marchant's death, began by helping her when she could no longer do the manual labor. A plant list of the garden, compiled by FOG, covers three single-spaced pages.

Owners of the cottage at 221 Filbert, who had intended to demolish their small building and replace it with a larger one, destroying part of the garden in the process, have put their plans in abeyance while FOG, with the help of the Trust for Urban Land, is raising funds to purchase the threatened site.

When you reach a wooden sidewalk that juts off the steps to the north, you are at Napier Lane, a compound of sea-stained cottages that may include some of the oldest houses in San Francisco. For the last eighty years, it has been a haven for cats, artists, and other denizens of Upper Bohemia.

At the northern end of Napier Lane, another garden has been created parallel to the Greenwich Street steps by Mrs. Desmond Heslett, Grace Marchant's daughter.

Digress if you wish, but return to Filbert Steps and continue upward until you reach Montgomery Street. If the famous art deco apartment building at the corner of Filbert and Montgomery seems familiar, it may be because you have seen it in an old Bogart-Bacall film. The sgraffito murals, glass block and sandblasted glass designs were a tour de force in 1938 when Irvin Goldstine designed the building.

Notice the continuation of the Filbert Steps across the street, but turn right instead and walk for one block along Montgomery Street. When you reach Julius Castle Restaurant, walk to the railings at the end of the street and look over the cliff to see another sheer face hidden behind new construction.

Take the brick steps upward near 303 Montgomery. Soon you are at Pioneer Park, which surrounds Coit Tower. Linger as long as you like, enjoying the views, the murals, and the sighing trees.

When you are ready to return, come back to the top of the Greenwich Street steps where you emerged and make a sharp turn south, following the walkway between red-rock walls. When it reaches the first houses, turn left to go down the Filbert Steps again.

You'll see more as you walk downhill, including a charming refugee cottage, a gilded statue that seems to be a ménage à trois, the Shadows Restaurant, and a dozen more little gardens that might have come right out of the Italian coast.

If it isn't as good as a vacation, walk slower, for Telegraph Hill has the kind of charming details people travel around the world to see.

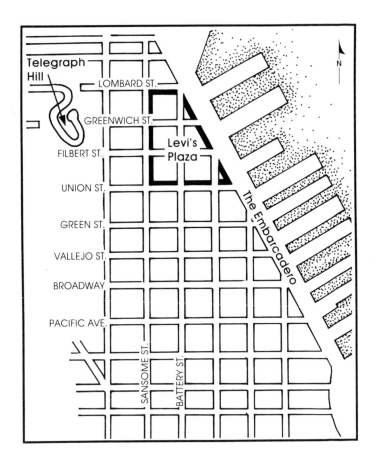

LEVI'S PLAZA

WALKING TIME: Ten minutes.

DISTANCE: Two blocks.

PUBLIC TRANSPORTATION: Muni buses 15, 32, and 42.

PARKING: Lousy on weekdays.

CLOTHES: YUP is de rigueur.

San Francisco has a wonderful new waterfront walk. Its heart is the eleven-acre Levi's Plaza, where the low, terraced red-brick buildings are scaled to human proportions, where half of the area is generously given over to well-planned open space, and where San Francisco Bay seems to be restored to the city, it is so close at hand.

"We wanted it to be as warm as a college campus," Peter Haas, president of Levi Strauss Company and scion of one of San Francisco's most civic-minded families, said as he showed me the prospect from his office terrace. "Levi's had its warehouse and office on Battery Street before moving farther downtown. We used to ship out of here. For us, it's like coming home again."

To make this walk, put on your favorite old Levi's, transport yourself to the corner of Sansome and Lombard streets, and prepare to be agreeably surprised. What was once an old warehouse district is now a vibrant urban mix of condominiums, offices, commercial space, and a privately developed area that is, in effect, a gift to the public.

Before The Embarcadero and its piers were built, sailing ships nuzzled up to Pier 27, fronting the number 1 Lombard building, which began as an icehouse; they were loaded from the open warehouse doors. "During reconstruction we found permafrost at the lower levels from long storage of ice here," architect Pat MacLeamy of Hellmuth, Obata, and Kassabaum, who designed Levi's Plaza, told me. The developer was Gerson Bakar.

Walk south along Sansome Street to reach Building B of Levi's Plaza at the Greenwich corner. For reference, look uphill to locate the Greenwich Street steps, and then about a hundred feet from the corner, bear left at an angle through the arcade, which suddenly opens between what seems to be another warehouse. Actually, it is the "back door" of the plaza, designed as a little neighborhood shopping center.

A sudden glimpse of a flowing fountain beckons one into the open space beyond. Watch those two sets of shallow steps as you descend into the broad corridor. Just before you leave the building, pause a moment to look uphill on your right. There the arcade unexpectedly soars to two stories, revealing Coit Tower in all its phallic glory.

As you emerge into the sunlight, the fine old Italian Swiss Colony warehouse, whose cornices and balustrades were face-lifted and earthquake-proofed, is on your left and houses a restaurant facing the plaza. Centerpiece of this urbane part of the plaza is a stone fountain with water flowing over many faces. Walk up into their midst via the stepping stones to enjoy the music of the water, then loop back via stones through the lawn area to return to the paved center of the plaza.

An expansive glass-roofed atrium ties together the two halves of Building A, the Levi Strauss headquarters, whose step-backed, zigzagged terraces, as classic as a Hopi cliff dwelling, seem to reflect the hillside homes above. Walk toward it, but stop on the red-brick walkway mid-plaza to discern the Filbert Street steps on the right and below them the plaza's main entrance from Sansome Street.

Bear left on the brick paving, which is actually Filbert Street, now an uncommercial pedestrian-only mall, toward the second fountain sur-

rounded by berms of earth and green lawns off toward the Bay. Enticing as it seems, resist it for a moment and, once across Battery Street,
walk south again to follow another arcade under a bridge connecting
the two halves of Building C.

When you emerge at Union Street, bear right until you can see the
little Cargo West Building, an historic landmark that has been surrounded by the larger building as sensitively as a jewel in a fine setting.
The setback facing the neighboring Ice House Alley is another delicate
architectural touch. "We think the spaces in between are every bit
as important as the buildings themselves," architect Bob Canfield
told me.

Retrace your steps along Union Street toward the tugboat lying at
Pier 19 at the foot of the street. Then, just shy of the Belt Line Railroad
tracks, cobbles and a sweet jolt of greenery make an introduction to
the plaza again.

Bear left and when you are again parallel to Filbert Street, go down
the steps on your left until you are abreast of another fountain, then
bear right. Like the rest of the plaza landscaping, the second fountain
was designed by Lawrence Halprin and interprets a Sierra headwater
source, with a mountain stream coursing down through a little natural
amphitheater disguised as a mountain meadow. Both stepping stones
and a bridge cross the stream. Take your choice, then continue northerly to linger on a second bridge overlooking a little island that could
easily serve as an impromptu stage. All that is missing in this charming
conceit of a meandering mountain rill are water plants and trout. On
the opposite side of the bridge, the creek seems to join the Bay. Actually
its waters are recycled back to start their melodic journey again and
again.

Idle in this welcome green oasis as long as you like. The restaurant at
its end is reminiscent of an earlier, lustier waterfront made more
romantic by the passage of time.

NOB HILL

WALKING TIME: All your life.

DISTANCE: As far as democracy will let you go.

PUBLIC TRANSPORTATION: The Big Four used the cable cars.

PARKING: That's the chauffeur's job.

CLOTHES: Sable, Savile Row, or forget it.

Nob Hill, a legacy from the nabobs who out-Horatioed Alger to the expense-account princes of our Affluent Age, is synonymous in San Francisco with rank, swank, and status. Its crest is an altar of the American cult called business to the goddess Sweet Success. It is also our best-known hill and pleasant indeed to walk about.

For Nob is a man's hill, with power in the air, privilege in a stair, and prestige in a chair. Its square heart is a stolid old brownstone mansion built in 1886 by bonanza king James Flood to prove he'd made the grade from corned beef to caviar. Its periphery is a wreath of establishments that could be grouped under one word, singular.

Begin this walk, as history did in 1856, at the corner of California and Powell streets, the crossroads of two cable cars. Here, on the site of the Fairmont Hotel, Dr. Arthur Hayne built a home for his bride, actress Julia Dean, after cutting a trail uphill through chaparral. Men of wealth soon followed his trail. Within a few years, Leland Stanford, Mark

Hopkins, Charles Crocker, Lucky Baldwin had all constructed elaborate palaces. The steep block that goes uphill on California to Mason Street will show you why they waited for the arrival of the California Street cable car to build them. Horses found the pull as steep as the walker will.

All the vainglorious display, except the Flood mansion, now an exclusive men's club, went down in the 1906 fire. The foundations of the palace James G. "Bonanza Jim" Fair had planned to build to outshine all the rest were later incorporated into the Fairmont Hotel. "Tessie" Fair Oelrichs built the hotel in 1906 and rebuilt it in 1907 to immortalize her father, and it is still the grandest tiger in the jungle.

Across the street, the Mark Hopkins mansion was first replaced by an Institute of Art, which now lives on nearby Russian Hill, and later by the hotel whose tower view tourists treasure. Walk around the Pacific Union Club to reach Huntington Park, once the site of another millionaire's showplace, and now a much-used breathing spot. Grace Cathedral Close, across the street, a gift from the Crocker family, replaced the redwood homes that once stood here. The Masonic Temple, whose stark white seems paradoxical next to the Gothic of the cathedral and the Edwardian architecture of the Flood mansion, is on the sites of more bygone glory, the homes of A. N. Towne (whose portals are now a garden ornament in Golden Gate Park), Robert Sherwood, and George Whittell. All, all are gone, the old familiar houses. Today Nob Hill has halls, church, lodge, club, apartment buildings, and hotels, and Lo! it equals the pomp of yesteryear.

HUNTINGTON PARK

NOTE: *For map, see Nob Hill, page 159.*

WALKING TIME: An hour.

DISTANCE: Four and one-half blocks.

PUBLIC TRANSPORTATION: Any cable car.

PARKING: Very little and very expensive.

CLOTHES: Cashmere sweaters, lizard shoes.

Huntington Park, the urbane one-and-three-quarter-acre park on Nob Hill, San Francisco's most glamorous enclave, has been renovated. Colorful new play equipment has been installed. There are new paving blocks and plantings.

The copy of *Fontana della Tartarughe,* the turtle fountain that Mrs. William W. Crocker donated thirty years ago to grace the center of the park, has not only had its long-missing turtles restored, it has had an infusion of spring waters flown from the original in Rome, which certainly must make it wetter than plain old Reservoir Hetch-Hetchy water.

Not surprisingly, on this apex of rank and swank, $500,000 of the $600,000 needed for the renewal came from what we call "the private sector"; the rest of us, through the San Francisco Open Space Fund, provided the other sixth. The five-hundred-member Nob Hill Association, which raised most of the funds, also provides a gardener to keep the new shrubs well groomed.

For most of us, the high life of Nob's posh hotels, restaurants, clubs, apartment hotels, and townhouses is to dream about, but it doesn't cost a cent to walk around the hill.

To make this walk, transport yourself, as the nabobs known as the Big Four did, to the corner of Mason and California streets.

The square heart of Nob Hill is the exclusive Pacific Union Club, the solid old brownstone mansion built in 1886 by bonanza king James Flood. Walk alongside it on the Mason Street side until you are midblock, then pause for a look east at one of our most civilized Beaux Arts panoramas.

To the left is Sacramento Street, which began as the path hacked through the chaparral by Dr. Arthur Hayne in 1856 when he built the home on the hill for his bride, actress Julia Dean.

Men of wealth followed Hayne's trail. Within a few years of the completion of the California Street cable line, mansions stood on the hill.

The elegant bow of the Fairmont Hotel's carriage entrance is enhanced like an architectural leitmotif by the corner entrances of the Mark Hopkins Hotel on the right and the Brocklebank Apartments on the left. Although created by different architects, other details on the three buildings are complementary as well.

Save the Fairmont lobby, one of San Francisco's most impressive indoor public spaces, for a later time, and for the moment return to California Street. Across from "the Mark," the handsome French-Baroque Morshead Apartments at 1001 and, next door at 1021 "The Jewel Box," a townhouse built for patent medicine millionaire Herbert Law in the style of a French *petit palais.*

Walk west on California, following the well-wrought fence as far as the stairway. The brownstone of the Pacific Union Club was resented as "foreign" when it was imported from Connecticut, but Flood had the last laugh when it survived the 1906 fire. Willis Polk's renovation in 1912 added an extra floor of bedrooms.

Continue walking toward the stunning rose window of Grace Cathedral. Once across the Pacific Union driveway, you are at Huntington Park, site of the mansion of David D. Colton, built in 1872. Colton—the chief lawyer for the Central Pacific Railroad, owned by Crocker, Hopkins, Stanford, and Collis Huntington—was known with derision as the "Half" of "the Big Four and a Half."

In the most sensational trial of the Gay Nineties, the Big Four sued Colton's widow, claiming her recently deceased husband had embezzled railroad funds. Mrs. Colton produced six hundred "Colton Letters" from Huntington, proving that her husband had been directed to use the money to buy politicians for the railroad in Washington and Sacramento. Triumphant at the exoneration of her late husband, Mrs. Colton sold the house and left San Francisco.

In 1892, Collis P. Huntington bought the Colton house for $250,000. Like most of its neighbors, it didn't survive the 1906 fire. His widow, Arabella Duval Yarrington Worsham Huntington Huntington (whose last husband was Henry Edwards Huntington, donor of the Huntington Library) gave the park to the city in 1915.

Pause at the stairway into the park to look across California Street at the discreet facade of the Huntington Hotel. The Masonic Memorial Auditorium at 1111 California Street has been softened by trees on the upper level, but its shiny white marble facings seem oddly contemporary. Before the 1906 fire, this was the site of the A. N. Towne home, whose surviving pillars, known now as "The Portals of the Past," stand by Lloyd Lake in Golden Gate Park.

Walk up the steps into the park. The first tangible indication of renewal are the lower shrubs. Many of the improvements—like new plumbing, underground sprinkling system, and lighting—are out of sight. The bronze *Dancing Sprites* on your right was created by French sculptor Henri Léon Greber. James Flood's daughter made a gift of it to the park in 1942.

Continue walking straight ahead to reach the Fountain of the Turtles, whose figures were made by Taddeo Landini, with the marble portions fashioned by Giacomo Della Porte in 1585. The original stands between the Piazza Venezia and the Via del Corso in Rome, not nearly so well displayed as the copy is in Huntington Park.

When Mrs. Crocker discovered this copy in a villa outside Rome, it was about to be destroyed to make way for one of Benito Mussolini's housing projects. She rescued it and took it to her home, Sky Farm, now the Burlingame Country Club. Two of the Crocker family homes stood across Taylor Street on what is now the Grace Cathedral Close.

Diocesan House and its neighbor Cathedral House, the Episcopal office building in front of the cathedral, resemble the seventeenth-century Mompesson House at Salisbury, England. Diocesan House stands on the site of an infamous forty-foot-high "spite" fence built by Charles Crocker to shut out a Chinese neighbor. No remnant of the fence remains, but the ensuing flap resulted in legislation that keeps fences in San Francisco to six feet in height.

The Sacramento-Taylor street corner was once the scene of a demonstration led by Dennis Kearney demanding "The Chinese must go" after railroad workmen found themselves replaced by Oriental laborers.

After the fire of '06, the Crocker family donated the entire square block to the Episcopal Diocese. Lewis Hobart was the architect of Grace Cathedral and took his inspiration from Notre Dame in Paris. The newest building on the close is Cathedral School for Boys.

Look north, past the pergola fronting the new play equipment, to see another of Nob Hill's architectural jewels, 1172 Sacramento. The charming little townhouse and the highrise next to it were built in the late 1960s for Edward T. Haas.

Find a bench and tarry as long as you like, enjoying the sunlight, the happy children, and the fresh feeling of a garden renewed.

Imposing though the surroundings may be, without Huntington Park to set it off, Nob Hill would be infinitely diminished. Like white space in an ad, this smidgeon of open space gives the hill its added shot of class.

GRACE CATHEDRAL CLOSE

NOTE: *For map, see Nob Hill, page 159.*

WALKING TIME: Six minutes. Allow one to three hours to explore the cathedral.

DISTANCE: A very square city block.

PUBLIC TRANSPORTATION: California Street cable car or Muni bus 55 Sacramento.

PARKING: Masonic Temple garage.

CLOTHES: Ladies will be more comfortable in hat and gloves.

CHILDREN: For most services, tots may be parked at the nursery.

When the stunning tintinnabulation of "Adeste Fideles" rings out loud and clear over Nob Hill on the Grace Cathedral carillon, to anyone within earshot—scrooges, sourpusses, overworked salespeople, and atomic scaremongers to the contrary notwithstanding—Christmas once again takes on its historical dimension as the hope of the world.

"O come, all ye faithful," the bells sing, and the rush, bustle, spangles, tinsel, and tawdriness of our affluent commerciality diminish like the piping of a penny whistle. This, the mind says, is the real thing, the world series of religion, Christendom's annual big birthday party, miraculous and nearly two thousand years old. Joy to the world. Unto us a Child is given.

Whatever his denominational persuasion, the walker who explores Grace Cathedral Close, which is the square block bounded by California, Sacramento, Taylor, and Jones streets, will find it alive with a phenomenon of our times: the resurgence of interest in vintage religion.

Begin this walk at the corner of Taylor and California, as early as you please, for life at Grace Cathedral takes hold of the wings of the morning while most of us are slug-abed. At the outset, examine the Ghiberti Gates, which stand between the twin to Coulson Bell Tower and the extension of the cathedral nave. The munificence of many citizens, among them W. W. Crocker, whose family also gave the land on which the cathedral stands, made this construction possible. Inside the north "Singing Tower" are forty-three bells with names like Sympathy, Isaiah, and Loving Kindness. Richard Purvis was the genius

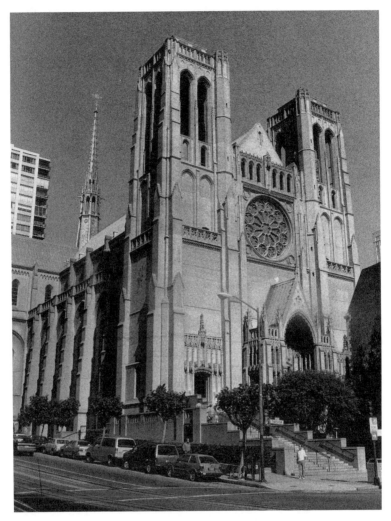

Grace Cathedral.

who first brought them to exuberance, sometimes on such a secular
occasion as the winning of a baseball pennant.

The soaring cathedral beckons the beholder with a taste for grandeur. Resist for the present, if you can, and walk along Taylor Street
instead. On one side is Huntington Park, whose fountain is a replica of
the Tartarughe Fountain in Rome. Diana Crocker can recall when it
stood on her grandfather's estate, now the Burlingame Country Club,

and had turtles in the basin. On the other side are the Cathedral and Diocesan houses, elegant office buildings of the church, both reminiscent of the seventeenth-century Mompesson House of Salisbury Cathedral Close. The juxtaposition of close, castlelike hotels, exclusive gentlemen's club, and the park has led one wit to call this area "that corner of San Francisco which is forever England."

Bear left uphill along Sacramento, past the wrought-iron gate. The playing field at the northwest corner belongs to the Cathedral School for Boys and tops a contemporary school building. Pause at Jones before turning south and look back to see one of our most civilized cityscapes.

From Jones, east on California will take you to the main entrance of the cathedral. For many years the cornerstone, now incorporated into the new construction, stood here beside the steps, a monument to the impatience of Bishop William F. Nichols, who laid it in a drenching rain in 1910 before blueprints were drawn.

Inside, the cathedral is many splendored. It is also busy. On Christmas Eve, it is busiest of all, when strangers, the weary, and those whom The Very Reverend David M. Gillespie calls the unchurched are welcomed in resonant tones in honor of a Child born in a stable.

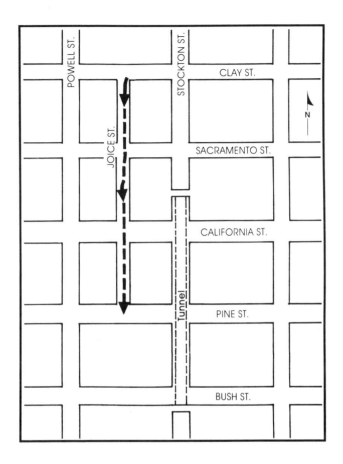

JOICE STREET

WALKING TIME: Six to ten minutes.

DISTANCE: Three city blocks.

PUBLIC TRANSPORTATION: Powell Street cable car going; California Street cable car returning.

PARKING: None.

CLOTHES: Last year's suit.

Threading the lee of Ern Hill, Fern Hill, or the Hill of Golden Promise as Nob Hill was known for the first twenty years of its civic existence, is an obscure three-block-long shelf called Joice Street, where Time, like any other climber, stopped to take a deep breath before going on to the top.

It is a modest street, uncommercial and almost unknown. For 140 years the frantic life of downtown San Francisco has swirled about it madly. In all that time, the changes have been so reassuringly few that any walker can retrieve the threads of continuity that link the surreal present with the more civilized past.

Begin this walk in Chinatown on Clay Street below Powell, across from the Commodore Stockton Grammar School. It was down Clay Street at 5 A.M., August 2, 1873, that Andrew S. Hallidie, his partners, and a gripman named Jimmie made the historic test run in the first cable car ever built. By the time they reached Joice Street, they were in a dense fogbank, tense and eager to stop rolling. The trip was a success. The Clay Street Railroad Company, since absorbed by the Muni, had launched San Francisco's best-loved anachronism.

Look down Joice Street before you begin to walk it. It has a noticeable backdoor ubiety, narrow and appropriate to service entrances and stable-door accesses. San Francisco's first exclusive residential section grew up just downhill on Stockton Street. Children who walked to Dr. Ver Mehr's Episcopal Parish School along this lane in 1850 must have watched with excitement as "Gold was found" (according to Soulé, Gihon, and Nisbet in *The Annals of San Francisco*) in "the sand taken from a great depth in sinking wells in Stockton Street."

Two years later, Soulé *et al.* record, "Stockton Street was being ornamented with many handsome brick tenements, which were intended for the private residences of some of the wealthier citizens." One of the finest, 806 Stockton, was the home of Francis L. A. Pioche, pioneer financier and bon vivant credited with giving San Francisco an appreciation of fine food. He imported many French chefs and a cargo of vintage wines. His stables fronted Joice Street, as several carports and tree-shaded parking areas do today.

One parking lot formerly held the refuge house of the Presbyterian Chinese Mission, long a sanctuary for broken lilies from old Canton. Cameron House, at the southeast corner of Sacramento and Joice, is named in honor of Donaldina Cameron, whom the Chinese call "Lo Mo," the mother, for her lifetime work freeing singsong slave girls. Her longtime assistant, Loran Logan, once told me that the last slave came to the community center in 1934. Go inside to see beautiful old carved cornices, calligraphy, and paintings.

As you cross Sacramento, look north along the line of the Stockton Street tunnel where the Chinese Six Companies, Chinatown's unofficial city hall, is headquartered. Kong Chow Temple is on the roof of the Chinatown Post Office beyond it.

At California, before you reach the corner, look for the formal little garden that gives a lift to this city eyeline. Across broad California Street, which led grandly to the mansions of the "nabobs" who gave Nob Hill its name, Joice Street eases along quietly for another half block, then drops precipitously in broad splendid steps to end at Pine in a gardenlike oasis with another surprise. There in the heart of the city, shyly hidden in the shrubs that line the steps, is a well-tended wayside shrine. It was built, with love and devotion, by Ronald Telfer, who lived on Joice Street for many years. Long after his death, it is still tended by friends, relatives, and admirers.

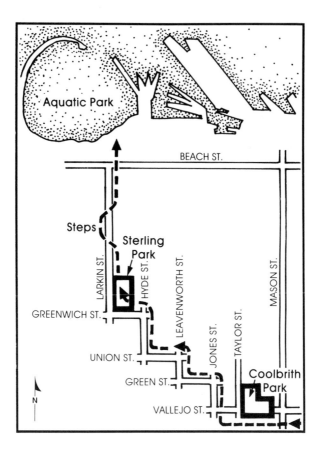

RUSSIAN HILL

WALKING TIME: Half an hour.

DISTANCE: A steep mile.

PUBLIC TRANSPORTATION: Hyde Street cable car and Powell and Mason cable car.

PARKING: Tight.

CLOTHES: Urbane.

Waterfronts, hilltops, and open spaces are what give San Francisco its exhilarating quality. We all enjoy the perception of space, interpreted as freedom, on a walk. Given the choice, almost anyone will opt for the clump of green trees or the glint of blue water visible in the distance as a destination for a walk.

Coincidentally, our city is famous for those unexpected glimpses of the Bay framed between buildings, the ever-widening perspectives as one climbs a hill, the sense of achievement at the top, the breathtaking reward of a distant vista from a summit, the rounding of a corner to find the whole open horizon. One of my favorite city walks touches two hilltops, a beach, four small parks, and has at least seven surprise vistas. There's public transportation handy to both ends. It follows the dogleg ridge of Russian Hill through our most "San Franciscan" neighborhood.

Begin this walk at Vallejo and Mason streets. Look around for the green oasis, then start uphill toward it on Vallejo. In a trice you leave the barren urban desert of stark North Beach to find the lush informality of Alta Vista Terrace. Take the steps alongside that lead to Ina Coolbrith Park, a memorial to the famous librarian who inspired Jack London. Once there, sit a moment on one of the park benches to look below at North Beach before crossing Taylor Street for a climb to even loftier heights.

With each ten feet you climb on the Vallejo Street steps, pause briefly to assess the widening vista. To Ambrose Bierce, Will and Wallace Irwin, Gelett "Purple Cow" Burgess, Charlie Dobie, and Frank Norris this flight was an aerie of Bohemia. The Mediterranean-style balustrades at the top of the hill were designed by architect Willis Polk, who lived on the south side of the 1000 block and divided his house rather than sell it after his divorce. For one of the all-time fabulous views of the East Bay, punctuated by Telegraph Hill, walk over to the end of the parking circle. This was the site of San Francisco's first gallows.

Russian Hill Place and Florence Place are so entrancing a neighborhood, you may want to linger forever, but for this walk start west again to the balustrade opposite at Jones Street, the site of the Russian graveyard that gave Russian Hill its name. When the ramps and balustrade were built in 1912, road cuts unearthed skeletons.

Bear right, down the ramp to Green Street, ignoring the soaring Eichler Summit highrise if you can, and cross to the north side for another of those great surprises, a view of Golden Gate Bridge. Then zig west on the "Paris block of Green Street," the most varied in the city, to enjoy its architectural mixture of firehouse, octagon, farmhouse, Beaux Arts, Art Nouveau, French, and Italianate buildings. Zag right again on Leavenworth and walk on the east side for the fun of a glimpse down Macondray Lane, one of the hill's best-kept public secrets. The Union Street corner view north is another sheer drop-off whose steepness gives a thrilling glimpse of infinity. Bear left on Union, and at Hyde Street there is another distant vista, revealing Pacific Heights with the Presidio as a backdrop.

A cable car may rumble past as you approach Hyde Street. If you can resist the original Swenson's ice-cream shop, follow the car tracks to the right until you reach Greenwich Street. Look east for a great vista of Coit Tower, but walk left up the red-brick ramp past the tennis courts into George Sterling Park, named for the poet whose home overlooked it. On the northern steps, start down and go right through the gap into a broad tree-lined *allée*. Short of its end, bear left through another gap in the hedge to the next lower terrace and look for the concrete staircase in the northwest corner of the park, a great place to see the mountains of Marin or watch a winter sunset.

Follow the steps down to Lombard Street. To the right, the site of the old Rolph estate now accommodates the Lombardia, a small group of townhouses happily conforming to neighborhood standards. Walk north on Larkin to Chestnut Street for a spectacular western aspect toward the Palace of Fine Arts.

Follow Larkin toward the trees on the west side of the street. Another surprise! Hidden steps go down at Francisco with a view of the whole northeastern waterfront. Look both ways as you approach the curve before crossing Larkin to reach a middle lap of the steps that lead to Francisco Street's lower section. You soon arrive alongside the Hyde Street Reservoir, the unpaved pathway of which borders the upper edge of the Bay Street Park, a favorite dog run for all of Russian Hill.

Near the charming vegetable garden, look for an even lower level of the steps, which parallel North View Court to end at Bay. Cross Bay Street with the stoplight, continue one block downhill on Larkin to reach the instant vacation known as Ghirardelli Square. Linger for lunch, browse, shop, or rest, for every bench has been placed with a masterful eye for the stimulating outlook. Then work your way downhill to Beach Street, cross it, and you are at the Golden Gate National Recreation Area's Aquatic Park Beach, the Hyde Street Pier, the National Maritime Museum, and the beginning to our grandest waterfront walk, the Golden Gate Promenade.

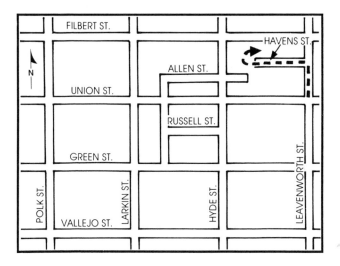

HAVENS STREET

WALKING TIME: One-half hour.

DISTANCE: A city block.

PUBLIC TRANSPORTATION: Muni bus 41 Union.

PARKING: Very little.

CLOTHES: Whatever.

Like a web cast by an inspired spider, little public lanes and stairways encircle Russian Hill. The lanes began as footpaths in a more gracious, leisurely time. Some led to houses still located deep in the middle of a block, others to places long gone. Always quieter than the nearby streets, many of the lanes have pathside vines, trees, or shrubs that soften the passageways, make agreeable shadows on patrician buildings, and provide natural foregrounds for the distant views visible from the fine old neighborhood.

Among them, Havens Street has emerged as one of the most charming, thanks to the cooperative gardening by its nearby residents. Barely three-fourths of a block long, the walk up through the gardens that surround the seventy-six steps of Havens Street and back down again can be done in a leisurely half hour.

Begin at Leavenworth Street to enjoy this walk. As you start walking north, the lordly view of the Bay from this steep hill is exhilarating. It may also distract you from the unimposing setback entrance to Havens

Street. Look for the steps about halfway downhill on the west, alongside 2033 Leavenworth. HAVENS 000, the street sign says, but unless you are climbing uphill from Filbert Street, you are past the sign before you are aware that you have arrived. Victorian box trees farther downhill were planted by the San Francisco Friends of the Urban Forest, a complement to the late Friedel Klussmann's organization, San Francisco Beautiful.

Look north for a vignette view of Alcatraz before you start to climb the concrete steps on your left. In November 1986, when tax attorney Edward Dean moved into an apartment next to the lane, Havens Street's steps were so overgrown with weeds and strewn with trash they were nearly impassable. Almost a year later, on Labor Day weekend in 1987, he and a neighbor began cleaning out weeds and trash, revealing the old fig, loquat, and olive trees.

By the time the lower fourth of the Havens staircase was cleaned out, they had removed thirty trash cans full of debris. Fortunately, the city will remove at no cost debris weeded from public lanes. Underneath, when the lane was clean, Dean found a gardener's treasure—a festoon of scallop-shaped red-brick terraces decorating the north side of the stairway and landings.

"A family named Bagnasco owned the building until 1980," Dean told me, "and from the trees, mirror plant, and perennials we found, they must have planted an elaborate Mediterranean-style garden here at some time." Making the most of the north light that filters between the surrounding buildings, Dean and Jeff Graham of Las Baulinas Nursery in Bolinas have created a tropical little Eden.

Inspired by the late Grace Marchant, who long ago began gardening the Filbert Street steps on Telegraph Hill with one pot of baby's tears, Dean began his efforts on the Havens Street steps the same way. His baby's tears originated from a pot ex-Mayor Dianne Feinstein had discarded.

The baby's tears ground cover, also called Japanese or Irish moss, grows so lushly from terrace to terrace that it looks like lava flow, standing in sharp contrast to the curved retaining walls.

As you start climbing, notice on your left the Balinese carving, which originated as the lintel of a temple and was designed to ward off evil spirits. Wild ginger, bromeliads, bamboo, agapanthus, clivia, and at least six kinds of ferns enhance the tropical feeling. Tempting as it is, turn left with the stairs and hug the building on the south side of the walkway; for this tour, follow the paving on the north side.

If there is a seductive tropical odor, look for blooms on the jasmine that grows on the fence on your right. Now that the Havens Street side garden is nearly completed, Dean says he "intends to do more with the lower garden," visible on the right under a bower of pittosporum trees.

After you pass the end of the fenceline, you reach the garden of Ted and Nancy Rademacher. Longtime residents, they redid their deck and garden many years ago, after heavy rains pushed an earlier deck down 430 feet into the yard below.

Turn right and walk north along "Kitty Cat Lane," as neighbors have nicknamed the walkway that approaches their deck. En route, you will pass a Royal Anne cherry tree, Victorian box, and camellias. Try to envision what this little hidden wonderland must look like on festive nights when the Rademachers illuminate the trees for a party or holiday. Lighting the tropical section is also in Dean's plans for the future.

When you have walked as far as you can, return again to Havens and continue uphill. Number 6 Havens, on your right, began as an "earthquake shake," or refugee cottage, after the 1906 earthquake. Architect William Wurster did the renovation years ago.

Friends of author Armistead Maupin, who once lived in an apartment overlooking Havens, believe that this pathway, rather than nearby Macondray Lane, was the setting for his book *Tales of the City*. My guess is that it was a composite of these and several other lanes on the hill.

White choysia, or Mexican mock orange, is the charmer near the telephone pole bearing the numbers 02.

Keep walking uphill and the ambiance changes as you reach the upper part of Havens, gardened by Catherine Allan. In sharp contrast to the tropical section below, it has a distinctive Mediterranean feeling, but Allan modestly told me, "Oh, it's just a little hodgepodge."

Ultimately, you arrive at a gate that closes off the upper end of Havens, which may have originated as a backdoor path to Leavenworth Street from the midblock house on your left. Peek through the fence to see a sunny west-facing garden boasting a big datura bush, bird-of-paradise plants, roses, tulips, and grape hyacinths. This is the side garden of the home of Minnie Huber, number 10 Hastings Terrace, whose front door is uphill from Hyde Street. Long ago, the path continued around this hidden house to emerge next to Verne's Shoe Repair shop on Hyde Street.

When you have enjoyed this glimpse of a secret shoulder of the hill, return downhill to Leavenworth Street, hugging the buildings on your right. The return trip will give you a completely different understanding of the hillside gardens. The love, planning, and thought that have gone into this little lane—as narrow in some places as a Japanese *ryokan* garden—demonstrate to the walker that neighborly cooperation has kept Russian Hill livable for so long, despite the incursions of that dubious factor sometimes mislabeled "progress."

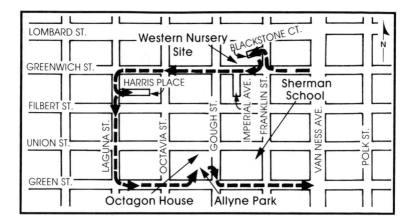

COW HOLLOW

WALKING TIME: An hour.

DISTANCE: One mile.

PUBLIC TRANSPORTATION: Muni buses 42, 47, and 49.

PARKING: Forget it.

CLOTHES: Your best casual cashmeres.

One of the joys of the city is that you can walk around a corner and find a different world. Cow Hollow, once an idyllic retreat of market gardens, pretty dairymaids, dunes, springs, and orchards, is such a world.

You will not find Cow Hollow on the map, but Union Street between Van Ness and Lyon is the heart of it. The walker who brings perceptive eyes can still find the droll, bucolic neighborhood of folklore clinging to Union, as incongruous as telltale wisps of straw on a Hattie Carnegie gown. Union is a woman's street, with flowers in her hair, fripperies in her boutiques, and a fancy selection of goods for conspicuous consumption, among them a plethora of pies, pre-Columbian fetishes, potpourri, and copper pots in her shops. As the carpoolers from Marin have discovered, it also has the prettiest girls and young matrons shopping or waiting for the buses.

Hundreds of cows and the dairies that served the city gave Cow Hollow its name. Charlton Court, a cul-de-sac that juts off Union, is reputed to have been a milk-wagon loading yard for one of these.

"Even though it has been seventy years since a cow set foot in Cow Hollow, and its pastures have dwindled to a vacant lot or two," wrote

San Francisco Chronicle columnist Robert O'Brien in 1948, "there are plenty of Native Sons who will say that Cow Hollow, San Francisco, is heaven on earth, and that's where they want to go when they die." Cow Hollow, Old Hollow, and the Marina—all of which lie within the little shell of land bounded by Russian Hill, Pacific Heights, the Presidio, and the Bay—are neighborhoods in the area originally known as Golden Gate Valley. The name was bestowed on the valley in the early nineteenth century, when it was a patchwork of dairies, nurseries, pastures, and market gardens surrounding Washerwoman's Lagoon, or, as it was sometimes called, Fresh Pond or Laguna Pequeña. It was on the shores of this lagoon that Juan Bautista de Anza and his exploring party camped on the night of Thursday, March 28, 1776.

Old maps show that Washerwoman's Lagoon was three little spring-fed, freshwater lakes shut off from San Francisco Bay by a large barrier sandbar. The largest of the three lakes, and the one that lasted the longest as San Francisco grew, had the "paisley shape" of an amoeba. It lay between what is now Filbert Street on the south and Lombard Street on the north, Franklin Street on the east and Laguna Street on the west. Indeed, this was one of the two lagoons that gave Laguna Street its name. The other was Laguna de Manantial, another of Anza's campgrounds, near what is now Mission Dolores.

When San Francisco had only three roads, one of them passed along the northern shore of Washerwoman's Lagoon, connecting Portsmouth Square with the Presidio. Remarkably, a piece of the old road is still visible. Along it are several buildings and many plants that once overlooked Washerwoman's Lagoon. The place to find them is Blackstone Court, which has been designated the city's smallest historic district.

Thousands of commuters from Marin pass Blackstone Court daily without suspecting that one of San Francisco's special secret places hides just off busy Franklin Street near Lombard. For the city walker exploring the area, there are other charming remnants from the era before Washerwoman's Lagoon was drained. Once, this area had all the scenic appeal of Oakland's Lake Merritt.

To make this walk, transport yourself to Golden Gate Valley at Van Ness and Greenwich Street and walk west downhill one block to Franklin Street. You have now reached the corner of the square block that once contained the Western Nursery, established in 1880 by Charles Abraham, for whom the flowering apricot is named. In 1886, when Abraham moved his nursery here, the lower part of his tract was still under the waters of Washerwoman's Lagoon. According to *Vignettes of Early San Francisco Homes and Gardens*, published in 1935 by the San Francisco Garden Club, "Abraham, with the aid of his old

mother and niece, gradually, one wheelbarrow at a time, filled in the
lower part of the property."

Cross Franklin Street with the stoplight and turn right. Three-
quarters of a block down, you reach a street sign that reads, BLACK-
STONE 000. Blackstone Court angles, on the same diagonal as Market
Street, behind the Rancho Lombard motel. Turn left alongside the
dentist's office and you are suddenly on the original Presidio Road.

When pioneer journalist Bayard Taylor came this way in the fall of
1849 to fill a donkey cart with water casks, he wrote, "Several tents
were pitched on its margin; the washmen and gardeners were dili-
gently plying their respective occupations. . . . The washerwomen, of
whom there were a few . . . had established themselves on one side of
the pond, and the washmen on the other. . . . It was an amusing sight
to see a great burly, long-bearded fellow kneeling on the ground, with
sleeves rolled up to the elbows, rubbing a shirt on the board with such
violence that the suds flew and the buttons, if there were any, must
soon snap off."

Even before the Gold Rush, the land adjoining the lagoon seemed
choice. In 1847, when William Eddy surveyed the area, he laid out
twenty-four double-sized lots, each aligned to look toward the Golden
Gate, rather than along the east-west line of later streets.

According to John L. Levinsohn's book *Cow Hollow* (San Francisco
Yesterday, 1976), "It was the surveyor's plan in time to align all lots in
this manner [and] most interesting was his placement of the survey
adjacent to the inland water, much as contemporary developers of
recreational land have frequently done." Every house in the north-
western part of the city would look toward the Golden Gate if the
surveyor's plan had been executed.

Walk toward the welcome spot of greenery at the end of the court.
Much of it was planted in the heyday of Abraham's Western Nursery.
At number 11, you are at Blackstone House, named, like the street, for
pioneer Nathaniel Blackstone, a member of the 1856 vigilantes. Blackstone actually lived next door at number 7, now demolished; number
11 may have housed servants or family members.

It is possible that number 11, a two-story Gothic frame house with a
rare veranda, is the oldest residence in the city. It began life as a cottage
and in the oldest oral history of the neighborhood "was moved here
from some ranch by a Mexican." The *rancho* could have been that of
Don Benito Díaz, once owner of two leagues of land running from
Washerwoman's Lagoon to Point Lobos. Díaz built "a small house for
servants" in 1845.

Look behind the Blackstone House to locate the original stable, long
since refaced for a garage. Twin Canary Island pines are visible tower-

ing over it. These are hidden from Lombard Street by a monster billboard.

Peek over the gate at number 30, where an attractive enclave of small homes includes the original Abraham House, set among the trees and shrubs that he imported. Botanists have identified more than fifty plants from Abraham's nursery still thriving on the grounds. Visitors staying in the adjacent motel can see the bougainvillea, first imported into this country by Abraham, which still blooms along his fenceline, and his Australian Peppermint tree towering over the gate.

Five glass houses, a tall glass palm conservatory, a water tower, tank, and windmill once stood on the property. Water was so precious during the hectic days after the fire of '06 that for three days Abraham's niece Charlotte Goesch ladled water out to people who had been waiting in lines. Guards from the Presidio were then detailed to relieve her.

Retrace your steps to Franklin and Greenwich streets, then turn right on Greenwich. Midblock, you are standing in what was the middle of Washerwoman's Lagoon until January 1879, when the municipal sewer line was completed, piping much of the lagoon into the Bay. The handsome Victorian at number 1649 was moved here after the lagoon was drained. Imperial Court is another of San Francisco's secret enclaves.

Head for Octavia and Greenwich, where O'Connor's Grading Camp once stood, handy to the lake bottom he was filling. Go one block farther on Greenwich, past other Victorian homes that survive like jewels among the plainer modern buildings, and turn left on Laguna Street.

In half a block you reach Harris Place. Architectural historian Anne Bloomfield said it was originally Harry's Alley. Stroll to its end. The old geraniums and trees—many of which may have come from Abraham's nursery—give the alley the feel of a suburban lane.

Return to Laguna Street and walk south uphill to pass chic Union Street, once bucolic and now a Yuppie paradise of shopping, dining, and entertainment. Ernest Coxhead was the architect for the handsome Golden Gate Valley Branch Library at Octavia Street, built in 1916.

When you arrive at the welcome green oasis in the next block, go through the picket gate to enjoy Allyne Park. On this sunny spot of lawn once stood the home of the Allyne sisters, Lucy and Edith. When I visited them in the 1950s, there was still a four-foot-tall porcelain vase in the garden that their father, Captain Allyne, had brought from the Orient on one of his many voyages. One of the sisters told me, "Our cow used to drink from it." That cow may have been the last cow in Cow Hollow.

Look northeast past the trees for a great view of Octagon House, which stands on land given by the Allynes to the National Society of Colonial Dames. Built by William C. McElroy in 1862, the house stood across the street and was donated to the Colonial Dames by Pacific Gas & Electric Company, on whose property it had been located. Both sites once overlooked Washerwoman's Lagoon.

Octagon House is open to the public on the second Sunday of each month and the second and fourth Thursdays from noon until 3 P.M. For a modest fee, visitors can inspect this classic "Fowler's Inkwell," named for Orson Fowler, who popularized the style.

If it isn't open, return to Green Street and walk east to pass, across from Sherman School, the Burr Estate, the parklike enclave midblock. Within this beautifully gardened private complex are eight buildings, all designed by distinguished architects, including Henry Gutterson, William Wurster, and Elizabeth Austin. Several are visible from the street.

Continue one more block to Van Ness Avenue to see the Holy Trinity Russian Orthodox Cathedral, built in 1909. Gleb Ilyn is the artist of its murals.

If you are eager for more walking, head seven blocks north to Fort Mason to enjoy all the bayside pleasures of the Golden Gate National Recreation Area or the adjoining National Maritime Museum ships.

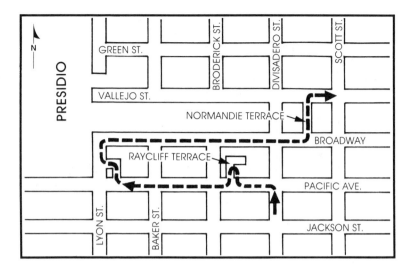

PACIFIC HEIGHTS

WALKING TIME: A morning.

DISTANCE: About a mile.

PUBLIC TRANSPORTATION: Muni bus 3 Jackson to arrive, 22 or 41 Union to depart.

PARKING: Not much.

CLOTHES: Gucci or Bill Blass, if you have them.

Little lanes, culs-de-sac, and public staircases are among the amenities that give cachet to San Francisco's stable old neighborhoods. Protected geographically from noisy through traffic, such places have the privacy and quietude most of us yearn for as an escape from the hectic modern world. This sweet serenity is one of the choicer things that money can buy.

To see for yourself, consider a walk along some little lanes in that stronghold of rank, swank, and status: Pacific Heights. May is a good time to walk it, when the streetside gardens are at their best.

Those who would like a close look on this walk, begin at the corner of Jackson and Divisadero. Walk north, uphill on Divisadero. If it seems steep, remember that climbing one uphill block can do your heart as much good as a fifteen-minute jog along level ground. Actually, the grade here is less than 10 percent.

At Pacific Avenue, you reach one of the lookout points that gave Divisadero, one of the first three roads in San Francisco, its name. Originally, this was an Indian path, and later a Spanish trail from the Presidio to Laguna de Manantial (now the valley of Mission Dolores). The name Divisadero means "to descry objects in the distance."

Look east beyond a consulate on the northeast corner for one of the finer views of downtown. North gives an equally patrician vista of the Bay. All of the large homes on this crest command views. Some also look south to San Bruno Mountain, and west to the greenery of the Presidio.

Turn left alongside the handsome brick house faced with fine old wisteria. Pause a moment on one of the park benches, which philanthropist Lee Herbst Gruen has thoughtfully placed around her home, to the everlasting gratitude of walkers.

Walk west. Farther along the street, the English-style mansion belongs to artist Weyman Lu. When you reach the lush garden at number 2820, listen for exotic birdsong. According to *Here Today*, the Junior League Historic Sites book, published in 1968 by the *San Francisco Chronicle*, "Willis Polk designed this grand house in the style of an Italian palazzo" in 1912. It was for Miss Alice Griffith, founder of the Telegraph Hill Neighborhood Association. Take a good look at the house behind the greenery, for you will see it three more times on this walk.

In a few more steps, you reach Raycliff Terrace, which dates to the 1950s. Turn right to enter one of Pacific Heights's secret enclaves. Architectural buffs will find the houses interesting as a compatible group, designed by different architects. Credit for number 1, which was designed in 1951, goes to Gardner Dailey. Joseph Esherick designed number 75; Germano Milono, number 55; and Wurster, Bernardi, and Emmons, number 15, the last to be built.

When you are in the deepest interior of the cul-de-sac, look east to see a sidewall of the same house you first located at 2820 Pacific. Unless there is a chainsaw whining somewhere in the area, this court is remarkably quiet.

Return to Pacific Avenue and look across the street, as you continue west, to notice how tastefully the pink rhododendrons at 2889 Pacific show off against the gray shingles. Arthur Brown is believed to have been the architect.

Across Broderick Street, the green-and-white awning of El Drisco Hotel on the southwest corner is so discreet that it could almost be a private residence. For many years, El Drisco has been Pacific Heights's secret place for housing extra guests during weddings and such. Diane Weaver, a longtime Pacific Heights resident, told me El Drisco's Sunday brunch, complete with harp music, is a community tradition.

At midblock, you are across from the former site of the U. S. Grant Public Elementary School. Generations of schoolchildren climbed the elegant concrete staircase on the north side, which exits onto Broadway. When my eldest son attended first grade at Grant School, a copy of the Social Register was among the books on the principal's desk.

The farmhouse-style gray-shingled house overlooking the block was once owned by a member of the Newhall family, who built the San Francisco and San Jose Railroad. New construction across from the Grant School site has been repeatedly stopped by residents of the area who believe another hotel would change the neighborhood from residential to commercial.

Cross Baker Street and continue west. The Egyptian consulate has been housed in number 3001 since 1959. The Mediterranean-style house at number 3035 was originally a firehouse; now it has great gardens and its own pool. When you arrive at number 3070, you have reached another of Pacific Heights's secret lanes. To the confusion of cabbies, delivery people, and first-time visitors, this little interior street has no name. The houses on the short N-shaped lane have Pacific Avenue street numbers.

Turn right to walk through it and left at its northerly end, past gardens and houses one wouldn't suspect existed, from Pacific Avenue. You will emerge on Lyon Street, alongside the eastern border of the Presidio. Turn right, downhill.

As you descend, try to envision Juan Bautista de Anza and his pioneer party of explorers en route from Mountain Lake, where they camped in March of 1776, riding along this ridge to Laguna Pequeña, or as later San Franciscans called it, Washerwoman's Lagoon. Surely Anza came this way to see all that he could. The view is even more spectacular in our time, with the Golden Gate Bridge defining the Bay, the encircling hills, the islands, and, in the middleground, the confection of the Palace of Fine Arts.

To drink it all in, pause when you reach Broadway. The wrought-iron gate to the Presidio on your left is usually closed to traffic, but the smaller pedestrian gate admits walkers. The Lyon Street stairs that descend to Green Street are used by University High School students for workouts in their physical education classes.

Inviting as the steps and surrounding garden are, save them for another time and turn right on Broadway. All the houses in the block on the north side are blessed with lordly character. Those on the south side, sited higher on stilts to achieve that superb view, are the houses the entrances of which you saw from the unnamed lane uphill.

Just past the Baker Street steps, you'll find 2898 Broadway. Dutch Colonial in style, it was designed in 1899 by Walter Danforth Bliss for his parents. Bliss was also the architect of the St. Francis Hotel and the Metropolitan and University clubs. Willis Polk was the architect for the next cheerful villa, the residence of Grove Weidenfeld president Ann Getty. Up the lofty steps, catty-corner across the street, are private tennis courts and, underneath, a private chapel.

The house on the southeast corner was built by Joseph Strauss, the structural engineer of the Golden Gate Bridge. Notice the lower steps that emerge midblock from the Grant School site, but continue east on Broadway between Broderick and Divisadero. See if you can pick out Miss Griffith's house again.

To find one more secret enclave, cross Divisadero and go downhill half a block. Turn left when you reach Normandie Terrace. This pleasant hillside ledge was built in 1938 and remained a private street until 1976. At the north end, steps descend to Vallejo Street.

Pacific Heights has other inviting secrets to find on the east-facing slope, but the walking is steep.

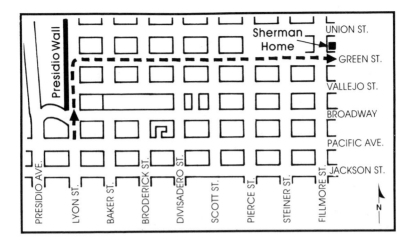

PRESIDIO WALL

WALKING TIME: A leisurely hour.

DISTANCE: Sixteen city blocks.

PUBLIC TRANSPORTATION: Muni bus 3 California going; 41 Union returning.

PARKING: Fair on weekdays.

CLOTHES: Cashmere sweaters and Coach handbags.

Pacific Heights is a state of mind bounded by Ambition, *Vogue* magazine, Dun & Bradstreet, and the Social Register. Its physical borders are equally rubbery. It began in 1893 as a real estate tract along the ridge between Broadway, California, Fillmore, and Van Ness, and has been inching northward and westward ever after.

No matter. If a house stands in that vast north-facing amphitheater where one can count the walkers on the Golden Gate Promenade as they pass Crissy Field, it surely stands in Pacific Heights.

The Presidio Wall, an elegant stone fence along Lyon Street and Pacific Avenue, holds two of the lines on this striving quarter and offers some of the most pleasant walking any citywatcher could desire.

For starters, the stroller might begin his explorations at Pacific Avenue and Lyon Street, at 360 feet above sea level, one of the high points of the ridge Juan Bautista de Anza rode along in 1776. The contemporary house you see was built on the high point after a water tank was removed about ten years ago. Originally it was an Indian lookout. When you have enjoyed the view, start walking north on Lyon Street.

Once a part of the Presidio, the eighty-foot strip that makes up Lyon was named for Nathanial Lyon, captain of C Troop, First Dragoons, who was killed at the battle of Wilson's Creek, Missouri, in 1861, fighting for the freedom of slaves. It was given to the city of San Francisco in 1876 when a fence that stood on an earlier survey line was moved west. About 1897, the beautiful stone wall on your left replaced the fence.

At Broadway, if you can take your eyes from the stairside garden, look at the dome of the Palace of Fine Arts in the middle distance and keep following the steps down toward it. Designed by Bernard Maybeck for the Panama-Pacific International Exposition of 1915, the Palace was his interpretation of Böcklin's painting *The Island of the Dead*. The redwood trees were also planted in 1915 for the Panama-Pacific Exposition.

The walk downhill gives glimpses of one of the most splendid panoramas in the city—the scene-stealing international orange bridge, the blue Bay dotted with white yachts, a backdrop of green islands and tawny hills, and in the middle distance, the romantic dome.

If your knees quiver as you descend, pause to rest on the benches. Notice how well-coordinated the stairs, balustrades, court, landings, and lampposts are with the residence entryways. They were all details perfected at the grand old École des Beaux Arts, on Paris's Left Bank.

At the foot of the steps, the little oval park began life as the *Ojo de Figueroa*, or Eye of Figaro, a spring where Spaniards watered their horses while en route from the Presidio to El Paraje de Yerba Buena, as the village that became San Francisco was first known. The Italianate villas on the left stand on part of one hundred *varas* (a *vara* was as long as a tall man's walking stick) of land granted in 1838 to Apolinario Miranda.

As you approach the southernmost stucco villa, notice the blended coloration of its walls, believed to be the work of Beaux Arts colorist Jules Guerin, who coordinated the colors of the Panama-Pacific Exposition. The villa facing Green Street itself has an attractive double-curved Beaux Arts staircase.

Bear right on Green Street to pass a medley of French chateaux, English manor houses, Victorian fantasies, and more Italianate places. The brown-shingled apartments are reputed to have started as a country inn to serve world travelers who wanted to be near the Exposition. Other lavish buildings sprang up in the preincome-tax era when land was cheap and labor cheaper.

When you reach Pierce Street, try to imagine it as a country road. It led through vegetable gardens and dairy farms in 1865 when Henry Casebolt built carriages in Cow Hollow. Now his home at 2727 Pierce is one of the architectural treasures of the city.

Another is the home of Leander P. Sherman, founder of Sherman, Clay and Company, and coincidentally godfather of the San Francisco Symphony. Built in 1877, the home at 2160 Green Street is one of the most spectacular mansard-roofed Victorian homes standing in San Francisco. Now a bed-and-breakfast inn, it has fifteen rooms and gardens all embellished by different decorators and designers and is often used for weddings and receptions. If you are invited, go.

Unless you were to the manor born, it's one sure way to get inside and roam around one of the lordly homes of Pacific Heights to see how life "upstairs" was lived.

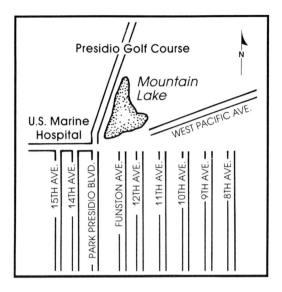

MOUNTAIN LAKE

WALKING TIME: Allow a morning.

DISTANCE: The equivalent of fourteen city blocks.

PUBLIC TRANSPORTATION: Take Muni buses 44, IA-X, and IB-X to California and 8th streets.

PARKING: Excellent on weekdays on the avenues between Lake and the park.

CLOTHES: Casual sweaters and play clothes.

Mountain Lake is that unexpected flash of blue fresh water that can sometimes be seen by motorists just southeast of the General Douglas MacArthur Tunnel on the Park-Presidio Golden Gate Bridge approach. From Lake Street, to which it lends its name, Mountain Lake cannot be seen at all.

Surrounded by a well-equipped park, also named for it, Mountain Lake is very much there, however, behind the houses lining the north side of Lake Street between 7th and Funston avenues. It can only be explored on foot and the walk is a delight to all who live nearby.

The logical place to begin this walk is dead center, at the end of 8th Avenue where a flight of stone steps goes up to a bench, a drinking fountain, and parcourse equipment. The first parcourse in the nation was erected here. A broad footpath runs east and west behind the houses that front on Lake Street. Bear left past the fountain, then follow the fork of the path that leads through bishop pines and leptospermum trees to a flagpole.

Pause at the flagpole. To the left is a secluded mountain meadow, full of daisies, kite flyers, sunbathers, touch-tackle players, and migrating ducks at different times of the year. Straight ahead is a three-sided shelter furnished with tables and benches and known locally as "The Cardhouse," where as many as ten pinochle games may be in progress. So enrapt are the old men in their games that they rarely look up.

The path meanders over a low, rolling ridge. From its crest one sees the spring-fed waterhole where Juan Bautista de Anza camped on March 27, 1776, an occasion commemorated by a marker in a grove of trees on the south shore. Anza called the lake Laguna de Presidio and decided it held enough water to supply a garrison. It did.

It also partially supplied San Francisco with water between 1852 and 1870. Part of an old conduit support from the Mountain Lake Water Company can still be seen leading, like giant steps, to the water.

Yellow lupine grows along the sandy beach of the near shore. Ducks nest on the far shore, which is a U.S. game refuge and was twice as large before the bridge approach was built. A leg of the Presidio Golf Course can be seen across the water. Sometimes, at water's edge, is a scene reminiscent of George Bellows's famous painting *Forty-two Kids*, in which boys, half-hidden by the tule reeds, have contrived a raft.

From the lake, the path swings up past playgrounds and tennis courts and loops around to follow the gardens of Lake Street houses. There is egress from this part of the walk at every street from Funston to 8th. At any of them, a walker can be back on city streets in twenty paces, feeling not unlike Alice when she emerged from the Rabbit Hole, "eyes bright . . ." and able to find pleasure in ". . . simple joys, remembering her own child life, and the happy summer days."

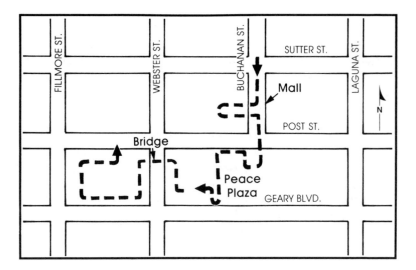

JAPANTOWN

WALKING TIME: Half an hour to cover the ground, half a day to browse.

DISTANCE: About a mile.

PUBLIC TRANSPORTATION: Muni bus 2, 3, or 4.

PARKING: Under the Kabuki Theater.

CLOTHES: Suitable for the city.

Shibui is the Japanese word for that mellow patina age brings to things that wear well. An old stone lantern moss-softened by time is a good example. However chipped or cracked it may be, there is character in it and an integrity that has survived adversity. Its scars are part of its beauty.

Japantown, with its two radically diverse parts—*wabi,* the old, and *sabi,* the new—on opposite sides of Post Street between Laguna and Fillmore streets, is finally, twenty years after redevelopment, developing some *shibui.*

Perhaps the most handsome, best-planned, and certainly most romantic of San Francisco's many ethnic communities, Japantown is pleasant to walk any time. While the annual *Sakura Matsuri,* or Cherry Blossom Festival—in the spring, or midsummer's Obon Odori Festival—is under way, Japantown is especially fun, for the community generously shares its rich cultural heritage. During festivals, Post Street is blocked off between Laguna and Webster streets.

Begin this walk at Buchanan Street and Sutter, where the Kyoto Inn on one side and the American Fish Company on the other alerts you that this neighborhood is different.

The torii gate is unmistakable. Walk to the center of it and look down this charming little street that represents a mountain village with a meandering stream in its center. This "river" of rocks swirls between two metal sculptures, one an origami chrysanthemum bud, and the other the flower in full bloom, both by Ruth Asawa. On either side are benches, overhung by cherry and plum trees, the flowers and leaves of which offer a fine contrast to the dun-colored buildings. A happy juxtaposition of shops and restaurants, all with compatible architecture, gives unity to the pedestrian-only street. The interiors are as authentic as the facades.

So is the merchandise and cuisine, with one recent exception: a twenty-four-hour fast-food purveyor at the corner of Buchanan and Post streets open, of course, twenty-four hours a day. This newcomer gives lip service to ethnicity with some "wanna-be" Japanese meals on the menu.

Survivors of fifteen lean years of redevelopment are Benkyo-do Pastry, Japan Trading Company, Gosha-do bookstore, Nichi Bei Bussan department store, Uoki Sakai grocery, Seiki Imports, and Soko Hardware. It is reassuring to find these pioneers from the pre-World War II era here, although no one is apt to bow you to the door these days and bid you "*Sayonara*" as the proprietors of Soko Hardware did when I first entered their shop in 1961.

Follow the swirl of stones in the river. Halfway the length of the outdoor mall, look to the right to find a little lane that leads to the parking lot. Continue south past the *koban*, or "cop-in-a-box," which maintains the safety and serenity of this community.

Japanese-Americans make up about a third of San Francisco's Asian population, but during festivals, visitors from the hinterlands may quadruple this number. Downhill, parallel to the Japantown Bowl, is the Ginza of Japantown. Teenagers love it.

As you cross Post Street, look uphill toward the Miyako Hotel. A satellite Korean community is emerging on the north side, much as a subsidiary Japantown has attached itself downtown to the Chinatown gates.

Step onto the south side of Post and you have left *Nihonmachi*, the *wabi* side, and entered the *sabi*. This is the Japan Center, a five-acre complex designed by Minoru Yamasaki, one of America's foremost architects.

Go under the handsome copper roof, past the empty ponds, and down two or three steps to the Peace Plaza, a public space with the eye-catching five-tiered pagoda, given to San Francisco by the people of

Japan in 1968. The adjacent stage is the center of many festival activities.

To find another, more informal community gathering place, walk west under the copper roof into the Kintetsu Building. Bear left at the first opportunity and turn right at the next corner. Japanese shops overlook a pleasant little interior street here, surrounding a street cafe under a skylight. The favorite quick snack here is tea and a *tai yaki*, a fish-shaped waffle stuffed with sweet bean filling.

If chocolate is your preference, Murata's Floral Design carries flowers of the elegant Joseph Schmidt brand. Linger as long as you like, visiting the nearby shops, then continue to the next corner, where the windows of the Ikenobo Flower Arranging School feature prize-winning arrangements.

Go around the corner and you are faced with two choices. On your right is a restaurant row. Turn left instead and you are on the Webster Street Bridge. Crossing it you will pass the Kimochi Senior Lounge and Library, where there are always a few handmade treasures for sale. The health food shop sells, among other goodies, a seafood jerky made from shark.

As you leave the bridge, Kinokuniya Bookstore, the largest in San Francisco, is on your left. Kinokuniya has been so successful in this location that it has bought the building and opened a second store featuring paper products, just across the central court on the upper level.

Whatever your desire, be it sushi or pearls, beer or antique kimonos, *futons*, *shiki-butons*, *tansus*, or *tatami* mats, some place in the building sells it. Look around, explore, and prepare to be delighted.

If you enjoy walking around *Nihonmachi* and Japan Center by day, plan to come again for an evening. Like Tokyo, Japantown engenders its own entertainment, including bowling at the Japantown Bowl and bars where the clienteles sing along with live piano or recorded music. (Look for these places tucked into unlikely corners.)

Don't miss the baths—notably the Kabuki Hot Springs, where a soak can include a *shiatsu* massage—and films at AMC Kabuki Theater, where eight movies run concurrently.

And, of course, there is a score or more of authentic restaurants. By night Japantown is as lively, and every bit as romantic, as it is by day.

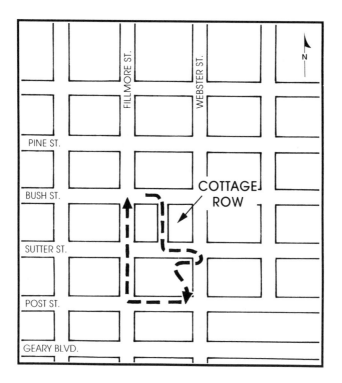

COTTAGE ROW

WALKING TIME: An hour.

DISTANCE: Three-quarters of a mile.

PUBLIC TRANSPORTATION: Muni buses 1, 2, 3, 4, 31, and 38.

PARKING: Not much.

CLOTHES: Casual.

For rural charm and big-city convenience, plus that elusive quality planners call "livability," it's hard to beat a one-block-long pedestrian-only lane in the Western Addition called Cottage Row.

Glimpse it from Sutter Street, a half-block east of Fillmore Street, and its trees and rich, red-brick pavement seem to beckon. For the most San Franciscan elements of its character, however, begin this walk uphill, at Fillmore and Bush streets, where Pacific Heights has been pushing its traditional boundary southward toward a new "Yuppieville."

MINI-BOOM IN WESTERN ADDITION read a headline in the *San Francisco*

Chronicle on July 19, 1976. The story described how prices of the old Victorians had soared in what was once known as Western Addition Redevelopment Area A-2.

They are still soaring. This fact is no surprise to anyone who knows how convenient and "livable" the Western Addition can be. Our forebears bestowed on this part of the city those things urbane people have always wanted: houses with high ceilings, spacious rooms, cozy open hearths, and big gardens, all located within walking distance of shops, schools, theater, museums, playgrounds, and a place of work.

Where does one find such pearls? The Yuppies who can afford it find them in the periphery of Japantown—an area that was once a slum, then a daring redevelopment experiment, and in the long run, a noteworthy success.

Signaling just how upscale the neighborhood has become is the elegant French bakery Patisserie Delanghe, at the southeast corner of Fillmore and Bush streets. Come along at the right time and see owner Dominique Delanghe, who once worked as a pastry chef at Buckingham Palace, creating *pain au chocolat* or lush berry croissants.

Walk east, and within a few steps, old and new stand side by side in startling contrast. Alongside a modest, clean-lined contemporary house that seems to adjoin the Bauhaus-style bakery is a row of six false-front Italianate Victorians at 2115–2125 Bush, little changed from the time they were built in 1874.

There were hundreds of other distinguished rows of Victorian houses in San Francisco's first Western Addition redevelopment plan, but they were relentlessly torn down, bulldozed away, displacing fifteen thousand people in 1960.

In an unprecedented move, the late Justin Herman, then director of the San Francisco Redevelopment Agency, offered homeowners of the second section, Area A-2, the opportunity to renew and rehabilitate their own property, giving them the same financial breaks big developers get when creating a redevelopment project.

Stop before you pass by this elegant line of Victorians. END COTTAGE ROW says a sign on the brown-shingled house. Look down it to discern a genuine "mews" built as servants' quarters for the larger, more elegant homes on Bush Street. The slightly later houses numbered 2103–2107 prolong the Victorian flavor of Bush Street; but turn right, if you will, down the steps of Cottage Row.

Notice the trees and greenery that give this lane a country look. A mini-park, built the length of the row on the lot immediately on your right, has ensured that this handsomely simple group of houses, all sharing common walls, will continue to look onto an attractive space.

When you have reached the first of the mini-park's gates, walk in and go as far as the pergola. Then turn around so that you can take in Cottage Row as a composition. Walk downhill from the pergola to enjoy this little oasis, which has been arranged like a series of outdoor rooms. Unusual in the lower park is an *allée*, a double row of trees, in this case Benjamin figs, which seem to be thriving outdoors in our benign climate. At the southernmost gate, return to the Cottage Row sidewalk.

As you step out onto Sutter, look west to see, on the far side of the street, three unusual establishments. The closest is Yamada Seika Bakery, which sells authentic Japanese pastries, many with sweet bean filling, that are baked on the premises. Mieko Yamada told me that she and her husband, George, have been creating the authentic desserts for nearby Japantown for twenty-eight years. Its next-door neighbor, Bon Temps Restaurant, specializes in Cajun food, revealing another of the neighborhood's ethnic influences. At the corner beyond it, Henry Calhoun's Sidewalk Books and Records, a mecca for collectors of old wax pressings, materializes magically on the street corner most mornings.

Turn left a half-block to cross Sutter at Webster Street. Walk south on Webster Street alongside the attractive two-story brown-shingled townhouses until you reach a lane. Designed by architect Frank L. Hope for the Redevelopment Agency as equal-opportunity housing, this community of homes has taken a cue from Cottage Row. Turn right on its internal lane. When you reach the parking lot, turn left and in another hundred feet you reach an attractive green lawn and the rental office/community center of this handsome complex. Turn left to pass it and you'll find, at its far side, a continuation of the lane leading south again to Post Street.

At Post and Webster, you have reached Japan Center. Enticing as it is, for now turn right, away from it, on Post Street. The eye-filler in this block is the splendid glass roof of the AMC Kabuki Theater. In a few more steps, you are at Fillmore Street, where fast-food places have sprouted like weeds.

To escape this modern plague, turn right. In half a block, you reach Victorian Square, a cluster of big Victorians moved to this location to make way for new apartments. On their journey here from lots scattered throughout the Western Addition, the houses lumbered through the streets, usually in the early morning hours before traffic picked up, with linemen cutting and resetting overhead wires in each block to let them pass. This, too, was part of the innovative Western Addition A-2 Redevelopment Plan.

Within the Victorian Square houses is a remarkable mix of enterprises, including Marcus Books, devoted to publications about the African-American community, May Sun Restaurant, which sells both

Japanese and Chinese food, the Hoky Vacuum Cleaner Shop, and the Bearly New Thrift Shop. As you cross Sutter Street, the ambiance becomes even more upscale, with shops offering designer clothes for kids, bejeweled belts, collectibles, flowers, and Belgian chocolates, all within steps of an outdoor cafe named Trio, which offers such unusual fare as homemade granola, country pâté, and the mouth-watering French sandwich called *croque-monsieur*.

If there is a chair vacant, pause to reflect. Within a two-square-block area, you have glimpsed five of the many little worlds that make San Francisco so livable.

POST ST.

GEARY BLVD.

CLEARY COURT

St. Mary's

LAGUNA ST.

ELLIS ST.

GOUGH ST.

N

FRANKLIN ST.

ST. MARY'S CATHEDRAL

WALKING TIME: Allow an hour.

DISTANCE: From here to eternity.

PUBLIC TRANSPORTATION: Muni buses 2 Clement and 38 Geary.

PARKING: So-so.

CLOTHES: Hat for women.

"O come, all ye faithful. . . ." blaring jubilantly forth on the trumpets of the big Ruffati organ in St. Mary's Cathedral is a true sound of Christmas. Forget silence. Forget ringing cash registers and shopping-center tapes, lutists and flutists, carolers and wassailers. When "Come and adore Him, born the King of Angels" fills the great dome of St. Mary's, everything else fades as though confronted by Gabriel. "*Laeti triumphantes* . . ." rings out, and once again Christendom takes on a world-shaking dimension.

Regardless of religious persuasion, anyone is welcome to visit St. Mary's Cathedral at Geary and Gough streets. The glorious architectural crown of Cathedral Hill sits in a close that can only be described as open. Nothing in San Francisco—possibly nothing nearer than Coventry, England—compares with this great cross in the sky set in a two-block square that overlooks all of San Francisco. If you have not walked around it, you are in for a surprise.

To make this walk, transport yourself to the southwest corner of Geary and Cleary, dearie. Elsewhere, Cleary Court is Octavia Street. Pause there a moment and discover how well located within the city St. Mary's Cathedral really is. Unitarian, Lutheran, Presbyterian, and Baptist are among the neighboring church spires visible as you scan the skyline.

Across Geary to the west is the Japanese Cultural and Trade Center, with *Nihonmachi* just beyond. Near at hand, apartment towers and townhouses of redeveloped Western Addition are a legacy from the late M. Justin Herman, a genius among redevelopment planners. Farther away, Twin Peaks, the San Miguel Hills, Pacific Heights, Parnassus Heights, Nob Hill, and Russian Hill seem like subtle ripples of color in a Japanese landscape painting.

Turn your attention to the soaring shape of the cathedral. It seems massive when seen from afar and intimate when you are beside it. This imaginative sleight of hand is the result of a collaboration among architects Pier Luigi Nervi, Pietro Belluschi, and the local team of Angus McSweeney, Paul Ryan, and John Lee. Looking down from a jet plane, there is no missing this great cross, centered on a second cross of red brick, as dominant a landmark as the tower of the Golden Gate Bridge.

Bridges over the hidden parking lot approach each entrance and form the plaza and pediment for the stunning building, creating a jewellike setting for the soaring hyperbolic parabaloids of the dome. Enter the upper plaza bridge on Geary. Suddenly, you become aware of the parking lot below, concealed from the street.

Walk to the western rail to discover in a far corner the bell of old St. Mary's surrounded by fragrant ceanothus. It hung in the steeple of an earlier St. Mary's on Van Ness, destroyed by fire on September 7, 1962. The oldest St. Mary's in San Francisco, dedicated on Christmas Day 1854 by Archbishop Joseph Sadoc Alemany, stands at the northeast corner of Grant Avenue and California Street.

At the main entrance, an impressive sculptured overdoor panel, the work of Professor Enrico Manfrini of Milan, depicts in bronze the risen Christ surrounded by men seeking the Kingdom of Heaven. The doors are a network of vines, the handles of which are serpents with goat, eagle, and alligator heads.

Go into the cathedral, preferably for the 10:30 A.M. or 12:15 P.M. Mass. Before you find a seat, look at the impressive doors, backed by a

sun-colored stained glass. Breathtaking exhilaration is the first re-
sponse of most visitors as they look upward at the vast interior of the
coffered cupola. The stained-glass abstractions are by Gyorgy Kepes in
colors of earth, sky, fields, fire, and sea.

Find a place in a pew if you can, then look around you. The altar,
which faces the congregation by Vatican decree, has the archbishop's
coat of arms over the largest central chair, but you are not likely to
notice it once you discover the baldachino. Sculptor Richard Lippold
wrought the mobile, symbolic of prayer ascending, which shelters the
altar. It vibrates on the stillest day and is as fascinating at the end of a
long service as at the beginning.

When you can take your eyes from the mobile's shimmer, a glance
out spacious corner windows will make one feel that inside and out are
merged. The massive pylons near them extend ninety-four feet into the
ground and each carries nine million pounds. The cathedral ceiling, at
the point where the stained-glass windows form a cross, is 196 feet
high.

With its 4,842 pipes, the organ, on its pedestal to the right of the
altar, seems like a *Star Wars* flower that has somehow floated down
from outer space to bloom here. Acclaimed as one of the finest, it is an
eighty-nine-rank, seventy-stop electro-pneumatic wonder of solid-
state circuitry. After Masses, little crowds often gather around in admi-
ration of this splendid instrument.

Between services, stroll around the periphery to see some of the
cathedral's other treasures. On the wall near the organ hangs "The
Black Madonna," an icon of Our Lady of Czestochowa, presented to
Archbishop John R. Quinn in August of 1982 by Cardinal Francis
Macharski from Pope John Paul II. In a niche just beyond it is an
aluminum sculpture of St. Joseph, St. Francis, and St. Patrick, co-
patrons of the Archdiocese of San Francisco, surmounting Mission
Dolores.

Just to the right of the altar is a little chapel of Our Lady of Guadalupe, which has a beautiful mosaic of St. Francis beside it. On the left
of the altar is the shrine of the Blessed Sacrament, a sunburst by artist
Peter Traphagan, enclosed in rich red marble. Walk around to the
southeast niche to see the patroness of the cathedral, Our Lady of the
Assumption, executed in bronze by Professor Manfrini. *Alae erecta*
create her shining aura. Manfrini is also the creator of the pastoral
candle holder near the entrance alongside the baptismal font.

The views of the city from inside the windows are every bit as noble
as those from the gallery that surrounds the cathedral outside. As a way
of ending this walk, take your choice of the perimeter walks, depending on the weather.

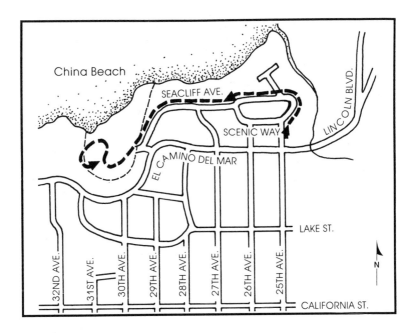

China Beach

SEACLIFF AVE.

SCENIC WAY

EL CAMINO DEL MAR

LINCOLN BLVD.

LAKE ST.

32ND AVE. | 31ST AVE. | 30TH AVE. | 29TH AVE. | 28TH AVE. | 27TH AVE. | 26TH AVE. | 25TH AVE.

N

CALIFORNIA ST.

SEACLIFF

DISTANCE: A sophisticated mile.

PUBLIC TRANSPORTATION: Muni bus 29.

PARKING: Fair.

CLOTHES: Worldly casual with sweater.

Seacliff perches where its name indicates, on the brow of a sheer rock face above the sportive, slate-colored eternity we call the sea. It is a Raoul Dufy watercolor in Mediterranean pinks and whites by day, in which the utility wires are happily out of sight underground, the garages inconspicuously placed, and the demi-mansions located for neighborly view-sharing. By night, it is a twinkling hill-sprinkle of lights.

Aboard ship in the watery funnel between Point Lobos and Point Bonita, it is not the Golden Gate Bridge but modest Seacliff that melts the heart of safe homecomers or brings an unswallowable lump of the *tristesse* to outbound passengers. Home, conceived by Madison Avenue with an assist from slick-magazine fiction, emerges symbolically through the rose-colored glasses of heart's desire looking much like Seacliff. Sometimes it also sounds like it.

This cliché image may have been imposed on thousands of Americans by an almost interminable network radio series called "One Man's Family," by Carleton F. Morse, which began in 1932. Seacliff was the aerie for its nest of emotional shorebirds, the Family Barbour, genus *histrionicus*, commonly known as the Much-Troubled Cliff-stalkers. "I think I'll take a walk!" a member of the Barbour tribe would announce when beset by trials that would make the Perils of Pauline seem pale. Then off he'd go to sob along the seawall. Two generations of housewives sobbed sympathetically into the sink.

To examine this paragon of landfalls on foot, or to walk off your troubles as the Barbours did, begin at the seawall where El Camino del Mar and Seacliff Avenue meet. Stroll downhill, away from the palm-studded boulevard, toward China Beach, a part of the Golden Gate National Recreation Area, to an irregular crescent of sand where Chinese fishermen once camped. Their nightly bonfires created the myth that the beach was a pirate lair. It is now a sunbathers lair.

About twice a year at dead low tide, it is possible to walk from this beach to Baker Beach, hard by in the Presidio and separated by a steep cliff. According to early deed records, much of this land once belonged to Colonel Edward Dickinson Baker.

John Brickell opened the development of the seventy-six lots of Baker's property before World War I. El Camino del Mar was then West Clay Street, and 25th Avenue was a red-rock road. It was Brickell's successor, the Harry B. Allen Company, that created the sound residential planning. One member of the firm recalls that, shortly after a survey by William B. Hoag, poles were put up at various elevations to determine height restrictions.

Architectural buffs will find that most of the Mediterranean-inspired houses were designed by Appleton and Wolfard. Three residences, 9, 25, and 45 Scenic Way, were designed by Willis Polk. A handsome contemporary house at 850 El Camino del Mar, designed by Wurster, Bernardi, and Emmons, is also worth seeking out.

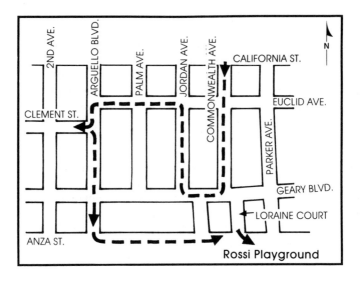

JORDAN PARK

WALKING TIME: An hour's amble.

DISTANCE: Eight square blocks.

PUBLIC TRANSPORTATION: Muni bus 1 California or 2 Euclid.

PARKING: Tough.

CLOTHING: Your most elegant casuals.

Jordan Park may not be on your map of San Francisco, but the eight square blocks within its boundaries include one of our choicer neighborhoods. Its streets are wider and its lots are bigger than anywhere in the city. Like a gracious old part of Cuyahoga Falls, Ohio, or Hannibal, Missouri, it seems almost as though a little flying carpet of the Midwest had magically managed to land in the Richmond district.

The living room windows of its venerable houses have no panoramic views of the Bay. No value-enhancing parks protect it. Nevertheless, Jordan Park houses are seldom for sale, and when they are, the prices match those of Pacific Heights.

This paradoxical paragon of places lies distinctly, with no rubbery borders, on the exceedingly flat land fronting three two-block-long streets—Commonwealth, Palm, Jordan, and the northern two blocks of Parker. Outside these well-established lines of demarcation you are no longer in Jordan Park and the difference is immediately apparent.

202

James Clark Jordan, the developer for whom the land is named, could come back tomorrow and feel at home. A Bostonian, he filled the tract once known as Kelly's Pond. A patriotic and generous man, he offered the U.S. War Department free use of the land for assembling military outfits during the Spanish-American War of 1898. "The offer was accepted with gratitude by Major General E. S. Otis, United States Volunteers, commander of the expeditionary forces, who voted it 'most convenient for this purpose' and thanked Jordan for 'his courtesy and generosity in helping us out of a dilemma.' " At that time, few people wanted a military camp next door.

When it was no longer needed by the Army, Jordan used some of the land to build his own home at 51 Commonwealth and designed the nearby lot sizes to attract the kind of people he would like for neighbors, a pattern sure to create what planners today call a "livable ambiance." Eighty years later, Jordan Park is still a pleasant place to live, and for the walker, charming to stroll.

To enjoy it, go to the corner of California and Commonwealth, where Children's Hospital is located. French Hospital, a few blocks west, on the site of the old racetrack, is close by. The proximity to them has given Commonwealth the nickname of "Doctors' Row." In fact, all three Jordan Park interior avenues, and Euclid Avenue, which transects them, are doctors' rows. It is so convenient to both hospitals that some of the medical families residing here are in the third generation of the original owners.

For a fair sample of the neighborhood, begin at California Street and walk south on Commonwealth. Roller skates, skateboards, tricycles, bicycles, toy automobiles, toy tractors, jump ropes, and all the other paraphernalia of happy childhood are often in evidence on these broad streets and front yards. If yours was an urban Midwestern childhood, this will seem like a ramble through yesteryear. The big houses, each different from its neighbor, are set far apart and well back on their frontages, like those of the prairie towns. The flatness of the land enhances the illusion.

By 1915, a city guidebook listed Jordan Village among those residential areas "protected from stores, saloons, bars, and the cheaper class of homes." It is still protected in this way. James Jordan gets credit for the city's first effective zoning.

When you reach Geary Boulevard, pause a moment to look uphill toward Lone Mountain, formerly a girls' college but now the site of the University of San Francisco's upper campus. Its earliest use was as Laurel Hill Cemetery. Colonel Edward Dickinson Baker, whose name is memorialized in a San Francisco street and beach and in a Marin County fort, dedicated the cemetery in 1854. As extraordinary as it may seem to us in this age of motorcars, funeral processions often came on foot, with mourners following the undertaker and his horse-drawn hearse all the way from downtown, which then surrounded Portsmouth Square, a distance of about three miles.

As you turn west on Geary, notice the Coronet Theater, a "first-run house" that has thrived in this comfortable enclave. Turn north on Jordan to examine another of these well-designed old streets.

At Euclid Avenue turn west, pausing at Palm Avenue to find that it really does have some stately "feather duster" palms to warrant the name. Despite the palms, it has never been called Los Angeles Street, although it has borne the names Chicago and Michigan.

When you reach Arguello Boulevard, pause to look uphill to the north to the rich green area that forms the entrance to the Presidio. Then look south, where the green border is that of Golden Gate Park.

Walk half a block south and you will be at Clement Street, where Jordan Park residents go for groceries and early morning coffee. In the last few years, since the Richmond district has become a satellite Chinatown, they also go there for dining out. By barring shops in Jordan Park, its founder inadvertently zoned the periphery of the eight-block oasis as well.

In 1877, according to Langley's *Guidemap to San Francisco*, Golden Gate Racecourse was a little to the southwest, Odd Fellows' Cemetery to the immediate south, and Laurel Hill Cemetery just to the east of what is now Jordan Park.

To see another vestige of an earlier time, unique in San Francisco, cross Geary and continue south on Arguello to Anza Street, across from Rossi Playground. Turn left on the north side of Anza and walk to Loraine Court. At the far end of the street, at number 1 Loraine Court, is the Columbarium, erected in 1898 by the International Order of Odd Fellows when this land was Odd Fellows' Cemetery.

This burial vault for ashes is the largest on the West Coast and the only existing structure of its kind in San Francisco. A young British architect, Bernard J. S. Cahill, designed the building in all its classic dignity. Homesteading of the surrounding land exempted it from demolition when the city passed a law outlawing cemeteries in San Francisco in 1937. Since 1980, it has been operated by the Neptune Society.

When you have admired its classical lines, stay a while and enjoy the green oasis of Rossi Playground and the easygoing ambiance of this cultivated slice of the city.

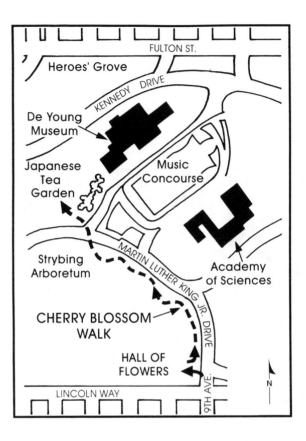

CHERRY BLOSSOM WALK

WALKING TIME: Two hours.

DISTANCE: Optional.

PUBLIC TRANSPORTATION: Muni bus 44 O'Shaughnessy goes through the park; 16, 71-X, and 72-X go to 9th Avenue and Lincoln Way.

PARKING: Fair on weekends.

CLOTHES: Subdued and casual.

SEASON: Spring.

> *The cherry-flowers bloom;*
> *We gaze at them,*
> *They fall, and . . .*
>
> Onitsura

205

And ... the world seems a better, happier place for a moment ... reason enough to hie oneself to Golden Gate Park, which now has close to two thousand cherry trees along its meadows and drives, for a cherry tree walk.

Half of the flowering cherry trees were a bicentennial gift from Emperor Hirohito and the government of Japan. The others were

Cherry blossoms in springtime at the Japanese Tea Garden, part of Golden Gate Park. *San Francisco Convention and Visitors' Bureau.*

donated during the last few years by Ikebana International, which planted its thousandth tree with a *Senbonzakura* celebration.

In Japan, *hanami*, or cherry blossom viewing, is a national pastime that almost amounts to a mania. From March through May, Japanese newspapers give daily listings of trees in bloom all over the country. At least fifty major resorts—with a distinguished old cherry tree or lane, meadow or mountainside of cherries as raison d'être—are listed in the official government guide to Japan. A dozen or more trees are so remarkable they are also listed under their own names. More than fifty varieties of cherry grow in Japan, including the *kiku sakura*, which has a chrysanthemumlike flower with two hundred petals, and *kongo sakura*, with yellow flowers. Devotees of *hanami* start their pilgrimages to these trees when the first bud breaks, and work their way as the season progresses from Nagasaki or Shimonoseki, to Kyoto, Nara, Yoshino, and finally to Tokyo, visiting the famous trees as they come into bloom. The romantic pattern for cherry-bloom watching is to take a picnic, a candle-lit lantern, and your light-of-love and watch from beneath the tree as dusk falls with petals sifting gently downward.

The more venerable the tree, the better, of course. Japan has one tree, named Yamataka Jindaisakura, which is reputed to be eighteen hundred years old, and four-hundred-year-old trees are not uncommon. While San Francisco can't boast any cherry trees as old as redwoods, the first trees planted in 1969 by Ikebana International along Martin Luther King Jr. Drive have now attained substantial size and make for the best show.

To make this walk, transport yourself to the corner of 9th Avenue and Lincoln Way. At the outset, go into the Strybing Arboretum through the main gate. Notice that inside, in the median strip, is the Knot Garden of Herbs. Pass the information kiosk and the last ornamental gate to find its fan-shaped counterpart. Both are colonial classics, much like those at Williamsburg, Virginia.

Bear left behind the Helen Crocker Russell Horticultural Library. Within a few steps you will be at the Takamine Garden, a memorial to Dr. Jokichi Takamine, a chemist noted for his work on adrenaline. He was the man who assisted President William Howard Taft in bringing the first cherry trees to the Potomac Tidal Basin in Washington, D.C., a project that has grown into six miles of trees. The Takamine Garden here in Strybing is a gift from his daughter-in-law Katharyn Hedland.

As enchanting as the arboretum is at this time of year, save this walk for later. Retrace your steps back through the main gate and continue along Martin Luther King Jr. Drive. You will walk in glory all the way when the cherry trees are in bloom. As you stroll, observe how the four trees on the east side of the drive have been planted in front of taller green trees. When Faye Kramer, a founder and former president of Ikebana International, accompanied me on the walk, she pointed out that the trees are the single-petaled *akebana*, which the Japanese consider the most beautiful and fragile and are grafted on sturdy mountain cherry rootstock, which resists most pests. "They have been artfully planted in groups of random numbers to give a natural feeling, such as one might find in the wild," Mrs. Kramer said. "The Japanese prefer to see cherry trees on the side of a mountain or meadow surrounded by green."

The northeast corner of the intersection at Middle Drive would be ideal for *hanami*, flanked by its solid wall of green. Other groups are visible alongside the sign for the Garden of Shakespeare's Flowers. Look for a path that seems to go nowhere to discover where the thousandth tree was planted. Amateur archaeologists will recognize the path that ends at the fence as the original main entrance to the arboretum, now phased out by the more impressive gates near the Garden Center and across from the Tea Garden. Slender striplings on the side of the path nearest the street are the tip-off.

"The Tokyo police force have the *sakura*, or cherry flower, as an emblem on their badges," Mrs. Kramer told me as we approached the Japanese Tea Garden, "which doesn't seem effete to them because the samurai identified with the cherry blossom too." Go as far as the Strybing rear gate and cross South Drive at the crosswalk. It will bring you to a path that leads through a splendid stand of cherries toward the side gate of the tea garden, where the most venerable of all the park *sakura* grow. After visiting it for the springtime jubilation, if you still aren't sated, there are another thousand trees scattered at various parts of the park: a large group near the Rose Garden, another near Stow Lake, many more along South Drive near 19th Avenue, at Marx Meadow, and by Spreckels Lake, North Lake, and Middle Lake. One group of commemorative cherries has been planted in the Fuchsia Garden behind McLaren Lodge in honor of two plantsmen, Arthur Menzies and Norvell Gillespie, and Park Commissioner John Conway. Three more memorial trees have been added for Mayor George Moscone, Congressman Leo Ryan, and Supervisor Harvey Milk.

Don't count on a seat in the Tea Garden teahouse in cherry blossom time. Better to end this walk with a beer at the House of Piroshky, 9th Avenue between Lincoln Way and Irving. I can vouch for the mushroom piroshki.

MUSIC CONCOURSE

NOTE: *For map, see Cherry Blossom Walk, page 205.*

WALKING TIME: Allow an afternoon.

DISTANCE: A mile and a half.

PUBLIC TRANSPORTATION: Muni bus 21 to arrive, and bus 10 to return.

PARKING: None on Sunday.

CLOTHES: Comfortable.

"Is there anywhere in San Francisco that would remind me of the romantic Old Vienna of my childhood?" a gentleman from Mill Valley recently inquired by post.

We may not have the Prater, but the Concourse in Golden Gate Park on a Sunday afternoon is for him, and for anyone else who loves musical comedy, gaiety, rococo sculpture, and culture. Rustic McLaren Lodge at Fell and Stanyan streets is the place to begin this stroll. At the outset, imagine a bagpipe salute, if you will, of "Scotland the Brave" or "All the Blue Bonnets Are Over the Border" for John McLaren, the park's most vigorous developer. Uncle John lived in the Lodge like a country gentleman from 1896 until his death in 1943. More than once, he and his gardeners routed squatters or ripped up roads in the night and planted large shrubs in the roadbeds to divert misuse of the park. The tremendous cypress on the front lawn, Uncle John's Christmas tree, is decorated annually by the Park Commission, now headquartered in the Lodge.

Walk south along Stanyan Street to Alvord Lake. Go under Kezar Drive and walk west to see the Romanesque Sharon Cottage, a landmark of "little Rec," the first park playground of its kind in the United States and, to this day, one of the most civilized. Senator William Sharon gave $60,000 in 1886 to establish the Children's Quarters, as it was then called. The lilting wheeze of the calliope and dashing steeds of the carousel have delighted kids ever since. Once there were also goat carts and donkeys to ride. Now gymnastic equipment, a cable car, totem pole, swings, elaborate sliding boards, and sandboxes amuse young visitors.

Beyond the parking lot, follow the road that bisects the lawn-bowling greens. A road that cuts from the De Laveaga dell will bring the walker out on Middle Drive at the rear of the Academy of Sciences.

Go around the south side of the Academy to find an underpass for pedestrians. Echoes later, the walker will emerge near the bandstand at the head of Music Concourse. The lighthearted strains of "The Blue Danube" have resounded over the pollarded plane trees in concert valley on many a Sunday afternoon. Viennese will recognize it as a counterpart to the classic prado, Prater, or plaza.

Look around this sheltered, tree-laned amphitheater, which is a legacy from the Midwinter Fair of 1894, an exposition successfully designed by *San Francisco Chronicle* publisher M. H. de Young to scotch a business recession, much as the WPA did years later. Imagine, if you will, a lacy iron structure over the center fountain. The Electrical Tower was the name of this early space needle. On an upper level there was the Belvista Cafe, comparable in its time to Seattle's Eye of the Needle. Instead of a gas torch, a beam from the Electric Tower spotlighted Strawberry Hill, the island in nearby Stow Lake.

North of the concourse, the De Young Museum and the Japanese Tea Garden, both built as part of the Midwinter Fair, have survived to become better loved with each passing year. Both are good walks in themselves, so popular that one must arrive at odd hours, off season, and early in the week to avoid crowds.

Worth seeking out are the Doré vase entitled *The Poem of the Vine,* in front of the De Young Museum, and the winepress in bronze in the concourse. The homesick Viennese can conclude his walk a few blocks away at Fantasia Bakery on California Street, where the *linzer torte* and *baumkuchen* are as lush as they were in *Alt Wien.*

JAPANESE TEA GARDEN

NOTE: *For map, see Cherry Blossom Walk, page 205.*

WALKING TIME: Allow a morning.

DISTANCE: From here to serenity.

PUBLIC TRANSPORTATION: Muni bus 44 O'Shaughnessy.

PARKING: None in the park on Sundays.

CLOTHES: Casual.

After eighty years of almost continual daily use, the Japanese Tea Garden, next to the De Young Museum in Golden Gate Park, could still ask, "Mirror, mirror, on the wall, which is the fairest on the mall?" with assurance that the right sycophantic answer would be forthcoming.

Planted originally by George Turner Marsh as the Japanese Village of the Midwinter Fair of 1894, enlarged with a "Peace" lantern and garden given in 1953 by Japanese cities, renewed even more recently through the efforts of the late Mrs. Frank Gerbode and the San Francisco Garden Club, the Tea Garden is the most exquisite three acres in the park. It is also the most popular, to which busload after busload of visitors can attest.

For many of them, it is all they will every know of Japan. For others, it is a way to recapture Kyoto. Whatever the reason for the visit, the Tea Garden does not disappoint them, for like any good garden in Japan, there is more here than meets the eye.

Plants, plans, artifacts, skills, and laborers were all imported to create authentically this oasis from a mundane world. The unities, verities, and a few of the foibles of a thousand years of gardening arts are all at work to delight and refresh the stroller.

In a way, the Tea Garden is a temple. Not as in the redwood groves, which are like Gothic cathedrals, but in the Buddhist way, meaning that man and nature are one. Any alert walker will realize, and so he should, as soon as he goes through either gate, that his connection with the outside world has been broken; for he is on the *roji*, the garden path to the teahouse, and also, as Kakuzo Okakura describes it in the *Book of Tea*, en route to "the first stage of meditation—the passage into self-illumination."

If this seems an ambitious route to travel on a morning's walk, all the Tea Garden really requires is that a walker put one foot in front of the

211

other and follow the path.   It leads beside still waters, over the irregularities of stepping stones, under the dappled light that filters through evergreens, past moss-covered granite lanterns to reflecting pools, a teahouse, a moonbridge, a Buddha. The paths are irresistible. Something beckons beyond each bend. Around each corner something ever more enticing presents itself. For the knowledgeable, the symbolic rectangle, triangle, and circle can be discerned from each contemplation bench, although sometimes the viewer is the circle.

Long ago, the family of Makota Hagiwara lived in the Tea Garden, maintained it, baked the tea cookies, fed the carp, prepared and served the tea, and at least one member died here, all in a manner suitable to the highest traditions of Grand Kabuki theater. An exquisite Ruth Asawa plaque on the left of the main entrance salutes the Hagiwara family's contribution. When the War Department exiled San Francisco's Japanese population, a dashing Australian, Alan Agnew, and his wife became hosts. Today, Japanese are again hosts at the teahouse and gift shop. Park Department gardeners feed the carp, clip the bonsai, prune the cherry trees, and clean the coins from beneath "the wishing bridge."

To find the Buddha "that sits through sunny and rainy weather without shade," walk uphill from the teahouse. This is Amazarashino-hotoke Buddha, cast in 1790 in Tajima-ken, Japan, and reputed to be the largest Buddha ever imported—a gift to the park in 1949 from Gump's.

Using the five-tiered, wooden Shinto pagoda as a landmark, walk away from the *torii* gate to locate the "Peace" lantern and garden regarded as modern in Japan since the style is Muromachi, only five hundred years old. While the rest of the Tea Garden has *sabi*, an appearance of antiquity, rusticity, and emphasis on natural textures, the new garden is known for *wabi*, a sense of quietness, astringency, good taste, and tranquility.

If you don't dig it all the first time you walk it, like Zen, try again.

STRYBING ARBORETUM: SUCCULENT GARDEN

NOTE: *For map, see Cherry Blossom Walk, page 205.*

WALKING TIME: A morning.

DISTANCE: One-half mile.

PUBLIC TRANSPORTATION: Muni bus 44 O'Shaughnessy.

PARKING: None on weekends.

CLOTHES: Wear comfortable shoes.

TIME: Open 10 A.M. to 5 P.M. weekends, 8 A.M. to 4:30 P.M. weekdays.

"In reality, San Francisco is different from America," David Wickers wrote in the London *Sunday Times*. "So richly is this Babylon-by-the-Bay endowed by nature that it could have succeeded without trying." He didn't dwell on earthquakes.

Climate is one of those natural endowments that make our city different. Almost anything will grow here—and does. At this moment, the twenty-foot-tall split-leaf philodendron growing happily in my south-facing garden on Russian Hill has flowers and fruit on it. Better known to horticulturists as *Monstera deliciosa*, it is a native of the tropics.

Indeed, the horticultural possibilities available to the Bay Area gardeners are so vast that Strybing Arboretum, the seventy-acre park-within-a-park, located just south of the Japanese Tea Garden in Golden Gate Park, takes "Plants of the World" as its theme.

The arboretum is a legacy that Helene Strybing left to San Francisco. The widow of silk merchant Christian M. Strybing left $100,000 to create the public arboretum when she died in 1926. Helene Strybing also gave the city six emeralds and a handful of rare coins, thereby creating one of our longtime unsolved mysteries.

The emeralds, which banged around City Hall in an unlocked brass-bound box for eighteen years before they were appraised, turned out to be paste, while the coins were judged to be worth $48. If a gypsy switch happened, nobody has been willing to talk about it.

At any rate, the Strybing Arboretum is a living library of scientifically labeled plants, containing a score of specialized gardens. Admission is free.

One of Strybing's least known gardens is the Eric Walther Cactus and Succulent Garden, named for the arboretum's crusty first director. A little jewel, it is so beautiful it looks like a three-dimensional painting laid on the land.

Gardeners who resolved during the drought of 1988 to convert a water-guzzling backyard or hillslope into something more tolerant of dry weather will find inspiration here. But whether you know a sepal from a stamen, or a pistil from a petal, the succulent garden is well worth seeing.

To make this walk, go to Golden Gate Park, to the point where Martin Luther King Jr. Drive crosses Tea Garden Drive. Walk north about one hundred feet on Martin Luther King Jr. Drive until you reach the north gate of Strybing Arboretum. The gate itself, with its tall wrought-iron grillwork alternating with squarish stacked concrete columns, is a tribute honoring former Park Commissioner Eugene L. Friend.

Once through the gate, you have arrived in Eastern Australia, or so one familiar with that country might think, because of the trees and shrubs. The seductive scene of a duck pond, broad lawns, and a little bridge will beckon you southward. Resist this impulse for the moment, and digress to your left to study the map of the arboretum on a wayside exhibit stand. When you have observed the interlocking pattern of Strybing's succession of gardens, return to the gate.

Facing the little planting circle, go right, or west, on the paved walkway nearest to the bordering fence. Within a few steps, you are abreast of a red-flowered bottlebrush. Cathay Loadman, a friend from "down under" who made this walk with me, said Aussie school kids gather the little seedpods that encircle the stems, which have a wonderful smoky taste, and spit them at one another, much as American children do with paper wads.

When you are abreast of the Joan Bostwick Powers Rock Garden, walk through it on the path beside the memorial bench, then continue on the "Burma Road," as Strybing gardeners have long nicknamed the broad path that goes through greenery typical of the South Pacific. En route, I recognized the feijoa tree, a huge mango tree, several palms, a large shelf fungus, and the powder-puff and cup-and-saucer vines.

Soon you will be at the Jennie B. Zellerbach Garden, a memorial that Jane Coney, a longtime president of the Strybing Arboretum Society, built to honor her mother. The gazebo was intended by designer Edward Williams to be an ideal viewing spot for the Strybing Fountain.

A few more steps along the broad walkway will bring you to a junction. The road to your right leads you, by way of a collection of Malaysian rhododendrons, past several of Strybing's beautiful magnolia trees, to the John Muir Trail, a favorite walk for those who enjoy the illusion of woodland in the city.

Take the low road to your left, which goes between the charming Moonviewing Garden and the Old World Cloud Forest, a garden in the process of renewal. Go to your right at the next junction and you will arrive in the Southwestern Australia garden, amid plants that are very drought-tolerant.

Turn right again at the next crossroads, and suddenly, just beyond a huge tree-poppy, native to Mexico, you will reach the rich tapestry of plants that surrounds the big S-curve of the Eric Walther Garden of cacti and succulents. It will take your breath away.

Replanted by gardener Andy Stone in 1988, the land around the old stone wall is now as lively as any contemporary sculpture. The stones for the wall were salvaged long ago from the Hearst monastery, the remains of which lie behind the Japanese Tea Garden.

When you have absorbed the magnificence of this composition, take a closer look at the individual plants. Succulents are the fat-leaved ones that look like cacti without spines. They were the favorite genus of Eric Walther, probably for the same reason that many Bay Area gardeners fancy them—they have a rich variety, which appeals to collectors, and will survive occasional periods of drought.

If you thought all succulents looked like the low-growing rosettes of leaves known as "hen and chickens," which you find in the foreground here, look uphill. Here are big spiky aloes, huge cabbagelike whorls with curly leaves, giant snaky medusa heads, festoons of ropes or cables, and a wealth of tiny exquisites with leaves like fat pebbles.

Blooms in all the sunshine colors of red, oranges, and yellows have their counterpoint in leaves that can be blue, purple, red, or gray as well as mossy or spring green. Miniatures that grow out of the crannies of the wall are in sharp contrast to the huge cacti. Some have thorns as efficient as miniature anchors; others have mean little points on their leaf tips. Interplanted with them are many kinds of bromeliads.

Follow the path upward, weaving in and out on the double loop of the trail until you reach the plateau on top. On the way, you may discover a carpet of plants that must look the way a shag rug looks to insects or furry plants that could be miniature old men, hairy as chimps.

At the top of the garden, walk south and take the first informal pathway that descends through the garden. Many of the plants in this area were collected by fireman Gary Meltzer, head of the city's arson detail. A lifetime collector of succulents, he donated them to Strybing when development threatened his five-acre garden on the Peninsula. The black swans in the duck pond are also a gift from Meltzer.

Aloe arborescens is the clumpy plant whose bright orange flowers light up this part of the garden. Gardener Andy Stone thinks aloe would be a great plant for lining roadsides. "It's easy to grow, takes zero mainte-nance, and would make a soft cushion for cars that crashed into it," he told me. "Maybe it could even save some lives in freeway accidents."

If the Elysian Fields exist where great old gardeners repose and reminisce, Eric Walther must look down on the heavenly little spot in sweet contentment.

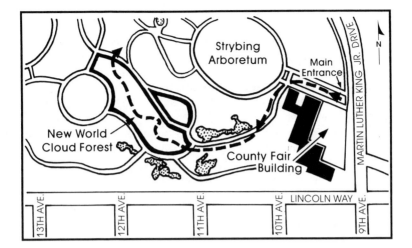

STRYBING ARBORETUM: NEW WORLD CLOUD FOREST

WALKING TIME: One-half day.

DISTANCE: Through cloudland.

PUBLIC TRANSPORTATION: Muni buses 29, 71, and 73.

PARKING: Some.

CLOTHES: Sensible shoes.

> *Monuments are reared and medals struck to commemorate events and names which are less deserving of our regard than those who have transplanted into the colder gardens of the North the rich fruits, the beautiful flowers and the succulent pulse and roots of more favored spots . . .*
>
> —ISAAC D'ISRAELI, 1843

Strybing Arboretum, San Francisco's world-renowned living museum of plants, is harboring some remarkable refugees from Central America. They are the 1,104 trees, vines, shrubs, ferns, bromeliads, and other plants of the New World Cloud Forest, a garden recently created on a plot of land that had been devastated by the furious storms of 1982–1983.

Destructive as those storms were, they don't compare to the frightening devastation in Central and South America, where forests are being cut down at an estimated rate of fifty acres every hour, jeopardizing the very air we breathe.

Even as Dr. Dennis Breedlove, an authority on Central American plants at the California Academy of Sciences, and his collecting crew were gathering plants now in the arboretum, a logging party dislodged them from their camp in a cloud forest on Cerro Boqueron on the Guatemalan border and began stripping the surrounding forest to the ground. By the end of this century, many specimens in the park, including the *Magnolia sharpii* that the crew brought back to San Francisco, may well be the only ones extant in the world.

The cool, damp foggy cloud forests on the coastal mountains of southern Mexico and Central America have conditions like those in San Francisco's own fog belt, which certainly includes Strybing Arboretum. It is hoped the rescued plants will thrive here, preventing their total extinction.

Spring is always a breathtaking time to visit the arboretum. If you'd like to include a walk around the New World Cloud Forest, here's one way to do it. Transport yourself to 9th Avenue and Lincoln Way to the County Fair Building, which was called the Hall of Flowers when architects Appleton and Wolford designed it. Paid for by pari-mutuel racing funds, it was created to provide a meeting place for the many floral societies in the city.

Walk past the Hall of Flowers to enter Strybing's impressive double gates, immediately beyond it. Stop at the information kiosk-cum-bookstore to pick up a map, provided free by the Strybing Arboretum Society.

Go past the Helen Crocker Russell Horticultural Library and through the second set of gates. The fountain visible in the distance, beyond the biggest cypress tree, commemorates philanthropist Helene Strybing.

Turn left at the first path and continue downhill to the left at the next fork in the walkway. The serene Japanese Garden on your right was designed by Mai Arbegast and commemorates Dr. Jokichi Takamine, the chemist noted for his work on adrenaline.

The "Emperor's Stone," the slab of Sonoma fieldstone a few feet along the way, was a gift from Dr. and Mrs. Samuel Kimura and other Japanese-Americans presented on the occasion of the visit of Emperor Hirohito and Empress Nagako of Japan to the garden on October 10, 1975.

Take a few more steps and you are parallel to Anelli Pond, named for a much more modest man, Joseph Anelli, who worked as a Strybing gardener. The surrounding trees include the *Magnolia campbelli,* Strybing's totem flower.

The larger pond you soon reach has been nicknamed "The Bamboo

Pond" for the bamboo clumps on its banks, among them a lush big-leafed variety. Like other ponds in this section of the arboretum, it is a remnant of a little lake that existed before 1870, when Golden Gate Park first took shape.

At the next curve in the paved walkway is the New World Cloud Forest. Leave the paving and walk straight ahead into the wooded area on the dirt path, which veers around to the right and soon reaches a broader path. Go right a few steps and pause.

One of the rare magnolias Dr. Breedlove brought from Chiapas is located downhill on your left. So is the remarkable Mexican hand tree, whose blooms look like a baby's hand. The big tumble of logs on your right, which looks not unlike an untidy giant's woodlot, is actually an "epiphyte pile." "Uncle John" McLaren, the uncompromising Scot who shaped much of Golden Gate Park, would have been delighted with this thrifty reuse of storm-torn trees as a home for plants.

Stop beside the epiphyte pile and take a good look. As in a natural forest, plants are emerging from every nook and cranny among the logs in the pile. Climb up the footpath steps that rise on your right to view many plants normally found only in the treetop canopy of cloud forests, among them fuchsias, begonias, and bromeliads that you may never have seen before.

When you reach the top of the path, turn left. This area, intended for a fern bower, has been left unfinished. It came to a dead halt when the gardener assigned was cut from the budget. Just beyond, look for steps that go down on the far side of the epiphyte pile. Among other rarities here is a relative of the African violet that grows in soil out-of-doors.

"In creating the New World Cloud Forest," Dr. Breedlove said, "first one had to find the cloud-forest plants. Now we must learn how to grow them here successfully. Finally, when we know how to grow them, we can display the plants for their unique colors, shapes, and other qualities."

At the foot of the pile, turn right again. Flashes of red on your left are from a member of the salvia family that blooms almost continuously. A little farther along is an unusual gesneria that is bright scarlet with purple calyxes.

Because most of the cloud-forest plants are new to our country, they have no common names. Look near the base of any plant to discern the arboretum's Latin name label.

Don't be surprised to hear many different foreign languages spoken on Strybing's paths as you continue through the forest. Bay Area Asians and Hispanics, among others, come looking for old friends— the plants they once loved in their native lands.

When you reach the next paved pathway, you have left the New

World Cloud Forest. For a quick return, turn right until you are back at the junction where you left the paving. Then turn left to retrace your steps to the main gate.

Better yet, wander as you wish. The arboretum has so many plants constantly changing that a nine-year-old child could find something different every day for the rest of a normal lifetime.

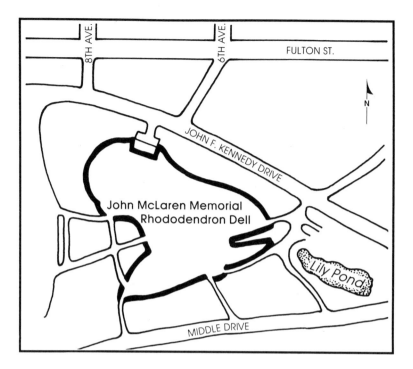

RHODODENDRON DELL

WALKING TIME: Allow a morning in May.

DISTANCE: Around twenty acres.

PUBLIC TRANSPORTATION: Muni buses 5, 21, and 44 O'Shaughnessy.

PARKING: Less and less.

CLOTHES: Comfortable.

The great all-time superspecial world-class Mother's Day walk is in San Francisco.

It is the John McLaren Memorial Rhododendron Dell, one of the botanical treasures of Golden Gate Park, located in a twenty-acre triangle that fronts on John F. Kennedy Drive.

Since rhododendrons like the same climatic conditions that people prefer, a walk through the sheltered dell is good anytime. In May, when the "rhodies" are at their peak, it is like strolling through the colorful Land of Oz. Nowhere else are there such lavish aisles of bloom. With the possible exception of an Oregon test garden maintained by the American Rhododendron Society, the dell contains the greatest collection of species and numbers of plants in the country.

To make this walk, begin at 6th Avenue and Fulton Street. Walk through Brayton Gate into the park to find, happily, that the extension of 6th Avenue into the park is blocked off to automotive traffic, a closure that makes this route pleasant indeed. Cross John F. Kennedy Drive and there you are at the graveled mini-court that signals the dell. If the court seems sunnier than in the past, it is because a dozen old pines have come down in storms during the last few years.

John McLaren, sculpted in bronze by Earl Cummings, stands overlooking the court, as green with verdigris as the leaves of "Pink Pearl," the rhododendron that surrounds his grassy plot. "White Pearl," "Mother of Pearl," and "Cynthia" are nearby.

There were only seven kinds of rhododendrons growing in Golden Gate Park when McLaren took over as park superintendent in 1887. It was soon recognized as his favorite flower. Six years later there were forty-four species or hybrids. Some came from Sir Joseph Hooker, director of Kew Gardens in London, following a visit here. Others were brought to the park from England in 1912 by John Robert Atkinson, longtime gardener for M. H. de Young. These and the Bowles's collection of Himalayan rhododendrons were planted on Peacock Lawn east of the Conservatory. Now their scions adorn many parts of the park.

The dell as we know it was started in 1942 with twelve acres and has expanded as enthusiasm for it grew. Today there are 140 species and any number of varieties. Facing the "stookie," as "Uncle John" McLaren called statues, bear right. As you walk, look uphill on your right to see another stookie. This one was "planted out of sight," by surrounding it with shrubs that grew to hide the statue. It was McLaren's method for making stookies, which he hated, disappear. Old-time gardeners say he would have planted out his own if he were alive to do it.

Bear left at the first fork. The luminous red rhododendron here is "Bulstrode Park," the purple is "Ponticum," a shrub that originated near the Black Sea. It is reputed by the Greeks to have saved them from an invading Persian army that ate wild Ponticum honey—which is poisonous, as is honey from other rhododendrons.

At the next fork, bear left around the base of Azalea Hill, then follow it around to the right. Forgo the steep path that climbs up the hill for the moment and take the next left fork through a pleasant aisle of the vanilla-colored "Burmanicum." The pale pink and white nearby is "Countess of Haddington."

Bear right at the next junction, past some deciduous yellow azaleas and the rhododendron "Tula Christopher." Gardener Ron Freitas pointed out that a bequest has supplied some new plants for this area to replace older ones lost to thrips and storms; as we strolled through the lush area, his colleague, Bill Collins, indicated that the paths in the dell make a big free-form horseshoe.

I asked the two men which of the flamboyant plants were their favorites. "Loderi King George" was Collins's choice. Freitas said he likes the creamy "Unique." My own favorite is the white "Fragrantissimum," mostly for its tantalizing vanilla fragrance.

At the next fork, bear right and make a digression from the big oval to climb Azalea Hill by the broad gradual path that goes up from this side.

Retrace your steps and return to the larger path, bearing right and right again to come alongside a big aisle of the Maddeni varieties. Continue past the white "Seagulls" until you reach a large "Countess of Sefton" at the corner. When a wall of the California Academy of Sciences Building is visible, bear right on the path that looks as though it will go to a green lawn. It doesn't. Stay on the path through the deep shade, with "Rainbow" making a great show dead ahead.

The path soon tracks back to the mini-court, bringing the walker full circle to the starting point for this leisurely stroll.

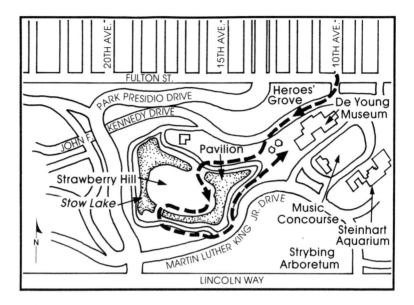

STOW LAKE

WALKING TIME: Half a day.

DISTANCE: Two miles.

PUBLIC TRANSPORTATION: Muni bus 5.

PARKING: Fair on weekends.

CLOTHES: Comfortable, unless you are newly wed and posing for your photo.

Stow Lake, one of Golden Gate Park's pleasantest spots, boasts a charming ornament, the Kinmon Pavilion. Lighthearted, airy, and decorative as a butterfly, it seems to float in green-and-red splendor on the water's edge at the foot of Strawberry Hill, like a little bit of old China cast up on this far shore. The best of times is to go when migrating waterfowl enliven the lake. Sundays are best for walkers because cars are forbidden in the eastern half of the park.

To make this walk, transport yourself to 10th Avenue and Fulton Street. Walk into the park on the west side of 10th and take the footpath that leads off to the right through Heroes' Grove, a fifteen-acre tract of redwood trees dedicated by the Gold Star Mothers of San Francisco to their sons and daughters lost in World War I. Though these redwoods are oddly truncated, you still experience the cathedral stillness of a redwood forest. In the rainy season, an unexpected little pond sometimes forms among the trees.

At the streamhead, you emerge from the grove near the Rose Garden. Cross John F. Kennedy Drive at the crosswalk and look for a sign behind the M. H. de Young Memorial Museum, which indicates a bridle path. Follow the macadam walk uphill. About fifty feet into the eucalyptus trees, the walkway comes abreast of the disassembled ruins of El Monasterio de Santa María de Ávila, built near Madrid by Cistercian monks in the twelfth century and shipped to America by William Randolph Hearst. This site had an unlikely use during the Midwinter Fair of 1894—it was the Forty-Niner Mining Camp.

Japanese fencing along the left identifies the Japanese Tea Garden. Entrancing as it is, for this walk pass it up and bear right on the paved pathway and staircase, which soon emerge at the long, easterly point of Stow Lake.

Cross the Stow Lake peripheral road to the shoreline walkway and begin walking to your right. Across the water, just past the little island in the middle distance, is your first glimpse of the bicentennial gift from our sister city Taipei, the Kinmon Pavilion, a setting for young bridal couples who want photos to send relatives in China. Dedicated on April 15, 1981, after six years of opposition from environmental groups who dislike buildings of any kind in the park, mayors of both cities were in attendance at the celebration, along with three hundred citizens and a score of lion dancers. Supervisor Carol Ruth Silver, who shoveled dirt at the pavilion groundbreaking, later had the pleasure of dedicating San Francisco's reciprocal gift in Taipei, a children's playground like the one at Hang Ah Alley.

For a closer look at the pavilion, continue along the lakeshore to the Roman Bridge. Cross it to Strawberry Hill, a natural elevation of 414 feet, named for the wild strawberries once found here.

Stow Lake is totally artificial, made on a base of clay hauled from a quarry that once stood at Turk and Divisadero streets. Crushed rock tops the clay under about 3½ feet or 15,331,700 gallons of water. Park Commissioner W. W. Stow is the lake's namesake, but the credit might well go instead to a hero of the Battle of Gettysburg, Captain Prichard, who served under Stonewall Jackson and who led his company valiantly during Pickett's Charge. Prichard was park superintendent from 1876 to 1881, when plans were being prepared for a reservoir atop Strawberry Hill and an overflow lake below.

Bear left and skirt the water from Stow Lake's biggest island. The retaining walls are a reminder of one of our lost tourist attractions, a gift from Collis P. Huntington. Until 1962, when storm damage collapsed the understructure, Huntington Falls cascaded 110 feet down the hill in two great leaps. Stepping stones once crossed the waters at its base.

When you reach the little redwood grove, the island seems totally Californian. Take a few more steps around the curve to three big Phoenix palms and there, with the pavilion standing behind its moat, the landscape is suddenly exotic, tropical, and Asian.

Go up the stairs to enjoy its marble stools and polished floors. Benches surround the little octagon, a painted ceiling overhead is almost jewellike. Carvings adorn the eaves and a richly carved wall surrounds the whole. The dedication plaque, inlaid on the travertine center table, reveals an unexpected poem, lauding the friendship between the States and the R.O.C., or Republic of China.:

Two sister cities were made, side by side and hand in hand. / Is people's well-being thus made.

Residing in this wide world, cooperating closely from our hearts / the universal brotherhood is thus made.

A scenic spot in the U.S.A. for ascending remained. / Easterly coming culture, a real friend cannot be wanting in this wide world.

A great ocean on R.O.C. for crossing lain / westerly looking from the Golden Gate.

The world, although so wide, becomes as near as the neighborhood.

When you have enjoyed its fresh ambiance, leave the pavilion by the opposite gate and cross the moat via the little bridge to see the waterfall. Then bear left again to continue around Strawberry Hill to the rustic bridge on the opposite side. By bearing left around the outside of the lake, one can complete this loop walk back to the steps leading toward the Tea Garden without ever destroying the illusion of a faraway Chinese landscape.

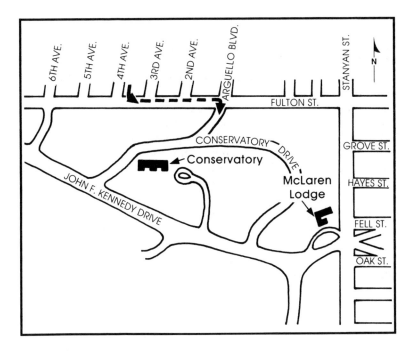

CONSERVATORY

WALKING TIME: Allow an hour.

DISTANCE: Three city blocks.

PUBLIC TRANSPORTATION: Muni bus 5 or 21.

PARKING: Fair on weekdays.

CLOTHES: Whatever.

Like a spun-sugar fantasy, or a stage setting for a musical comedy of Old Vienna or London, the Conservatory in Golden Gate Park seems to await joyous fiddles, ballerinas, a wedding party in morning clothes, or ice skaters with flowing red scarves and Hans Brinker blades. There it sits, ethereally, holding its breath for the curtain to rise. Except that you and I, fellow walker, are the cast members of this gossamer glass palace.

For more than a hundred years, a ramble through the jungle within has been San Francisco's favorite indoor stroll. Plant lovers go almost monthly to see the west wing's changing displays of showy blooms, chosen for seasonal color.

In the past, the seasonal blooms have been predictable—lilies for

Easter, poinsettias for Christmas, azaleas and cyclamen for Chinese New Year and Valentine's Day. These days you'll find something new has been added. Changing shows! For example, three hundred guzmanias, all in bloom. If you've never seen one, the blooms of guzmanias look like red stars on stalks; some are ten inches long. The guzmanias are a genus of bromeliads especially imported from Central America by Michael Rothenberg of Pacifica. As "tulip mania" swept Europe in the seventeenth century, so "bromeliad fever" has been surging across the United States, partly because the beautiful plants are survivors, withstanding neglect in either overheated condos or underheated lofts.

Begin this walk at 4th Avenue and Fulton Street. Walk into the park on the path between 3rd and 4th avenues. The Conservatory is open from 10 A.M. until 5 P.M. daily, and there is a modest fee to enter.

Before you go into the main entrance, pause a moment to look down on Conservatory Valley, where the pedestrian tunnel under John F. Kennedy Drive looks like a secret grotto surrounded by lawns and carpet beds.

This site is much more impressive than the Conservatory's first chosen location. Originally, William Hammond Hall planned to put it on Mount Lick, the little hill facing Stanyan near Fell. When a "Sand-Lotter" in the Legislature tried to kill the whole project, a location reshuffle was approved, with splendid results.

Glance at the plaque for Landmark Number 841, which explains that this lacy confection of a building is modeled on the glass house at Kew Gardens in London and came to the park in 1879. Shipped 'round the Horn under sail from England, it had been intended for James Lick's own garden in San Jose. After Lick's death, his heirs, the Society of California Pioneers, sold it to a group of public-spirited men who had it assembled here largely at their own expense. They couldn't have done San Francisco a greater favor.

When you enter, the freshness of refurbishing is immediately apparent in the foyer. As a one-hundredth-birthday present to the distinguished Victorian confection, the San Francisco Garden Club, which now maintains a sales gazebo in the entryway, helped raise funds for accurate historical renovation. Since the Conservatory is not only a city, state, and national landmark, but listed in the National Register of Historic Places as well, every scrap of work done on it must duplicate the original to maintain "the total design and integrity of the building."

Hanging baskets and floral displays in the foyer give a preview of what is to come. Go around the gazebo and you are in the main rotunda under the highest dome. Aficionados of the Conservatory will recognize some old friends here, especially the tall Chinese fan palm and two venerable philodendrons. Gardener George Marcoupolis told me that these huge vines, each more than fifty years old, are familiarly known as "Mom" and "Pop." There are also some red bananas, which bear fruit, near them. Wait long enough and you can see them peel themselves.

Go around to your right. When you are parallel with the door to the east wing, pause and look to your left at the center circle of Brazilian plants. Then walk through this path, perhaps the shortest jungle trail in the world.

Continue into the west wing. If it seems to you larger and more open than in the past, your perceptions are right-on. A glass wall has been removed to give the illusion of spaciousness. The first section has heliconias in bloom, little red bananas, rhizomatous begonias, and bromeliads—the neoregelia. There is also a great idea for gardeners—a large pottery crock in which to coil a hose so walkers won't trip on it.

When first-time visitors to the Conservatory, especially out-of-staters, reach the far end, they usually catch their breath over the lavish blooms here and exclaim, "Why, it looks just like a seed catalog cover!" or "Are they real flowers?"

When you recover from the impact of the massed blooms, look for two interesting garden accent pieces: a Mediterranean legacy from the Panama-Pacific International Exposition of 1915, adorned with cherubs and Della Robbia wreaths, and a wrought-iron display tree designed by Tom Bass, former director of the Conservatory.

On the raised platform overlooking Conservatory Valley, there is a porcelain bench that memorializes one of Bass's predecessors, Sidney Stein Rich, the only woman ever to hold this post. "We try to show and do things here you won't see in commercial nurseries," Bass told me, "hoping to encourage people to do them in their own homes and gardens." One such idea is the propagation of rare or old varieties of plants, such as a group of rhizomatous begonias in one of the propagation houses behind the main building. One day they will go on display. Also waiting in the wings is a collection of palms, many one-of-a-kind.

To see more varieties of bromeliads, continue down the garden path to the east wing. En route, you will pass anthuriums in bloom and some big cycads, one with cones three feet long. Flashy multicolored crotons flank them. The big yellow flowers over the door to the pond room are allemanda.

Go through the door and immediately look overhead on the glass wall to see a display of tillandsias, another kind of bromeliad, also donated by Mike Rothenberg.

Then bear right around the cloverleaf, currently a symphony in nature's rarest color—blue—largely tillandsias and vanda orchids.

Vrieseas and achmaeas, other forms of bromeliads, are also tucked in around the naturalized grotto to the rear of the cloverleaf. When you have circled around it, you are back at the pond.

Don't be tempted to dabble a finger in the pond or push your little brother in; those Amazonian fish are carnivorous.

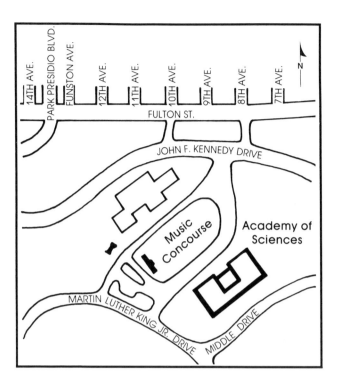

ACADEMY OF SCIENCES
MEYER HALL

WALKING TIME: An hour.

DISTANCE: As far as your imagination will take you.

PUBLIC TRANSPORTATION: Muni bus 44 O'Shaughnessy.

PARKING: None on weekends.

CLOTHING: Casual.

TIMES: Academy is open 10 A.M. to 5 P.M.; there is a fee.

We live in a greedy world. One morning, the growl of a bulldozer brings you to your window overlooking a hillside dotted with oaks. By the end of the day, the yellow iron monster has pawed the fragile skin of loam and wildflowers off the land, revealing bedrock in thirty-two places that a developer will call homesites.

231

Soon the gray fox you used to watch at dawn and dusk no longer crosses the meadow. Gone is the manzanita bush, along with the chipmunks that once frisked in golden ribbons on its branches. The song of the white-crowned sparrow that greeted your mornings is stilled. The tree where he nested has been felled.

Multiply this a thousandfold and you have an idea of the rate at which wilderness is disappearing, and what this loss means. Scientists at the California Academy of Sciences, the treasure trove of knowledge in Golden Gate Park, foresaw this seventy years ago.

The scientific world was rocked back on its heels when the North American Hall of Mammals opened in 1916. It was the first structure ever designed to display dioramas—large habitat groups of stuffed or simulated animals shown in their natural surroundings.

Now, the great vaulted hall has been renovated and renamed Meyer Hall. It contains a remarkable show called Wild California: A State of Diversity. It's a great walk. One can look in on the Lilliputian worlds of a square inch of beach magnified fifty times, or a teaspoon of water enlarged two hundred times—with a jaunt through the Farallon Islands en route. Science factual has outdone science fiction by the simple process of magnification.

Once you're through the door of the airy concourse, the temptation is to head for the fascinating Academy's store. Save this treat for last and turn right instead. Monarch, the grizzly bear, marks the entrance to Wild California. Pause to watch the stunning introductory video narrated by actor Peter Coyote.

A few steps to the first diorama and immediately you are at the floor of a young desert, somewhere near Cottonwood Springs in Riverside County. Pick up one of the telephones on your right to learn some secrets of this scene, one of the original 1916 displays renewed. Charles Bradford Hudson was the muralist for this and several others in the hall. If all the phones are in use, you can play "count the creatures" while you wait. There are more than forty in the spiky display of ocotillo, hairy cactus, and Spanish bayonets, including the creature that Californians call the "horned toad" and Texans the "horned frog." We're both wrong; it's the desert horned lizard.

In the next alcove, California's diversity is immediately apparent as you look in on five tule elk browsing at a tule marsh. Thanks to the combined efforts of Henry Miller, of the famous Kern County Miller-Lux Ranch, and Barton Warren Everman, one of the early directors of the Academy, tule elk are among the great success stories of the environmental movement. Reduced to a single pair by 1874, at last count California's tule elk population had grown to two thousand.

A few more steps bring one to the oak-madrone woodland, complete with poison oak. That heap of leaves in the foreground may look like your neighbor's brush pile, but it's really an active nest of dusky-footed wood rat.

The last verified sighting of a grizzly bear in California was in 1922, so the two in the next diorama are cousins who never heard of state lines. Both were shot with bows and arrows in the Grand Tetons of Wyoming. Plants, birds, and small mammals of the same kind also appear in the Sierra Nevada, however, so the Montane Slope, as this display is named, qualifies as Californian.

By now the grunts, gurgles, snorts, and growls of the two gigantic elephant seals will attract you to the creatures on your left. Without benefit of seasickness, you are at the Farallon Islands at mating time. This is one of Meyer Hall's new exhibits, designed to be walked through. Turn left by the boulders to meander through this sandy cove for a better look at the bulls challenging one another for dominance of the harem.

Double back under the flock of screaming sea gulls, past some more sea stacks to inspect a female elephant seal and her pup. Having walked around the lonely Farallon Islands several times, I can assure you the ambiance is authentic. The only things missing are the kelp flies and the all-pervading chicken-coop smell of the great seabird rookery.

The next diorama is of mule deer moving down from the Sierra after an early snowfall, a scene charming enough to be on a Christmas card.

The weather is warmer at lower elevations, like that simulated in the neighboring window, which portrays the Great Basin Desert of Modoc County, where pronghorn antelopes, the fastest land animals in the West, pause a moment.

Turn the corner to your left and it's spring again! You are back at the Farallon Islands, this time undersea in a new fourteen-thousand-gallon aquarium, complete with cabezon, salmon, rock cod, wolf eels, and any number of sea stars, anemones, and other marine life.

Swing around to your left to arrive twenty-six miles inland at the exhibit Between the Tides, depicting Point Montara. A few steps farther, prepare to dispense with your personal orientation to the world as you reach the Sea Meadow Exhibit, where a smidgeon of clean, pre–oil-spill seawater from just outside the Golden Gate has been magnified two hundred times. This "living soup" shows drill, crab larvae, anchovy eggs, copepods, and diatoms, all being sorted by the tentacle of a hungry feather-duster worm.

Next stop on this magical mystery tour of California is the Salt Marsh Nursery, a compressed view of Limantour's Estero in Point Reyes. Loyal Academy volunteers molded and painted thousands of stalks needed for each square foot of the intertidal zone.

Beach Wrack, the next window, lets you play Gulliver again, this time in a minuscule world magnified fifty times to show a rove beetle about to feed on a dead beach hopper. Nothing produced at George Lucas's Skywalker Ranch was ever scarier. Kids love it.

Now that you know all those things are there, maybe you'll never sit down on a beach without a blanket under you again.

DISCOVERY ROOM

NOTE: *For map, see Academy of Sciences, p. 231.*

WALKING TIME: All your life.

DISTANCE: From here to enlightenment.

PUBLIC TRANSPORTATION: Muni bus 44 O'Shaughnessy.

PARKING: Iffy.

CLOTHES: Comfortable.

TIMES: The California Academy of Sciences is open 10 A.M. to 5 P.M. daily. Discovery Room's hours vary.

The rainy-day walk par excellence in San Francisco is through the California Academy of Sciences in Golden Gate Park.

There is always something new to discover at this venerable museum, no matter how knowledgeable, bored, or blasé you may be. Only an insensitive person could fail to have his attention engaged at the Academy, and as the late, great physiologist Ajax Carlson said, "An insensitive person is a dead one."

For small fry, there is the Discovery Room, a charming "hands-on" gallery especially designed for kids. Created in 1978 with the inspiration and support of writer Janet Nickelsburg, it is supported by the royalties from her book *Nature Activities for Early Childhood*.

To discover the Discovery Room, bring your own tot, nieces, nephews, grandkids, or borrow a neighbor's bright five-year-old. Then transport yourselves to the Music Concourse in Golden Gate Park.

Once at the Academy, pay your modest admission fee (or better yet, purchase a family membership, which lets you in free all the time and provides other advantages as well), then stop inside Cowell Hall.

Walk left, past the 27-foot-long allosaurus, a meat-eater who lived in what is now Utah about 130 million years ago, and the geophysical globe, which shows how the Earth would look sans oceans. Enter Simson African Hall. Here is a modernized museum in a museum, for the traditional dioramas inside, which have been here since the 1930s, would be almost impossible to duplicate. Most of the animals were gifts of big-game hunting members of the Academy. Since many of the rare species are now on the endangered list, and gentlemen no longer consider big-game hunting a desirable sport, every display is a treasure.

Go all the way to the end to see the water hole, enlarged so that visitors can walk among the animals. Visitors see a daily cycle of changing light, which will repeat itself every twenty minutes to the accompaniment of appropriate background sounds. No, you won't age three days if you stand inside the exhibit for an hour.

From the water hole, bear right into the adjoining display of the African Origins of Man, replicas of old Lucy's bones and a graphic jigsaw puzzle of man's development. Just beyond is the African Annex, more birds and animals.

None of them could exist, nor could we, without the thin layer of plants busily making soil and oxygen for us, depicted in the next gallery, the Eastwood Hall of Botany, named in honor of prize-winning botanist Alice Eastwood, who was a curator at the Academy from 1892 until her retirement in 1949. This plucky woman saved most of the Academy's precious collection of botanic specimens from destruction during the 1906 earthquake and fire at an earlier Academy location at 4th and Market streets.

Just past the big redwood slabs, cut from a tree that was 1,710 years old (count the rings if you doubt it), look for two doors on the left. Behind them is the Discovery Room, a rich niche so successful that explorers are limited to twenty at a time and the time limit is twenty minutes per visit, if the crowd is large.

At first glance, the Discovery Room seems deceptively simple, until one finds that the barriers are gone and you can touch the jaw of a great white shark, heft the bones of a dinosaur, listen to the sea resound in a trumpet shell, or scrunch up the bag woven by a Zinecantan Indian of Chiapas. Behind a vestigial counter are several dozen big wooden boxes of specimens that can be checked out like library books and examined at the tables.

Mrs. Nickelsburg, whose system of teaching science to young children is very like that now used by Marin naturalist Elizabeth Terwilliger, taught for fifty years before endowing the room so her tradition could be carried on.

When your time is up in the Discovery Room, go out the way you entered and bear left into the Wattis Gallery, a long, narrow room featuring a handsome exhibition of primitive Polynesian fishing implements.

On your way out, you pass the Foucault Pendulum, swinging as the Earth turns. If it's about to hit a peg, the crowd of gathered kids watches tensely and cheers if a peg is knocked over.

FISH ROUNDABOUT

WALKING TIME: An easy hour.

DISTANCE: The long road to knowledge.

PUBLIC TRANSPORTATION: Muni bus 44 O'Shaughnessy.

PARKING: Fair.

CLOTHES: Casual.

> USED TROUT STREAM FOR SALE.
> MUST BE SEEN TO BE APPRECIATED.
>
> *"Where did the stream come from?" I asked.*
>
> *"Colorado," he said. "We moved it with loving care. We've never damaged a trout stream yet. We treat them all as if they were china."*
>
> *"You're probably asked this all the time, but how's fishing in the stream?" I asked.*
>
> *"Very good," he said. "Mostly German browns, but there are a few rainbows . . ."*
>
> —RICHARD BRAUTIGAN,*
> *Trout Fishing in America*
> (New York: Dell Publishing Co., Inc., 1989)

Dear Richard: Guess who bought that stream? The California Academy of Sciences, that's who. They got the hole, the head of the hole, the tail of the hole, the pool, the rapids, the waterfall, the banks, trees, and a couple of white-crowned sparrows to boot. Plus those browns and a few rainbow, cutthroat, and golden trout.

You could have bowled me over with a piece of popcorn when I went to Steinhart Aquarium to see if they had any geckoes (ever since I got back from Samoa I've been missing the gecko who hung out over my bed in Faga'alu) and found this trout stream installed in a long tank made out of three smaller ones.

The new trout stream flows along, clear as an ice cube, with continuously changing fresh water under skylights that make it look as real as the North Fork of the Yuba or the lonely reaches of the Upper Blackfoot. They say the trout can leap upstream in spawning time.

* January 8, 1984. After the late Richard Brautigan read about this walk, he immediately went fishing for trout at his Montana home. He caught some whoppers, placed them on a platter of ice, and hand-carried them by plane to San Francisco where we had trout for dinner that night.

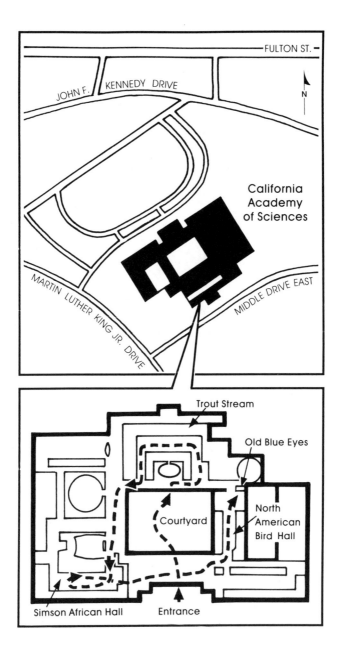

FULTON ST.

JOHN F. KENNEDY DRIVE

N

California
Academy
of Sciences

MARTIN LUTHER KING JR. DRIVE

MIDDLE DRIVE EAST

Trout Stream

Old Blue Eyes

Courtyard

North
American
Bird Hall

Simson African Hall

Entrance

238

It is like looking into a trout bedroom or something. The lunkers are revealed by glass along the sides of the stream. Those poor fish have no privacy. They see us too, of course. Some nine-year-olds were making funny faces at the fish through the glass. If fish had anthropologists, they could learn a thing or two here about their cleverest predators. It would be challenging to fish this new trout stream. To case it next time you come down from Montana, take any bus out to Golden Gate Park. The Academy of Sciences is on the southeast side of the Music Concourse, off John F. Kennedy Drive, about parallel to 8th Avenue.

If you are on the shorts, try to get there on the first Wednesday of the month. If you're flush, join the Academy and you can get in free all the time. Otherwise, the tab is two bucks for you, and another two for your lady friend. If she has a school-aged sprat, it's six bits for him. The Confederate General would have to pay a buck, like any other senior citizen.

When you get to the Academy, walk out into the open courtyard past Bob Howard's big *Mating Whales* statue to go into the aquarium. Save the alligator pond and the dolphins for later and go into the darkness between them. The trout stream is at the end of the aisle.

You'll see that there is a rock ledge big enough for one fisherman to stand on, but I doubt if there is enough elbow room for a graceful cast. We might consider trying something that fishermen do in Tonga. They talk the sharks right up to the side of a boat, then reach over and grab them. There's enough room on that rock ledge to lie down and talk up a trout. If he is under plate-size, we could throw him back with no one the wiser.

Don't confuse the trout stream with another stream just across the aisle. It is full of Jackass penguins, the *Spheniscus demersus,* from South Africa, and bears the highfalutin name of The Penguin Environment. But it looks like just another run-of-the-mill stream to me. It has a back-bar mirror to make everything look bigger. I counted thirty penguins, so there must be fifteen. Some of them were flying underwater like little paddle-propelled, side-wheeled waiters at a fish-grotto restaurant.

The only thing I missed was a handy place to sit down and study these streams. If you want to reflect a while, you could zip over past the Foucault Pendulum, which will reassure you that the Earth is still turning, and past the Planetarium to Simson African Hall. Forget what African Hall used to be, the differences since renovation will hit you like a sock full of wet sand.

There is a good place to sit in front of the watering hole. Two days passed while I sat there. Two nights, too. I didn't time it, but while I was looking over the renovated dioramas, it seemed like a day dawned and night fell about every ten minutes. Think of it!! You could age an extra year in just a few days of watching that tall, stuffed giraffe not move.

There were some thirsty teenyboppers crowding around that giraffe, but they decided not to chance a drink out of the water hole after some great jungly sound came out of the brush.

A good country tracker would go mad studying the animal footprints in the apron of floor that sprawls out of the water hole onto the rug. Yes, I said rug. Before it was done over, the cavernous place looked and echoed like a waiting room in the old Sacramento Train Station. No more. It now has sound-muffling panels overhead and sound-silencing wall-to-wall underfoot. A drunk Texas hawg-caller couldn't be heard in there. Even the benches are upholstered in rugs. It's like no jungle you'll ever see. More like the Botswana Hilton.

Who are all those guests in the see-through rooms off the lobby? The dik-diks are in one. The oryx in another.

When you're rested, cut back toward the aquarium. Just before you get to the tide pool, there is a tank you won't want to miss. In it is Old Blue Eyes, the coelacanth, *Latimeria chalumnae*, the fish they call the living fossil. This one is swimming in formaldehyde (some way to live!), but his fan club doesn't care. If you want to join, it's called SPOOF, the Society for Preservation of Old Fish.

As ever,
Margot Patterson Doss

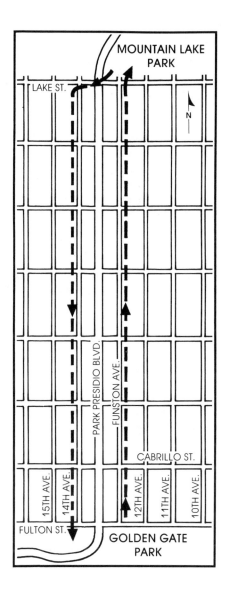

PARK PRESIDIO BOULEVARD

WALKING TIME: A morning.

DISTANCE: Two miles.

PUBLIC TRANSPORTATION: Muni bus 5 or 28.

PARKING: So-so.

CLOTHES: Take a jacket.

San Francisco has a remarkable outdoor museum of trees chosen for their good manners. Good manners in a tree are not so different from good manners in a teenager. The well-behaved ones know their space and they stay in it.

These trees don't mar foundation walls or sidewalks. They keep their feet out of the plumbing and their heads out of the power lines. They don't drop their leaves for someone else to pick up.

On smoggy fall days, it's also nice to know that trees are the most consistent, if not the only effective, way to clean up the air. They are nature's green machines for digesting airborne bilge. You can come in out of the smog, as you might the rain, by standing under a big old tree.

Real estate agents will tell you that planting a well-chosen street tree in front of your house can add as much as $5,000 to the home's resale value.

Whether you want to inspect this museum with an eye toward tree behavior or simply enjoy a pleasant walk, the place to do it is in section 13 of Golden Gate Park, the twenty-three acres bounded by Fulton and Lake streets and Funston and 14th avenues.

It is the one place where the park is wider from north to south than it is from east to west. Originally called the Presidio and Park Panhandle, it is better known as Park Presidio Boulevard.

When the land was purchased in 1903, at the unbelievably low price of $360,000, it was described as including "several blocks of land, each block 600 feet long and 240 feet wide, or nearly one mile extending from the northern boundary line of Golden Gate Park to the south line of the military reservations, at a point not far from the old U.S. Marine Hospital."

Park commissioners cheerfully predicted that "the new boulevard running through the main body of the Richmond district from Golden Gate Park to the Presidio will open up a new field of park life."

It also opened up a desirable place to live on either side of the lush green strip, a bridle path for horsemen cantering from the park to the Presidio, a traffic chute, and more recently the outdoor museum and test plot of street trees.

To explore Section 13 on foot, begin at Fulton Street and Funston Avenue. As you start walking north along Funston, notice how traffic noise and exhaust fumes seem to diminish as you approach the shelter of the fine old shady trees growing on the raised berm of earth along the eastern strip of boulevard.

Residents of the vintage townhouses on either side of the boulevard made an effective protest when park gardeners began removing the noise-reducing understory of shrubs from the median strips. The residents pointed out that when the boulevard was laid out, it had only two traffic lanes. Three lanes of concrete on either side were once lawn.

The banished grass, like shrubs and trees, was also nature's own consumer of the hydrocarbons belched by cars. Approximately one hundred trees are needed to consume the smog emitted by one car driving through San Francisco from the Golden Gate Bridge to the San Mateo County line.

Department of Public Works Assistant Melvin Baker, who is in charge of urban forestry, estimates that the city has between 175,000 and 200,000 street trees. "But, we certainly need many more," he says. Two ordinances passed by the Board of Supervisors, one on urban forestry in 1986, the other on "adopt-a-tree" financing in 1988, are helping the cause.

Walk along the west side of Funston Avenue. Here the demonstration plantings grow between the sidewalk and the street, and on the periphery of the berm. Labels on the trees were attached when they were planted in 1971, as a joint project of San Francisco Beautiful, the city street-tree department, and others. The first trees planted were maytens, with two on one side of the sidewalk and one on the other. The next little clump are Chinese elm reversing the pattern of three. They are followed by Victorian box, Indian laurel, and the tree almost everyone recognizes for its huge glossy leaves, the southern magnolia.

Weeping bottlebrush, glossy and wax-leaf privets, Brazilian pepper, Italian buckthorn, and Grecian bay all are on the first block. Because they are living unprotected, the trees show homeowners and other tree planters, better than any nursery could, how different varieties hold up in our climate through the years.

After you cross Cabrillo Street, there are four varieties to look for: Catalina ironwood, the Lily of the Valley tree, the Karo pittosporum, and the Silver Queen pittosporum.

Walk twenty feet farther west in this block, toward the older gnarled trees, and look along the red-rock bridle path that meanders gracefully through the east side of the park. Once much used by horsemen, it makes a fine promenade for walkers. Follow it north toward Mountain Lake, the Richmond district's choice historic spot.

A horseman friend told me that he used to pretend to be Juan Bautista de Anza, riding toward the night's encampment on the shores of Mountain Lake, when he came along this way. Horsemen could ride the bridle path again as a way to the Golden Gate National Recreation Area, he says, if only stoplights were coordinated at cross streets.

As you walk, it becomes apparent that the shade trees are planted in groups. One goes from a grove of contorted leptospermum, or "tea trees," reeling and writhing and falling in coils, to stalwart soldierlike pines alongside graceful "manna gums" tossing their long limbs.

Plantings were designed to thrive within the variations of Presidio

Parkway microclimates, which differ from street to street and from one side of the street to the other.

Landmarks outside the forest as you walk north are Sutro School, the classic columns of a Christian Science church, and the Congregation Beth Sholom (west side of Clement Street and 14th Avenue). Congregation Anshey Sfard (which means Men of Spain) is also nearby. So are White Russian, French, Japanese, Chinese, Vietnamese, Thai, Lao, Korean, Slovak, and German residential colonies.

If it is an average day, especially on the major shopping byways of California, Geary, and Clement streets, walkers will have to detour to stoplights to cross at corners; as you do, check out the nearby street trees.

Especially interesting near Cabrillo Street are two big Italian stone pines and the bronze-leafed dodenaea. There are shish kebab eucalyptus near Balboa Street. Near Anza Street, the big, naked gum trees are *Eucalyptus viminalis*. Monterey cypress near Geary Street are native Californians, as are the California pepper trees near Clement.

The original San Francisco Beautiful plantings continue on to Mountain Lake Park. As have other parks in the city, and indeed other streets, Funston Avenue has also been improved recently by the San Francisco Friends of the Urban Forest. The lively group's street-planting guide, *Trees for San Francisco*, won a national award in 1985 from the American Society of Landscape Architects. Copies are available for $6 each from San Francisco Friends of the Urban Forest, 512 Second Street, San Francisco, California 94107.

Linger as long as you like in Mountain Lake Park. When you are ready for more walking, return to Lake Street and turn west, crossing Park Presidio Boulevard to 14th Avenue with the light.

As you pass the western side of the green strip, notice how the bridle path that once approached the U.S. Public Health Service Hospital within the Presidio, along the western shore of Mountain Lake, has been "planted out" with grass.

Turn south and walk along the western side of the median planting strip, where two kinds of hawthorn, several tulip trees, and red-spotted gum trees are among the demonstration plantings. Cross California and the variety is even greater, with pink tea trees, escallonias, evergreen pears, and ornamental avocado trees.

Continue along the street side, enjoying the variety and benefits of these well-mannered trees as you walk.

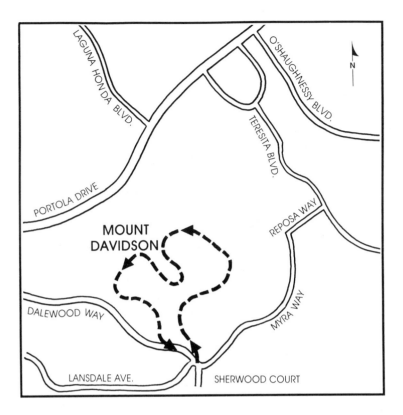

MOUNT DAVIDSON PARK

WALKING TIME: A morning.

DISTANCE: Two miles.

PUBLIC TRANSPORTATION: At the terminal of Muni bus 34. Special buses on Easter.

PARKING: Limited. Cars are towed on Easter Morning.

CLOTHES: Warm.

Bridges, towers, pyramids, radar fixtures, microwave relay station, Nike missile sites, and other recent soaring monuments notwithstanding, San Francisco's most enduring landmark for the last two hundred years has been a cross on a mountaintop. Although it hasn't always been the same cross, or the same mountaintop, the landmark has always stood near the sea.

The present cross, 103 feet tall, made of cast concrete, lighted at night and visible for fifty miles in fair weather, surmounts Mount Davidson, elevation 938 feet, the highest peak in the city. It is reputed to be the largest cross in the Americas. The sculptured Christ in Concrete of the Andes, by comparison, is only 26 feet high, although, at the elevation of 13,000 feet, it is undeniably higher in the air.

Father Francisco Palou planted the very first cross in San Francisco on Point Lobos in about 1774 in what has since become Lincoln Park. It stood about where the Palace of the Legion of Honor stands today.

Three years later, Don Manuel de Ayala had a cross erected on Cantil Blanco, the white cliff that guarded the south side of the point where San Francisco Bay meets Golden Gate Strait. Cut down to make a pediment for Fort Point in 1864, Cantil Blanco serves as an anchor for the south end of the Golden Gate Bridge today.

Down through the years, five crosses have stood on Lone Mountain, the first in 1862.

Four earlier, wooden crosses have also stood on Mount Davidson, which was named Blue Mountain by Professor George Davidson when he surveyed it in 1862. It was Lucky Baldwin who owned the land in 1911 and built the first trails on it, who renamed the mountain in honor of the incorruptible surveyor.

The walk up Mount Davidson is a gradual, exhilarating climb through sighing eucalyptus, climbing ivy, rambling wild cucumber vines, and peeping wildflowers. On any clear day, joggers, dog walkers, photographers, tots, and grandparents all make the climb to the broad clearing near the top. Wearing your hiking boots and a warm coat, transport yourself to the junction of Myra, Lansdale, Dalewood, and Sherwood Court to make this walk. Bring a friend.

Since 1923, thousands of people have made the climb in the pre-dawn chill, sometimes in heavy fog or pouring rain, to await the Easter sunrise sermons on the mountain. Impelled by the same conviction that has led pilgrims to walk to Rome, Jerusalem, Mecca, and up Fujiyama, they come on Easter Morning, flashlights in hand, giving the sinuous mountain trail an otherworldly quality as the undulating stream of walkers and flashlights makes its way to the top.

It was in 1923 that Dean J. Wilmer Gresham of Grace Cathedral delivered the first sunrise-service sermon at the urging of a fellow cleric, the Reverend Homer K. Pitman, a Presbyterian. Since then, the San Francisco Council of Churches, which sponsors the annual event, has supplied ministers from almost every Christian denomination in the city.

Since not all walkers make it to the top, on Easter Morning the Council of Churches also supplies a standby ambulance.

From the semicircular bus turnaround—marked by a nondescript pole labeled "terminal"—take the broad dirt road into the twenty-six-acre park to the summit of Mount Davidson. Stick to the broad road, no matter how many switchbacks, shortcuts, and side trails there seem to be. Recently renovated, the main upward trail is the safest and has the gentlest grade. All trails in the park lead to the top, but this one also offers spectacular views of the South Bay area as you climb.

Twinkling lights in the early morning outline city streets and the airport. As the trail swings around the eastern slope, the panorama widens to reveal San Bruno Mountain first, with its rows of box-roofed houses snaking their way up the hills, then McLaren Park, framed in peak-roofed older homes. Around the next curve is a view of downtown San Francisco.

Walk out on the bald northeasterly knoll to see the downtown towers—gilded in the dawn's early light if you make this climb Easter Morning. In any case, take time to enjoy the vastness of the scene. Brodiaea, malva, poppies, and vetch are all in bloom along the trail in springtime.

When you are on a line with Sutro Tower, bear left uphill. Soon you arrive beside two big rocks, and the square concrete vent of an old underground pillbox. From this angle, the cross is shielded by the towering eucalyptus and cypress trees. Walk to the far side of the clearing to get the long view of the cross.

Then, unless the service is under way and the path is impassable, walk up to the base of the cross itself, if only to perceive its massive size. Close up there is disturbing evidence of urban ills in this tranquil spot— racist and other unpleasant graffiti painted on the base of the towering cross.

A few years ago some mountain climbers, not content with climbing the mountain, continued up the cross and raised Old Glory on it. The climbers also reported back to groundlings that they had discovered the leather fern, *Polypodium soleri*, growing on the cross itself. Walkers who go for fun some sunny afternoon, rather than for reasons of faith on Easter Morning, will also see clumps of the hardy fern growing in crotches of old trees on the north side of the cross. Take the other broad trail downhill to find them. It descends by a big boulder near the approach trail.

Follow this trail down through the stately trees to arrive on Dalewood Way, about half a block from the beginning of this walk. Turn left to return to the crescent of blacktop that serves as the bus terminus.

If you enjoyed the shelter of the trees, send silent thanks to Mayor Adolph Sutro. Mount Davidson was as bare as nearby Twin Peaks until he had it planted. When Sutro owned Rancho San Miguel, which included Mount Davidson, schoolchildren came out annually on Arbor Day to plant seedlings from his private nursery on Clarendon Boulevard. Inadvertently, they also planted plum trees, which grew from the pits of plums dropped from their picnic lunches.

GOLDEN GATE HEIGHTS

WALKING TIME: An hour.

DISTANCE: Three-quarters of a mile.

PUBLIC TRANSPORTATION: Muni bus 6.

PARKING: Fair.

CLOTHES: Warm.

Charm is where you find it, and, in San Francisco, it is frequently on hilltops. Unlikely as it may seem, one of the more charming neighborhood parks in San Francisco hides on a peak in the Sunset, an area most people assume to be relatively flat. Now known as Golden Gate Heights, old-timers called it Larsen's Peak for its donor, the philanthropist Carl G. "Tivoli" Larsen, who left the land to the city in 1928. It has also been called Sunset Heights and is sometimes confused with Mount Moriah, or Grand View Park, another Sunset peak a few blocks northwest, which was also a gift from Larsen to the city.

By whatever name, Golden Gate Heights is a serene six-acre oasis, 725 feet above sea level, with spectacular views visible from the old ranch road that loops up to its crest. On those scintillating blue-and-gold days when the fog forgets San Francisco, Golden Gate Heights is a very pleasant place for a walk.

City lovers who like to think they have explored all the secret nooks and crannies of San Francisco will want to climb it at least once for the nobility of the view. To make this walk, go to the southeast corner of 10th and Pacheco.

At the outset, look north to see the hills of Marin beyond the towers of the Golden Gate Bridge and east for an intimate view of Twin Peaks, a smidgeon of Sutro Forest, and the sailing-ship-skeleton-in-the-sky that is the Sutro Tower.

Cross 10th Avenue and start uphill on curving Pacheco Street through this comfortable middle-class neighborhood.

The late historian Roy Graves, who lived in Golden Gate Heights, once told me it should have been called "O'Shaughnessy's Enlightenment," for this is the area where City Engineer Michael Maurice O'Shaughnessy, best known for his part in building the Great Highway and Esplanade, the Sunset Tunnel, and the Hetch-Hetchy Reservoir, rearranged the streets from the boring grid pattern common to much of San Francisco. In Golden Gate Heights, thanks to O'Shaughnessy, the streets acknowledge the hills.

Within half a block, look for Oriole Way, a broad concrete staircase that takes off uphill on your left. The "witch's hat" turret of the attractive house at 645 Pacheco peers down like a sentinel.

Turn left uphill and climb these ninety-seven well-maintained steps, pausing at each long landing to see that the distant perspectives seem to change with every ten-foot rise. Though the bordering gardens are green, no one in our time has reported seeing an oriole on Oriole Way.

At the top of the steps, turn right on Cragmont Avenue and follow as it curves to the complex corner where it meets 12th and Funston avenues and Rockridge Drive. You are now at the entrance to Golden Gate Heights Park, as a green sign on your left indicates.

Forgo the temptation to climb these broad cobbled steps, which lead up to two tennis courts in the park. Instead, cross to the west to Rockridge Drive. Walk about one hundred feet to find an asphalt-paved road that leads gradually uphill. Cross Rockridge Drive to enter the park here.

Soon you will be walking alongside a charming green meadow bordered by cypress trees, often used by Frisbee players. Closer at hand is a wild blackberry briar, which was full of chirping pine siskins when I strolled by with Kenny Mar.

"I discovered Golden Gate Heights Park because my sister lives nearby," said Mar, a driver for Concord Express. "She thinks this is the very best place to live in all of San Francisco."

Tivoli Larsen must have felt the same way. A Dane who came to San Francisco in 1869, he made a great success of a restaurant called the Tivoli Cafe, which stood on Eddy Street near the old Tivoli Opera House and was much loved by opera buffs. At the top of the menu was the slogan "Fresh Eggs from Tivoli Cafe Ranch Every Day." The ranch lay between 12th and 14th avenues and Quintarra and Pacheco streets. By 1888, Larsen also owned several other large chunks of the Sunset dunes, including the area where Shriners Hospital is located.

Turn left when you reach the fork in the path. Tennis courts on your left offer players a great view of West Marin. A few feet higher, kids on the jungle gym in the tots' playground have the same lofty panorama, visible through trees.

Turn right and, at the next junction, go left up into the grove on the knoll. Sun-filled, it makes a great picnic area. Just downhill on the south side is a rocky outcropping that seven generations of children have enjoyed as a fort, a lookout, an aerie, and, best of all, a shelter on windy days.

Larsen, a bachelor, loved children and left much of his land for children to enjoy. His niece, Mrs. Hedvig Eichner, recalled in an interview published in the *San Francisco Chronicle* in 1966 that "one of her greatest childhood pleasures was riding in her uncle's two-seater to the beach or to Strawberry Hill in Golden Gate Park."

When her uncle died in 1928, his body lay in state in the rotunda of City Hall and hundreds of mourners, including many children, attended the funeral.

Near the outcropping, look south for a fine panorama that includes San Francisco State University, the Harding Park Golf Course, Lake Merced, and much of the Sunset District, whose population increase was envisioned by Larsen. Each year he would throw a big party at the ranch, usually at chicken-hatching time, and guests would be shown the eggs in incubators, the broad chicken yards, and Larsen's gardens.

Posted in one part of the ranch was a sign saying "Twenty years ago this was drifting sand. Walk through it and tell me if you can, why all the great sand dunes in San Francisco were not reclaimed like this twenty years ago. Fifty thousand people could be living here today." The dunes are long-since gone, and Larsen's forecast of a hundred years ago has come true.

Return to the forked trail when you have enjoyed the view from this slope and climb the neighboring knoll to the west. Here, a grassy oval defined by a road, once a carriage turnaround, is marked with two large boulders.

The commanding view is west, overlooking all of the Sunset and the three miles of beach it fronts. Given clear weather, one can see from Fort Funston and the zoo north to Point Reyes and west to the Farallon Islands.

Take the broad trail leading downhill on the west side of the slope. It goes through trees and a leafy understory. As you descend, distant views will vie with wildflowers closer at hand for your attention.

Soon you will be back near the point of your entry into the park, having looped it in an irregular circle. It is easy to get lost on Golden Gate Heights's curving avenues, so the easy way back is the way you came.

There are many other staircases to find here. Be daring and seek them out, if you wish, but remember that they may drop you on the opposite side of the hill from the place where you wish to be.

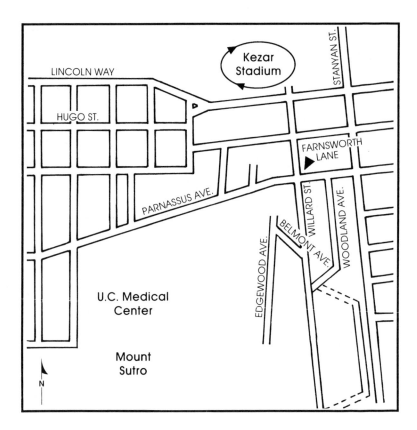

EDGEWOOD AVENUE

WALKING TIME: Six to ten minutes.

DISTANCE: Two city blocks.

PUBLIC TRANSPORTATION: Muni bus 6 Parnassus or N-Judah streetcar.

PARKING: Fair.

CLOTHES: Citified casual.

The lace-edged Valentine called Edgewood Avenue bursts into pagan pink glory one mild day irrespective of the weather bureau, the vernal equinox, the groundhog, or the calendar. Walk along this two-block ledge on the edge of the greenbelt at that time and winter is dead as a dinosaur.

See it bloom with sunshine filtering through the pale pink plum

252

blossoms onto the red brick of the paving below and you will never forget this double lane fronting stately old houses. It becomes a red-carpeted aisle transmuted into timeless but short-lived beauty. Through the alchemy of color it could be a backdrop for Makarova in a tutu pirouetting on the sunlit bricks. Kiri Te Kanawa bursting into something from *Cosí fan Tutte* would seem appropriate.

Farnsworth Lane is the special secret place to discover this remarkable spun-sugar fantasy. Most vantage points look down on a vista, but Farnsworth Lane looks up.

To reach it, begin at Willard Street at Parnassus. Walk uphill on Willard about eighty feet. The Farnsworth steps slip off inconspicuously uphill between two short squat obelisks, looking exceedingly private. It is public. Start up them and you climb to an unexpectedly green world of treetops. The hectic street below and the bustling University of California Medical Center nearby recede out of sight and sound as you ascend. At the apex, step out onto the roadbed of Farnsworth Lane, which forms a short platform at the foot of Edgewood, and look uphill. When the *Prunus pissardi* and *Prunus bleiriana* trees lining either side are in bloom, Edgewood is a moment of magic for every beholder.

At any time of year, Edgewood is handsome. This is no accident. Families whose homes face on Edgewood planted the purple-leaved plums because they liked the color interplay when this was an unpaved red-rock road, part of a horse trail that once led up into the hills of Rancho San Miguel. The trees cost six bits apiece and were planted ten feet apart at the urging of Rose Levy, a dedicated gardener who lived on the east side of the street. Long ago, a strong neighborhood association fought paving of any kind and red brick was the happy compromise. When the sun picks out the rich pattern of the brick in counterpoint to the redder leaves or pale pink blossoms, no one can doubt their wisdom.

Edgewood has been something of an artists' and writers' area as well as a doctor's row. Agnes Danforth Hewes, who wrote historical novels for young people, Hearst columnist Elsie Robinson, Margaret Parton, author of *Laughter on the Hill*, environmentalist Rosebud Preddy, sculptor Chris Mueller, Sr., and actor Holbrook Blinn were among the talented residents.

Then, as now, Edgewood encompassed a special world of nocturnal wildlife in Sutro Forest, which hugs the avenue on the south side as part of the greenbelt, and on the west, where Ishi the Indian made his final home. The last free coyote trapped in San Francisco came down from the ever-diminishing Sutro Forest in 1927 and was caught on the lawn of what was then called the Affiliated Colleges. Raccoons and skunks are still nighttime visitors. On hot days, a few San Francisco garter snakes, an endangered species, come out to warm themselves in Edgewood gardens.

Stroll up the street to its end, for this is a place for leisurely perambulation. Probably nothing closer than Prunus Walk at Dumbarton Oaks, Washington, D.C., has quite the same heady exuberant pink springtime ambiance.

To get the fullest pleasure, walk up the shady side of the street to the tall stand of eucalyptus. This greenbelt area is so lively with growing things that it could hardly be called a "dead end," though there is no through road for cars. The surefooted may want to try the footpath through the greenbelt. By bearing consistently right, the path through the forest will bring one to a U. C. parking lot. Downhill, through trees immediately behind the houses, the path loops back to Farnsworth Lane.

More entrancing is to return on the sunny side of the street three-quarters of the way down Edgewood. Bear right on Belmont to see how the plum tree persuasion has expanded. Bear right again on Willard to Woodland to enjoy more of this sunny pocket on the eastern slope of Mount Sutro. Woodland returns to Parnassus.

Inspired by the effect of Edgewood Avenue's annual two-week Valentine, residents on adjacent streets have also chosen to plant the purple-leaved plums as their street trees. The pink of the trees in bloom gives a festive air to the whole community.

It is an area so neighborly that it annually closes off streets for a block party. Like their neighbors on Edgewood, citizens along Belmont and Woodland believe that beauty is not only its own reward, but like liberty, well worth the extra effort.

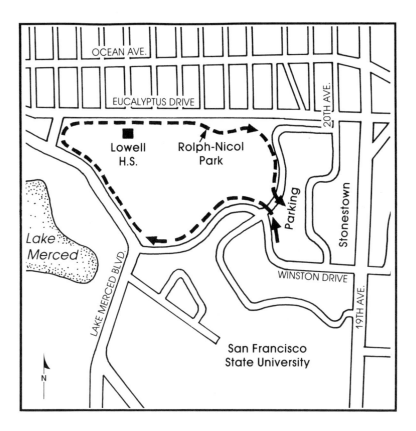

STONESTOWN

WALKING TIME: Allow half a day.

DISTANCE: Two miles.

PUBLIC TRANSPORTATION: M-Ocean streetcar and Muni buses 17 Park Merced, 18 46th Street, 28 19th Avenue, and 29 Sunset.

PARKING: Plenty.

CLOTHES: Suburban.

CAVEAT: Bring money.

The wilderness that once was San Francisco still peeks through the urban fabric of the city in unlikely places. One of these tattered remnants of the original wilderness still exists in the last district to be developed. You will find this genuine vacant lot between the Sutro

Library and Lake Merced out near the Pacific Ocean in the southwestern part of San Francisco.

The fifty-seven acres that have been labeled as the community of Stonestown on the city street maps since 1948 is bounded by 19th Avenue, Eucalyptus Drive, Lake Merced Boulevard, and the San Francisco State University campus.

This is where the malling of San Francisco began. For all practical purposes, it was suburbia when the first scoop of earth was remolded. When Henry and Ellis Stoneson, two brothers from Iceland, founded a construction company to build here, the area boasted golf clubs, gun clubs, Fleischhacker Zoo, Fort Funston, Stern Grove, and the little community of Parkside out in the sand dunes near the northern arm of Lake Merced.

Recently, the pioneer Stonestown Mall has received an impressive renovation, including a new glass galleria sheltering a concourse, a mezzanine full of trendy fast-food dispensaries, a branch of the Nordstrom Department Store, and some Yuppified boutiques. It is now possible to see the San Francisco of yesterday and tomorrow in one short walk.

The contrast won't last long. Tomorrow has the upper hand here. There are already truckloads of clean fill for some construction project on the vacant lot which was once a riverine watercourse leading to Lake Merced.

Make your way to Stonestown out in the southwestern corner of the city. Once there, go behind the mall and walk down to the sidewalk that borders Winston Drive and turn right toward Buckingham Way. Cross Buckingham and continue west on Winston, past the lowrise Stonestown Apartments. Like the rest of the original Stonestown, they were designed by architect Angus McSweeney.

Visitors from Sacramento may experience a sense of déjà vu when they arrive at the Sutro Library, 480 Winston Drive. Sutro librarian Gary Kurtz told me that during the restoration of the state capitol between 1976 and 1982, this building served as assembly chambers for the state senators and representatives. When it was no longer needed, the building was cut into twelve sections, trucked here, and reassembled.

Open every weekday from 10 A.M. until 5 P.M., the Sutro Library has a main reading room and a smaller special collection room for rare books. Part of the library of former San Francisco Mayor Adolph Sutro is housed here. Since it has a research center and labor archive, the Sutro Library has become a mecca for amateur genealogists, who come to trace their roots through employment records.

In another hundred feet, the concrete outside changes to an unpaved footpath. You have reached that rarity in San Francisco, the vacant lot.

This was part of the shoreline of Lake Merced when Captain Fernando Rivera y Moncada, Father Francisco Palou, and an exploring party of soldiers came this way in 1774. Continue on the footpath, past willows, coreopsis, acacia, fennel, French broom, and the pompous invasive pampas grass. Turn right alongside Lake Merced Boulevard. The last time I came this way, a red-tailed hawk swooped into the vacant lot. When he rose again, there was a rodent in his talons.

Laguna de Nuestra Señora de la Merced, which we have shortened to Lake Merced, was at least forty feet higher when the Spanish explorers came along its shores. At that time, its waters also flowed westward through a gap in the dunes to the Pacific Ocean. On the night of November 22, 1852, a temblor shook the area, and the water level mysteriously dropped thirty feet, letting seawater flow into the lagoon. As a result, there are small underwater creatures in the northern arm of the lake that have adapted to both fresh and brackish water.

When you reach the dirt road that admits trucks loaded with fill, cross it and walk within the median planter strip that parallels the Lowell High School Football Field until you reach Middlefield Drive. Walk past the Lake Shore Elementary School. The boxy suburban houses in Lakeshore Park on your left were built by Carl and Fred Gellert, once the city's largest house-building firms. They commemorated themselves in the first street name you pass en route.

Turn right again on Eucalyptus Drive walking toward Mount Davidson and alongside Lowell High School. The main entrance is marked by the Lowell flagpole and plaza at Forest View Avenue. Just past 25th Avenue, where the Lowell campus ends, the Rolph-Nicol mini-park begins. Cut downhill through the Lowell parking lot about a hundred feet to reach a soft park path that goes through the greensward following a line of benches and old eucalyptus trees.

Return to Eucalyptus Drive when the park ends and turn right. In a few steps, you will be abreast of the charming St. Stephen's Roman Catholic Church. Turn right and cut through its parking lot, which has an unusual freestanding tower.

The Emporium Department Store is visible on your left beyond a sea of parking just across Buckingham Way. In another half-block, you will be back at the junction with Winston Drive.

Turn left here and cross Buckingham Way to reach the Stonestown Galleria. Two boutiques are worth a look. One is a candy store at the top of the escalator that features little glass silos full of jelly beans, all graded by color. A sign warning snitches against tasting before buying reads, "Offenders will be turned into Jelly Babies and sold for 99 cents per quarter-pound."

The other intriguing shop is the Imaginarium toy store on the first floor. Huge tiles in the floor are imprinted with the footprints of deer, puma, and dinosaurs. Most amusing are the human footprints outside the corridor, with wee bare feet by the children's door and larger ones outside the adults' door.

Since it's your money, the walk through the rest of this mall is up to you.

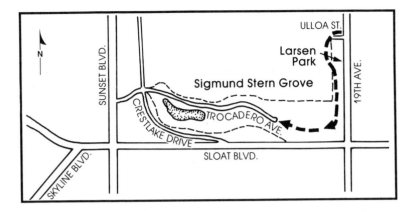

STERN GROVE

WALKING TIME: Half a day.

DISTANCE: Three miles.

PUBLIC TRANSPORTATION: Muni buses 28 19th Avenue and 10 Monterey.

PARKING: Fair, except during concerts.

CLOTHES: Bring a warm anorak.

"Nature's own music box" is the way the *San Francisco Chronicle's* late music critic, Alfred Frankenstein, described the secret glen that hides a hundred feet below street level out in the Parkside district. The occasion was the opening concert in the first Sigmund Stern Midsummer Music Festival. The year was 1938. A thousand people came to sit on the grassy canyon floor of Stern Grove and listen to the free music. They were sheltered then, as now, by what may be the oldest eucalyptus grove in California.

The attendance at that first musical afternoon was considered phenomenal. Now, many years later, twenty thousand is considered an average attendance for any of the ten concerts in the annual free summer series. The grove absorbs them all gracefully—students, professional people, merchants, parents, toddlers, octogenarians, the rich, and the poor.

For music lovers, at 2 P.M. on a Sunday afternoon during the season, no other walk in the city can compare with the stroll to the outdoor theater designed by architect William Merchant, partner of the better-known Bernard Maybeck.

Thanks to the generosity of Mrs. Sigmund Stern, who bought the grove as a memorial to her husband in 1931, added to its acreage throughout her life, and organized the festival association that still presents the concerts, programs for every taste are performed. The selection runs the gamut from ballet to blues, musical comedy, jazz, classic opera, Gilbert and Sullivan, and symphony.

As beguiling as the concerts are, Stern Grove and its periphery have their own charms for the walker who is also a naturalist, historian, aficionado of the city, lawn bowler, croquet player, golfer, tennis player, or horseshoe pitcher.

Begin this walk at 19th Avenue and Ulloa Street. Stroll southerly through Larsen Park to locate the bowling greens, a clubhouse used frequently for folk dance classes, and a spacious swimming pool. At least three footpaths wind their way to the adjoining grove. Another footpath leads to Vicente Park at 26th and Wawona Street, near the western end of the canyon containing Stern Grove.

Walk into the Grove from 19th at Sloat Boulevard. A trail downhill borders the asphalt road, a route established in 1847 by pioneer George M. Greene. It was his son, George, Jr., who planted the eucalyptus in 1871 from seeds sent to him by Bishop William Taylor of Australia.

Two roadhouses, Ocean House and Ingleside House, frequented by the crowds from the nearby racetrack, once overlooked the canyon. The most famous roadhouse of all, The Trocadero, still stands in this glen. You see its rooftop and yellow fish-scale shingles through the treetops as you descend. The charming Victorian building, built in 1892 by Greene, Jr., was the recreational rendezvous of an elite who came this way via horse and carriage when "The Troc" was in its heyday. Millionaire lumberman C. A. Hooper, sugar magnate Adolph Spreckels, and man-about-town Hiram Cook were among them.

Anglers once enjoyed trout fishing in the stream that carved this canyon. Water still trickles down from under 19th Avenue, but the fishing, a deer park, beer garden, and open-air dance pavilion are no more. Traces of them are still visible in the area on your right fronting The Troc.

When you reach level ground, turn right among the trees and walk toward the opposite side of the canyon to see that The Troc, well maintained, now serves for meetings, receptions, weddings, and such. The scene is appropriate to romance. When this land was part of Rancho Laguna de la Merced, Spanish señoritas flirted during the *bailes*, or parties, and barbecues held in the glen, triggering more than one spark of jealousy into gunplay.

Shots rang through the canyon a few years later when the family Greene defended their homestead against interlopers in one of San Francisco's early land grab battles. Old George Greene advised his sons,

"Shoot low, aiming for the belly, so it will take two men to carry off the wounded." Congress validated their land claim by a special act in 1887.

The most famous of the grove gun battles was the capture under the eaves of The Troc of political boss Abe Ruef after the Ruef-Schmidt political machine was smashed. Bullet holes still adorn the upstairs walls; unfortunately for history, others have been lost to renovations in the interior. If the building is open, go inside to inspect the handsome little bar, fireplace, and stained-glass windows.

Despite its romantic past, The Troc was never what was known as "a blind pig," or a place that sold bootlegged liquor. To use George M. Greene's own words, "I closed because of Prohibition, because I wouldn't have bootlegging here." He was living in the Trocadero when Mrs. Stern bought the property in 1931 and continued to live there until he died.

Walk to the east side of the building to find rare purple rhododendrons, the garrya and the *Lacula gratissima*. They were planted by the late Art Menzies, a direct descendant of Archibald Menzies, the botanist-surgeon who accompanied British explorer George Vancouver on his visit to California in 1792. Art Menzies ended his park gardening career as superintendent of acquisitions for Strybing Arboretum, where there is a wildflower garden named for him.

Stroll west from the building to pass the parking lot and reach the amphitheater beyond it. Traditionally during concerts, Mrs. Stern's picnic table was under a big tree on the meadow floor, as is that of her daughter, Mrs. Walter Haas, and granddaughter, Rhoda Goldman.

Blue jeans have long been de rigueur for concert regulars. Many of them can remember, as I do, when Walter Haas, the manufacturer of Levi's, used to walk toward his table through the crowd, checking out jeans with, "Yes, that's a pair of ours, and that's one of ours, and no, that one isn't." Once, I had to show him a label to convince him I was wearing the right jeans.

If you continue through the linklike meadows beyond the stage to the westernmost end, you will reach Silver Tree Day Camp, on the shore of Pine Lake. It was called Laguna Puerca, or Pig Lake, when the Greenes farmed here. At that time it was much larger. Sunset construction surrounding the grove has made the water table drop. Follow the path on its northern side to emerge at 34th and Crestlake Drive. By bearing left along curving Crestlake, you will once again reach Sloat Boulevard.

It is also possible to loop around the lake and return via the other side of the valley floor, especially enjoyable when the native polygonum, or knotweed, is holding its pink flowers up, like listeners awaiting the music that is sure to float on the afternoon breeze during concerts.

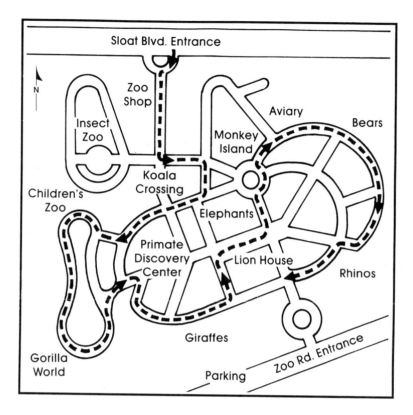

ZOO

WALKING TIME: All day.

DISTANCE: From here to Down Under.

PUBLIC TRANSPORTATION: Muni buses 10 Monterey and 18 and L-Taraval streetcar.

PARKING: Beautiful.

CLOTHES: Bring a jacket and money. Admission is free on first Wednesday each month.

TIMES: The Zoo is open from 10 A.M. to 5 P.M.

San Francisco's first menagerie, a far shriek, hoot, howl, growl, or yodel from today's distinguished institution at Sloat Boulevard and the Pacific Ocean, was a dingy basement at Clay and Leidesdorff streets, operated in 1856 by James C. "Grizzly" Adams.

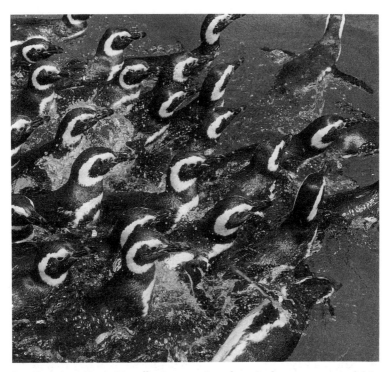

San Francisco Zoo's Magellanic penguin colony is the most successful in the world; fifty-five chicks have been hatched on the island since the birds arrived in 1984. *Brian Katcher.*

Those distinguished native Californians, *Ursis horribilis c.,* were the main attraction. As historian Theodore Hittell described the pioneer zoo: "In the middle, chained to the floor, were two large grizzly bears, which proved to be Benjamin Franklin and Lady Washington. They were pacing restlessly in circles some ten feet in diameter, their chains being about five feet long, and occasionally rearing up, rattling their irons, and reversing their direction. . . . At the rear, in a very large iron cage, was the monster grizzly, Samson. He was an immense creature weighing some three-quarters of a ton, and from his look and action, as well as from the care taken to rail him off from spectators, it was evident that he was not to be approached too closely."

By 1889, when Monarch, another huge grizzly, was exhibited at Woodward's Gardens and later in Golden Gate Park, grizzlies were growing rarer. The first animal in the San Francisco Zoological collection, Monarch, survived until 1911. Thousands of people went to the Golden Gate Park lily pond to gaze on him in wonder. Stuffed, he is now in the park's Academy of Science "Wild California" exhibit.

There are a half dozen other kinds of bears at the San Francisco Zoo. None of them is chained, but you won't see a California grizzly. The last documented California grizzly bear was shot by a rancher in 1922 at Horse Corral Meadow in Fresno County.

You will, however, see koalas, which could almost be a prototype for the teddy bear. You can call the cuddly creatures Bangaroos, Koolewongs, Buidelbeers, Colos, or New Holland Sloths, but it's unbearable (pun intended) to call them bears. They are marsupials, like the opossum. You will also see Magellanic penguins, black rhinos, capybaras, flamingos, François leaf monkeys, siamangs, douroucouli, muntjacs, puma, llamas, and 930 other creatures representing 240 species of mammals and birds—plus 6,000 insects, among them 64 species of arthropods.

Pick a fair day to visit the Zoo, especially if your goal is the new Koala Crossing, for koalas like sunshine as much as we do.

A graceful stone wall with inset benches surrounds the main entrance, Sloat Gate, at Sloat Boulevard and 47th Avenue. Go down either of its curving ramps past greenery, through the ticket booth into the main promenade. On your left is a broad lawn. On your right is Mother's House, which contains the Zoo Shop. A national landmark, the Mission-revival building was designed by architect George W. Kelham and completed in 1929. Herbert and Mortimer Fleischhacker commissioned the building as a memorial to their mother, Delia. Ultimately, it will be a museum. Stop on your way out if you want a zoovenir.

This is also an area to pick up a stroller if you brought a tot; board a Zebra train or the carousel; visit the Insect Zoo (one of only three in the United States), or enjoy the Children's Zoo and its barnyard and nature trail. All are situated in the northwest corner of the Zoo, on the site of what was once Fleischhacker Pool.

To reach Koala Crossing, turn left by the hot-dog stand when you are parallel to the castle that heralds the Children's Zoo. Stop short of the carousel, go left past the wildlife theater and the playfield.

Suddenly, you are in a smidgeon of Australian outback beside what seems to be an Aussie station that could be a stage set for *A Town Called Alice*. Turn right, step up onto the broad veranda, and you are in Koala Crossing. The $500,000 exhibit, largely financed by the San Francisco Zoological Society and private donors, takes its name from traffic signs posted in the outback.

If the light is on in the window at your right, there will be one or another of the Zoo's six koalas on view, usually one of the three-year-olds, Pat, Kay, Karen, or Yvonne, who are not taken outside during inclement weather. Interpretive panels with titles like "Firm Grip on Life" and "Womb with a View" are a few steps along.

Especially engrossing is an eight-minute videotape on koalas in the wild, adapted from David Attenborough's "Life on Earth" series and other footage from Film Australia. The Aussie accent is authentic, generously provided by the Australian consul. Visitors often watch the tape again and again. Don't miss the exhibit called Special Delivery, in which a newborn, smaller than a nickel, is shown as an embryo wriggling over the mother's fur into her pouch.

When you have absorbed the exhibits, step to the edge of the veranda to see whether you can spot the silvery fur balls that are Frosty or Clarry, the Zoo's six-year-old koalas, in the eucalyptus trees. Nocturnal creatures, they often sleep twenty hours a day and are fussy about the eucalyptus leaves they eat.

More than one thousand specimens of eucalyptus have been planted in the Zoo and other city parks to provide the red gum, manna gum, and swamp mahogany leaves koalas prefer. Keepers must harvest fresh leaves twice a day to keep this special salad constantly available.

Before you find yourself drowsing off watching the koalas munch or nod, say "g'dy mite" and come out from Down Under by stepping off the other end of the veranda. Turn right to reach the Primate Discovery Center, a prize-winning series of soaring glass vaults housing sixteen rare and endangered primates and subprimates. Like Koala Crossing, it is part of Zoo 2000, the Zoo's long-range plan to make a place in the wild where every visitor is an explorer.

Little by little, the plan is being accomplished. When you can leave the fascination of primate-watching in the soaring glass monkey house, descend to the ground level, walk past the Nocturnal Gallery, and turn left alongside the Discovery Hall. A sign directs you to Musk Ox Meadow, where a broad walk takes you safely over the Zoo's herd of rare white-fronted musk oxen as they browse in the 2.6-acre habitat below. You'll emerge at the innovative Gorilla World, a lush expanse of trees, rocky outcroppings, and waterfalls.

When you have passed the last informative panel at Gorilla World, swing past the giraffes to reach Penguin Island, another innovation. A lively colony of fifty Magellanic penguins welcomed several dozen fledglings that had just learned to swim when my grandson, Alex Doss, last took me to the Zoo.

Stop in across at the Lion House if you haven't called on Prince Charles, the rare white Bengal tiger, or seen the snow leopard, an animal that naturalist Peter Matthiessen sees as a metaphor for the Holy Grail because it is so rare.

From the Lion House, almost every visitor heads toward Monkey Island, after a pause to see the elephants perform. Just past Monkey Island, cross the bridge to reach the walk-through aviary.

Wolf Woods is a spacious forest containing American timber wolves. But if you seek bears, continue walking south, past the outdoor avian area. There, just beyond the sea lions, are the classic bear pits, designed by architect Lewis Hobart in 1934 and modeled after the famous Hagenbeck Zoo in Stellingen, Germany, the most advanced of its time. There are honey bears, polar bears, and brown bears—but most of Phil Franks's bear friends are cavorting at 5th and Mission streets.

Swing with the path past the lagoon and you will be at another of the Zoo's popular exhibits, the black rhinos, where the prolific sire Stonewall has brought forth his eight offspring, all chips off the same black block. Baby rhinos look like armored tanks and are even more preposterous than are their parents.

If you walk up an appetite, the Zoo offers ethnic food. The Terrace Cafe, always trendy, has an all-you-can-eat salad bar and gourmet

Greater One-Horned Rhinos at the San Francisco Zoo. *Jim Hildreth.*

sandwiches, but at the Plaza Cafe, near the Primate Discovery Center, you can get pizza, Polish sausages, *chimichangas*, fried wontons, pork buns, and cappuccino. Look around and you'll find hot *churros* for sale, and over in the children's cafe, there are stuffed baked potatoes. If you brought along a child—or he brought you—finding the food will be easy.

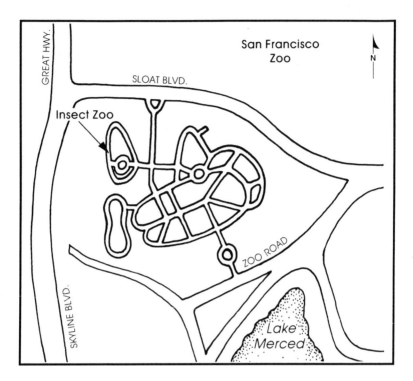

INSECT ZOO

WALKING TIME: A morning.

DISTANCE: One-quarter block.

PUBLIC TRANSPORTATION: Muni buses 10 Monterey and 18 and L-Taraval streetcar to the San Francisco Zoo.

PARKING: Spaces fill up quickly.

CLOTHES: Buy a buggy T-shirt there.

FEE: Zoo buffs buy an Animal Express card, a real bargain.

"Be's you got bugs?"
"Sure I are. Everybody do."

Not everybody has bugs to compare with the unusual ones in San Francisco's Insect Zoo. Here some fine specimens can spray like a polecat, mimic sticks or leaves, or roll over and play dead. Some have eyespots that glow like neon; others have marks on their underbellies that resemble little zippers.

All the charms of the big animal zoos of the world exist in Lilliputian scale at this unusual zoo within a zoo. For that matter, it is a zoo within two zoos, for it is located within the Children's Zoo, which in turn is located within the 125-acre San Francisco Zoo.

If you have never seen this unusual collection of small creatures, one of only three in the country, you are missing a special San Francisco treat. Entomologists come from all over the world to see it.

To make this walk, transport yourself, preferably via public transportation, to Sloat Boulevard and Great Highway. Go through the main gate on Sloat Boulevard. Once through the ticket booth, you are on the main promenade. The first big brick building on your right, dedicated to the memory of Mrs. Herbert Fleischhacker, was called "Mother's House" when this zoo also bore the family name. Sentinel sea gulls often perch on the red-tiled roof of the fine building designed by architect Lewis Hobart, in subtle counterpoint to the mosaic birds portrayed with St. Francis on the north side of the entrance. On the south side is another mosaic, this one featuring children playing with animals. Beneath it waits a flotilla of very real tot strollers.

Now operated by the Zoological Society, the building has a shop that is a treasure house of inexpensive scientific toys and books. Save it for the return trip.

Once you have passed the black-and-white-striped Zebra trains, look on your right for an Insect Zoo sign. Some of its letters represent insects, or are adorned with them. Turn right, pay another six bits (unless you can flash that Animal Express card for the Zoological Society membership) and go into the Children's Zoo.

Raptor shows, with hawks that are being trained for release into the wild, are often under way on your right. Stop if your timing is right.

Then continue along the walkway in either direction to the Children's Zoo courtyard, a favorite place for birthday parties. Pause a moment to look at this unexpected outdoor cafe, which certainly has a leafy charm. Parrots often sit in the trees alongside the tables, and the "Adopt-an-Animal" office gives the area an urban ambiance. Walk over to the office and look under the big dracaena tree to find the Twelve Stone Garden. "Insect Zoo Garden. Insects Only, Please," reads the sign, but it doesn't seem to keep out the guinea hens roaming this part of the Zoo. You'll discover the stones are numbered, one for each month of the year. As a way of introducing the Insect Zoo, it is fun for kids to pick up the stone that corresponds to their birth month. Curator Leslie Saul, who conducted me on this walk, picked up Stone 8 for my birth month and under it found sow bugs, ants, a rove beetle, a feather, and two leaves.

Go into the door to the left and you are inside the Insect Zoo itself. The room is organized in three sections, labeled Plant-Eaters, Predators, and Scavengers.

On your right, in a little habitat within a glass terrarium, is a darkling beetle, a tanklike fellow, a few inches long, who may live to be ten years old and can rear up and spray like a skunk. If you're lucky, you may see this "stinkbug" perform. One local psychoanalyst regularly brings his patients to see it.

Then look at the next glass menagerie on your left where Jiminy and some other lively crickets jump most of the day. As you make your way along the wall cages, you will see insects, millipedes, arachnids, centipedes, and crustaceans, the last three of which are also arthropods— bugs by a better name (although the only "true" bugs here are milkweed bugs and the giant toebiters). Many of them are common to the Bay Area or other parts of California. A favorite from the desert is the gray deathfeigner, who "plays 'possum" when disturbed.

Near him is a terrarium featuring the big lubber grasshopper depicted on the Insect Zoo's logo. Not only is this grasshopper a perfect food source, but he tastes good. "We always fry up a few for our Zoo fair each year," Leslie says. "The kids love them because they are crunchy like potato chips and have a nutty flavor."

A California native, the lubber has red underwings, which the males fan out and display to attract the females. Indians ate them long before the gringo came. Since the lubber eats lettuce or bean plants, gardeners who find their vegetable patch dispatched can harvest the lubber instead.

It is the katydid who looks like it has a zipper on its belly. Come to the zoo on a late sunny afternoon and this room is melodious with katydid song. Clever katydids hide in the hearts of bromeliads or under leaves and are so well camouflaged that they are hard to see. So are the mantids and the walking sticks; some are so fat they look more like logs than twigs.

Campers planning an expedition to unknown terrain may enjoy looking over the cages of the African scorpion, whose stinger glows in the dark. More unusual in this circle of cages is the whip scorpion, who has a black tail that squirts a vinegarlike substance.

If you've never heard a cockroach hiss, look for the hissing cockroach from Madagascar. Mehitabel's friend, Archy, may have written free-verse poetry, but there is no record that he hissed.

From the Bay Area, two creatures often have a crowd around them. These are the California tarantula, which lives under leaves near

A wide-eyed observer at the Insect Zoo. *Brian Katcher.*

Mount Diablo, and the Jerusalem cricket, which likes the open grassland on any sunny slope.

Another great favorite is ''Crazylegs,'' the Mexican red-legged tarantula with distinctive markings.

Many of the insects were collected in Costa Rica by Insect Zoo staffers. Others are obtained by trading with the Smithsonian Institution and the Cincinnati Zoo, which have the only other true insect zoos in the United States.

Just about the time you discover the educational displays of moths mounted on the walls or the remarkable photographs by Stennett Heaton, it will be ''time to go, Grasshopper,'' as Master Po used to say in the ''Kung Fu'' television show. But don't leave until you have sought out that strange Victorian necklace of the exoskeletons of beetles. At first glance, they look like scarabs but these are not carved. They are the real thing. So is this remarkable zoo.

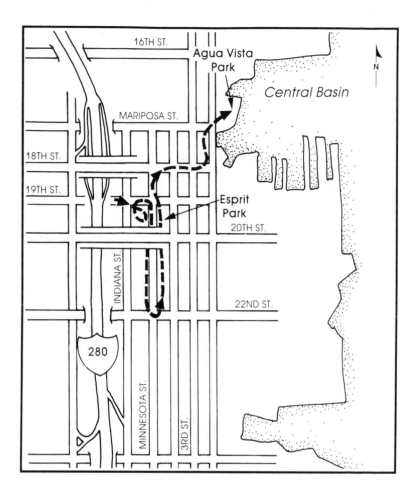

SOUTH O' THE SLOT

WALKING TIME: An hour.

DISTANCE: A mile and a half.

PUBLIC TRANSPORTATION: Muni bus 22.

PARKING: Catch-as-catch-can.

CLOTHES: Whatever.

"Whether you know your location or not, the heart of the city is South o' the Slot!" begins a poem by Miles Overholt, who was proud to be known as a South of Market boy. He was talking about the twenty-two square miles of San Francisco that lay beyond that 110-foot-wide "slot" through which streetcars ran in his time. The Slot is even deeper in ours, now that BART (Bay Area Rapid Transit) and Muni Metro run through it.

The rest of the city may have been known for romance and charm, but it was South o' the Slot where neighborhood people gave San Francisco its strength, sense of humor, resiliency, and punch. They stocked the factory boilers, slaughtered the cattle, poured the molten steel, built and sailed the ships. Most of them lived within walking distance of where they worked—places like Tar Flat, Happy Valley, Bay View, Butchertown, Central Basin, and the Potrero.

Unlikely as it may seem, people in this area—where marsh once fringed Mission Bay at the foot of Potrero Hill—are once again living within walking distance of their jobs. This time around, the South of Market is no longer only a brawny country cousin; it has considerable charm. To see for yourself, consider a walk around privately owned Esprit Park.

Start at the corner of 19th and Indiana streets. The green lawns and bordering trees make for an instantly welcoming oasis in a predominantly industrial area.

At the outset, look around and try to envision a time when this landscape was rural. Glimpses of Victorian homes, visible uphill to the east above the hanging gardens of Interstate 280, give an inkling of the past. If you're having difficulty envisioning this industrial landscape as bucolic, you might look at the California Historical Society, where an excellent painting of the scene in 1871, by artist David Kindleberger, is hung. It is reprinted in Jeanne Van Nostrand's *San Francisco 1806–1905*, published in 1975 by the Book Club of California.

In the late nineteenth century, the five hundred acres around Mission Bay, including the spot on which you are now standing, were soggy marshland. Industries, such as Pacific Glass Works, Union Iron Works, and Pacific Rolling Mills, began moving into the area after 1865, attracted by the new Kentucky Street Bridge over Mission Bay, the advent of the Southern Pacific Railroad tracks, and the deep-water harbor, Central Basin, at the eastern end of 19th Street.

Look south to locate the scene shop for the San Francisco Opera, snuggled between the Santa Fe Railroad tracks and the freeway, then walk up to Esprit Park.

At the entrance, you are greeted with some simple rules, as well as information on how to obtain a park pass. You will also see some nice street furniture and a grown-up jungle gym, known as "The Fitness Cluster, Series 3," part of a parcourse. Walkways within Esprit Park have a soft surface, especially good for runners.

Park designer Drew Detsch sought the illusion of a forest surrounding a meadow, and he brought off this conceit very well. The trees with metallic-colored leaves are copper beeches. In time, the giant redwoods in the center will tower over this pocket park. The north end of the park is bordered by the only grass tennis court in San Francisco. Reserved for employees of Esprit, it is so well shorn it looks like Astroturf. A greens mower goes over it three times weekly. When you are through, exit on the east at 19th Street. You will be facing Bill Graham's Winterland Productions. Bear right on Minnesota Street, cross 19th, and you are in a little street-tree lane of London plane trees, which seems like an extension of the park. Chinese evergreen elms adorn the west side of the block, with tulip trees on the east.

The commanding eye-catcher as you begin to walk south on Minnesota is a beautifully restored, old red-brick warehouse, entwined with Virginia creeper. Used in the past for many industrial purposes, including wine storage, this building now houses both factory and office operations. In sharp contrast is the cold, metal, high-tech building across the street, designed by John Evans. This schizy pair of buildings are both parts of Esprit.

Peer into the front door of the brick building to see the beautifully redesigned interior by architect Hanns Kainz. The reception area at ground level has been cleverly surrounded by an open, U-shaped working area one story higher.

The big wall-hanging at the far end of the reception area is part of a significant collection of Amish, Victorian, and Log Cabin quilts. Walking tours of the collection are conducted during working hours whenever a group of six or more people assembles at the front desk.

Continue along Minnesota Street to see some fine little "working men's Victorians" being perked up on both sides of the street, some by Esprit employees who have bought homes here.

The next unusual structure is the old wooden I. M. Scott School, now the home of a dozen community organizations under the aegis of the Potrero Hill Community Development Corporation and a concerned man named Jim Queen. The First Step project, the Potrero Hill Senior Escort Outreach Program, the Haitian Relief Program, and the Coalition of Conscience are just a few of the groups housed within.

At 22nd Street, notice the big log sculpture in front of the Muni car barns. Cable cars are renovated in the Muni repair shop beyond the little park in the foreground. Greenery farther up the hill surrounds the Potrero Hill Recreation Center. You may itch to change the spelling of "breakfest" on the W. and J. Cafe diagonally across the street.

If you are still eager for another of this area's pleasures, seek out

Agua Vista Park on the waterfront, five blocks east on China Basin Street. Runners from Esprit choose the 18th Street route.

At Mission Rock Resort, it is possible to sit on the deck and examine Central Basin and what is left of the Union Iron Works. Today, it is owned by Bethlehem Steel. The high jinks going on across China Basin Street from Mission Rock Resort is the Esprit outlet store.

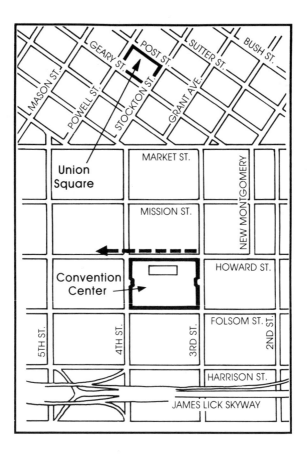

MOSCONE CENTER

WALKING TIME: Three days for conventioneers.

DISTANCE: Three blocks.

PUBLIC TRANSPORTATION: Taxicab or Muni bus 9, 15, 30, 76, or 81-X.

PARKING: It will cost you.

CLOTHES: Power ties.

There was a big semi, the kind Mike Nomad drives in the comics, in the middle of the floor when I first saw the main exhibit hall in Moscone Center, named for George Moscone, the mayor who was brutally assassinated in 1979. From the top of the escalator at the landing above, the semi looked as small as a child's toy. It wasn't until much later, after I walked closer to the semi, that I realized how big the center really is. As a yardstick a semi-truck is too small.

There can be three conventions of six thousand to eight thousand people, several banquets for three or four hundred, any number of meetings of fifty to a hundred people, and scores of smaller training sessions all going on simultaneously in the center. None of them feels crowded.

For thirty years, Yerba Buena Center was the hottest planning potato in the city. Justin Herman wrestled with it in the 1960s, Tom Mellon in the 1970s, and Roger Boas in the 1980s. To get some idea of the saga of the Yerba Buena Center Wars, tune your mind to some Wagnerian Sturm und Drang music. Over mountains of legalities, through marshes of red tape, hassles, impasses, morasses, and monetary embarrassments, our loyal civil servants pressed on through the years, sometimes at a snail's pace, sometimes on the run, toward dedication day, December 2, 1981.

Architects Hellmuth, Obata, and Kassabaum, Inc., who also designed the Smithsonian Institution's Air and Space Museum, have given the center a lofty feeling, convinced that although the building is underground, no one should feel locked in a dark basement when they come to a convention here. Through the magic of glass and superb design, nobody does.

Third Street at Howard is the logical place to start this walk. Walk up one of those curving walkways between trees and planted berms to get a sense of the area from the parklike top of the center. A glimpse of Twin Peaks is visible beyond the gaily flapping banners. Just across 4th Street is Yerba Buena West, with mirrored windows. Abreast of it is Woolf House, a nine-story contemporary concrete apartment complex for low-income elderly and handicapped residents.

Visible to the north, the Marriot Hotel, with fans of mirror windows atop a building that looks like an antique jukebox, creates a new background of a most charming view toward Old St. Patrick's classic brick church and the landmark Willis Polk PG&E substation. Other early San Francisco buildings along Mission Street front this side of the Meridien Hotel.

When you have surveyed the scene, go down via the steps, pass the taxi approach lane, and walk toward the banners, the flagpoles of which have a nice relationship to the big round trusses of the center. At night, the white neon and lights shining up on the ceiling make the roof seem to float on a sea of light.

If the lofty lobby is open, go in to enjoy its special lift of spirit. Custom-made joints connect the big glass panes suspended from the

trusses to minimize the transition from outside. Bridges lead to mezzanine meeting rooms. Three granite staircases, each as broad as the big
one at City Hall, and edged with escalators, lead underground. If the
function happening inside is public, go down and walk to the big main
hall. It will take your breath away. It is 37 feet high, 275 feet wide, and
880 feet long—a good healthy hike from one end to the other. Eight
graceful slotted arches of reinforced concrete braced under the flooring
by steel cables make this the biggest column-free room in the world.
Local architect Gyo Obata gets the credit for it.

After you've enjoyed the sheer magnificence of it, try to imagine it
divided with three conventions going on simultaneously. The dividers
are stored in plain sight. If you can't spot them, look along the walls,
where they seem part of the decor. Glance underfoot to find the squares
that hide outlets for that spaghetti of power cables, telephone, water,
waste, compressed air, and gas lines that are always in demand for
exhibit booths. Concessions, service facilities, rest rooms, and such are
on the Folsom Street periphery.

Trucks can drive onto the floor from the 3rd Street end. To locate the
ramps, bear left at the far end of the building, past the passageway
between the kitchen and the "swing space," a flexible area used in
dozens of ways. This is where the unloading bays for trucks have an
indoor one-way road system. Beyond the kitchens, near the lower
lobby, there are three ballrooms. More truck docks are at the far end,
along with an exit ramp.

The elevators are especially designed for the handicapped. The rest of
us use the escalators to return to the street-floor lobby. Cross the
bridges here. At either end of the upper floor you'll find handsomely
carpeted meeting rooms, convertible to large or small spaces.

If you don't come away with the feeling that Moscone Center has
restored San Francisco's reputation as "The City That Knows How,"
you've been listening to the critics who think Moscone Center is too
small.

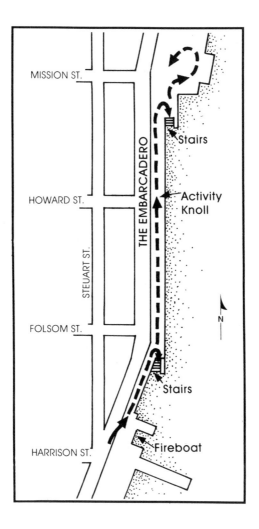

THE EMBARCADERO WATERFRONT PROMENADE

WALKING TIME: An hour.

DISTANCE: Half a mile.

PUBLIC TRANSPORTATION: Muni bus 32.

PARKING: Fair on weekends.

CLOTHES: Easy.

The Embarcadero Waterfront Promenade is a place to stroll, to dip a hand in the water, or to pull a fish from the depths. It has vast vistas and sunny benches, where one can linger a while by the Bay and dream the romance of this roadstead to faraway ports. It goes along Rincon Point by way of The Embarcadero from Harrison Street to the Ferry Building.

Harrison, at the waterfront, is the place to begin. Walk over to the water's edge and lean a while on the seawall ledge, designed at just the right height for that purpose, and enjoy this unimpeded view of the soaring Bay Bridge, Treasure Island, and Yerba Buena Island.

A hundred years ago, swank Rincon Point jutted out this far into the water, sheltering a sandy beach that curved back to 1st Street, defined at its northern end by Broadway, and then rounded Telegraph Hill. A much-eroded old sea stack called Sunken Rock was three feet underwater offshore, as more than one sailing ship captain learned to his dismay. Fine weather and good views made homes on Rincon Point choice indeed, until the 2nd Street cut brought instant property devaluation. Rincon Point's fashionable location was finished off when it became the western pediment for the Bay Bridge. Today it is chicly re-emerging as South Beach.

On your right, San Francisco's fireboat rocks in her berth, snuggled against an historic firehouse. A new fireboat pier is being planned for this area. Turn around and look back at the city where Hills Brothers' gracious old brick factory sent forth that odor of roasting coffee beans that tantalized us all for years. Green lawns will one day fill a park between Folsom and Howard streets at The Embarcadero, according to Vello Kiisk, chief harbor engineer for the Port of San Francisco.

As you reach Folsom Street, walk down to the water's edge to explore the "activity knoll" and "tidal stairs," which lead into the water. Here's a place to launch your kayak, canoe, or foldboat, row in from a yacht hanging offshore, or launch toy boats. If it's high tide as you come along here, the steps may be underwater. (The lighted flag flies day and night, a thrifty device however extravagant it may seem. It's cheaper to pay for electricity than a flag-raiser.)

When this was old East Street, the forerunner of The Embarcadero, it was the site of the Oregon & Mexican Steamship Wharf. At that time, there was a wharf at the foot of each Rincon Point street. By the time the Ferry Building had been completed in 1898, there were twice as many piers. Pilings visible offshore now, which supported Piers 8 and 16, have been deliberately left at Howard Street. The tall ones, on which gulls usually perch, protect a telephone company underwater cable. The short ones ultimately will support offshore sculpture.

Follow the balustrade westerly and you will be walking on a level lower than the street, nicely bordered by a broad sweep of bench, which is lighted from below.

Climb up to the higher level and you'll find equally linear street furniture, echoing the line at the curbside, and more street trees. During the week, at noon, both upper and lower benches are loaded with brown-baggers from the financial district.

As you approach the Agricultural Building, another historic landmark—like the firehouse it has kept its facade but was renovated within—notice how the Embarcadero Freeway darkens the whole area as it swings toward the shoreline. Renovation plans for the Ferry Building call for the freeway's removal—but the earthquake of 1989 notwithstanding, when or if it will ever be done is anybody's guess. When you reach the curved windbreak wall at the foot of Mission Street, go inside to see how benches have been built into the curve facing another set of tidal stairs. Scorch marks on the benches indicate where drifters have made improvised fireplaces.

Architect Arthur Paige Brown patterned the Ferry Building on the Giralda tower of the cathedral at Seville, Spain. It soon became the belle of the Bay. Scores of thousands of commuters surged through the handsomely arcaded building every twenty-four hours. At that time, the traffic was comparable only to Charing Cross Station's in London. Old timetables list 170 daily arrivals and departures of ferries in the eight slips on the water's edge. The charming old Audifredd Building, renovated across the street, watched it all.

Commuters to Marin can find a few trips daily from the slip that has been tacked on behind the Ferry Building. After you pass Sinbad's Restaurant, bear right to explore Ferry Plaza, climb its view promenade, and linger, if you wish, to fish, dream, or dine. Better still, continue walking The Embarcadero another block to find the recently completed Pier 7, the longest on this side of the Bay and elegantly urbane in its appointments.

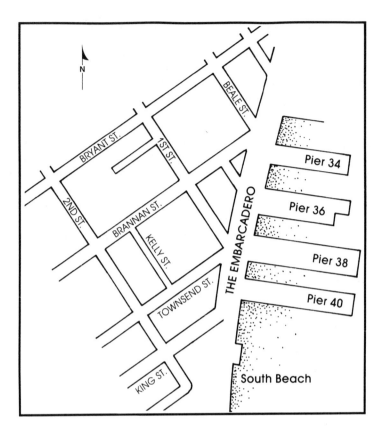

SOUTH BEACH: STEAMBOAT POINT

WALKING TIME: An hour or two.

DISTANCE: Two miles.

PUBLIC TRANSPORTATION: Muni buses 32 and 42.

CLOTHES: Casual.

Steamboat Point! Savor that name. Roll it on your tongue. Whether you remember Steamboat Point or not, it smacks of an earlier hell-for-breakfast time when the waterfront was Frisco, and without it, San Francisco was nowhere. Named for the nineteenth-century landing where the mail arrived for the first sixty years of San Francisco's history, Steamboat Point was once so important to the city that every streetcar would fly a little white flag when a steamer from the Pacific Mail Steamship Company was due to arrive. The point juts out from 1st and Townsend streets, the heart of South Beach.

Under a contract assigned in 1847 by the Post Office Department, the Pacific Mail Steamship Company maintained that long, thin haphazard thread of communication that tied the West Coast to the rest of civilization. In the process, the company became the largest private employer in the city. PMSS carried not only the mail, but passengers, treasure, and cargo to fill warehouses. Until 1922 most of the immigrants from the Orient arrived on PMSS.

In an 1872 report on the company's importance, the *Alta California* said, "What this city would be now as a shipping port, were it not for the past operations of PMSS Co., it is difficult to determine."

Still left from its heyday is the company's Oriental warehouse, built in 1867, where the silks, ivories, spices, and jewels from Singapore, Bangkok, and Tokyo arrived for "the China trade," as all Asian commerce was loosely called then. It is one of a scant handful of historic buildings in South Beach, an area of new apartments which stretches a few blocks to the northeast of the point.

The westerlies of change are blowing across this little chunk of waterfront now. If you have never walked around Steamboat Point and South Beach, this is a good time. The salty unsavory waterfront of old godowns, wharves, pier sheds, warehouses, gin mills, brothels, clothing stores, seamen's boardinghouses, eateries, harness shops, stables, shipping offices, gambling dens, and Chinese laundries is almost gone from San Francisco. Soon the dirty face behind that gap-toothed smile of piers we call The Embarcadero will be wiped clean.

To make this walk, head south from the Ferry Building along The Embarcadero to Piers 42 to 44.

The first eye-catcher at Pier 40 is the *Dolphin C. Rempp*, a three-masted topsail schooner set up on a platform like a mantel ornament. Built in Denmark in 1908 for the lumber trade, her colorful past includes carrying supplies to Europe in World War I and to the Pacific during World War II. Now she has come ashore as The Ship Restaurant. Her promenade deck is open to the public.

Resist the temptation to take a closer look and walk south. This is Steamboat Point, although the big San Francisco Redevelopment Agency sign calls it "South Beach Harbor, Rincon Point."

"It's an element of a larger project," explained community development specialist Barbara Amato. "In the course of redevelopment, Steamboat Point will become a seven-acre grassy waterfront park, stretching to Second and King streets."

Sunday sailors who had been on the waiting list for fifteen years for a berth at the Marina and at Gas House Cove were gratified to learn that a 780-yacht basin was created here. Look to the south to see the breakwater at the mouth of the 3rd Street Channel. Mayor Art Agnos wanted to put a new ballpark in this neighborhood.

Do an about-face and return to the schooner, climbing her surrounding platform. Walk around to the back to find yourself standing over the water. Comparable decking reaches the 3rd Street Channel.

Look to your left, where Pier 40 is shorter, and the concrete portion has been reconstructed to accommodate restaurants and marina-related services, an area open to the public.

Then walk around to the front of the decking and look across The Embarcadero. The trees conceal the nice little ILWU Building, surrounded with shrubs and grass of the "soft surface" park.

Twenty-six hundred units of medium-priced housing have replaced the mini-storage cubicles that stood beyond the Belt Line Railroad tracks. Amtrak cars often awaited the call to service on a spur along here.

Walk north on the water side of The Embarcadero to Piers 32 to 34. En route is an unusual view of the downtown skyline to your left and the Bay Bridge soaring off toward Yerba Buena Island on the right.

Red's Java House has been a breakfast hangout for stevedores since before the container ships were invented. White hats that cluster around it at 6 A.M. on weekdays are fewer today. Service Engineering Company, beyond, is due to move to Pier 36 as South Beach emerges in its new image.

Soon you reach Piers 30 to 32, where the "Santa" ships of Prudential Grace Line (later Delta) berthed until shortly before a fire destroyed the pier in 1984. Just short of the piers, cross The Embarcadero in the crosswalk to come out at Brannan Street, alongside the little green building that once served as a train station. Beyond it, blackberries once tumbled over the fence next to an old garment warehouse made of red brick and tile.

At 1st Street, you are equidistant from two fine old warehouses. One is the Cape Horn at 1st and Bryant. The other is PMSS Oriental Warehouse, to the left on 1st Street. Listed on the National Register of Historic Places, Oriental Warehouse was built over the water in 1867 of eight-by-eight redwood timbers.

Ships could sail up to the warehouse's big folding metal doors in those days. If you had tried to walk along 1st Street then you would have been standing in the water. In the same building, at the next doorway, was a firehouse in the era of horse-drawn fire engines.

Go back toward the waterfront, past the Captain's Table Restaurant, and zig or zag on Townsend to reach Colin P. Kelly Street, named for the first flying hero of World War II. Before that it was named Japan Street, fronted by the historic Japan Street Warehouses.

Walk to 64 Townsend to visit Bouncer's Bar, the liveliest remaining vestige of the brawling waterfront of yore. Will Antonik, owner for the last twenty-five years, calls his place "a workingman's bar." Stevedores, teamsters, and ironworkers, whose skills were always in demand along the waterfront, still make it their own. Open 365 days a year from 6 A.M. to 9 P.M., it is worth a visit to see the waterfront memorabilia and the brass memorial plaques dedicated to old customers.

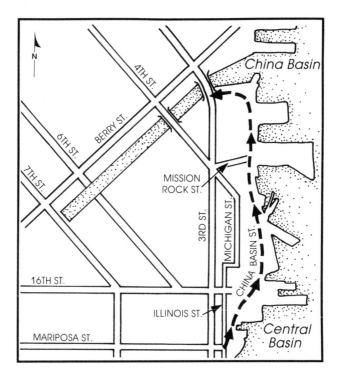

MISSION CREEK

WALKING TIME: An hour.

DISTANCE: A long half-mile.

PUBLIC TRANSPORTATION: Muni bus 15 to 4th and Channel streets.

PARKING: So-so.

CLOTHES: Casual.

Innocent barges
floating where you find them—

Dreams bob,
Harbor lights,
Double morning freeway competes
with rippling
upside down
cars:

Obscure adventure
plunked near Townsend
like a bright dime
in a storm drain.

—"WATER-BOURNE,"
by Sharon Skolnick,
from *Mission Creek*
San Francisco

Mission Creek is all that is left today of Mission Bay, but the snowy egrets and great blue herons nest along its shores as they did in 1775. It was in that year the first white men set eyes on Mission Bay. They were members of an exploring party under Second Mate Juan Aguirre, scouting in a launch from Juan Manuel de Ayala's packetboat, the *San Carlos*. Aguirre named it Ensenada de los Llorones, the Bay of the Weepers, for some Indians who were weeping on the shore. Why they wept, no one knows.

At that time, Mission Bay stretched from Steamboat Point, Pier 46-A, to what is now Mariposa Street, encompassing 4th, Brannan, Townsend, 7th, and lower Carolina streets in a sweeping curve. The Bay was filled by 1870, mostly by Mayor Frank McCoppen, a contractor who leveled much of Rincon Hill for fill and planned to do the same with Strawberry Hill in Golden Gate Park.

At the Pacific Mail Steamship Company's docks, at the mouth of Mission Creek, passengers arrived from China, giving the waterfront the name that has stuck—China Basin.

Since Mission Creek and China Basin are frequently in the news as possible sites for a new baseball stadium and a 185-acre Southern Pacific development of office buildings, condos, and shops, consider a walk to look at what remains of Mission Creek. It is sure to change soon.

On the shores of Mission Creek is a community of twenty or so houseboat owners, all enjoying a marina life so unhurried that the egrets sometimes walk fearlessly on their floating sidewalk. On a weekend, Mission Creek is surprisingly peaceful.

To see for yourself, look first at a tide table. High tide is the best time to walk Channel Street, which borders the creek.

Begin just west of 4th Street. Walk over to the creekside. Some of the old dock pilings were installed when the Channel, as Mission Creek is also known, was a place where vegetables and hay were unloaded from the scow-schooners out of Sacramento.

Arrive at the right time and you may see the trunnion bascule bridge over 4th Street go up. Designed in 1933 by Joseph Strauss, who also designed the Golden Gate Bridge, it and its companion at 3rd Street are the only drawbridges left in the city. This end of 4th Street began—before the fill—as the Kentucky Street Bridge, which extended four blocks past the Channel, then bent and continued another seven blocks to Mariposa Street. When the fill was completed, the last seven blocks of the wooden bridge were cobbled and named Kentucky Street. Now it is 3rd.

Look across 4th. This is the area proposed for a ballpark. The big blue China Basin Building across the creek began as a typical godown, or waterfront warehouse, and is now full of chic offices.

Bear left along the creek bank. If you had come along the opposite shore in 1870, a diamond-stack steam locomotive of the San Francisco and San Jose Railroad might have been tooting its high sharp whistle. The first tracks ran on what is now Brannan Street. Today railroad noises in the distance come from Southern Pacific trains en route to the 4th and Townsend station.

When you have walked the length of about a city block, pause a moment where a broad strip of greenery adorns the foreshore. Britton and Rey's city map for 1877 shows a two-block parklike green space here labeled Market Place. Draymen coming for hay for city livery stables, schoonermen from the Central Valley, and lumbermen from the Mendocino coast found this a welcome oasis. Members of the Mission Creek Harbor Association restored a vestige of the park several years ago, matching a grant with their own money and labor to bring in soil and plant trees and shrubs.

If the gate is open, go through, cross the bridge, and bear left along the floating dock that serves as a walkway for the houseboaters.

"I remember the first time I saw these boats . . . I couldn't get over that this place is really in San Francisco," houseboater Nancy Keller says in a sensitive little book, *Mission Creek San Francisco*, published by a nonprofit group named Mission Creek Conservancy under the sponsorship of the California State Coastal Conservancy. Keller's reaction is the same as that of most first-time visitors.

As you walk along the dock, look to the unused land under Interstate 280, where the egrets and herons nest. Night herons, grebes, and cormorants also come along here, especially when silvery streams of anchovies come into the Channel. Perch and bass are usually right behind them, followed by the sea lions and harbor seals. Flounder sometimes rise lazily like sluggish leaves off the bottom and, once in a while, the whiskery face of a sea otter pops up in the Channel.

Houseboaters would like to see a wilderness park here, with native shore plants and a clean channel to encourage such wildlife. "If the creek is ever lost or destroyed, a very important part of San Francisco and its heritage will be lost," says houseboater Bob Palm.

When you reach the next bridge, bear left up it, then walk through the next section of the little park. As many as four hundred people and three bands have shown up for the annual Mission Creek barbecue held here, according to boat owner Marvin Banks. They serve vegetables from the community garden at 6th and Channel. The ducks waddling in the grass will come if you quack at them.

Jog a little to the right to glimpse the garden (and find a portable privy), then take the last little bridge to see the pretty green residence of Harbormaster Ruth Huffaker, who has been a houseboater for more than thirty-five years. The houseboat next door sits on a scow-schooner much like the *Alma* in the National Maritime Museum fleet at Hyde Street.

When you have enjoyed the casual ambiance of the neighborly little enclave, stroll back, trying to envision a wilderness park in the city. It could happen. As the Mission Creek book points out, ". . . water is a great and soothing force, a universal therapy. No appointment necessary."

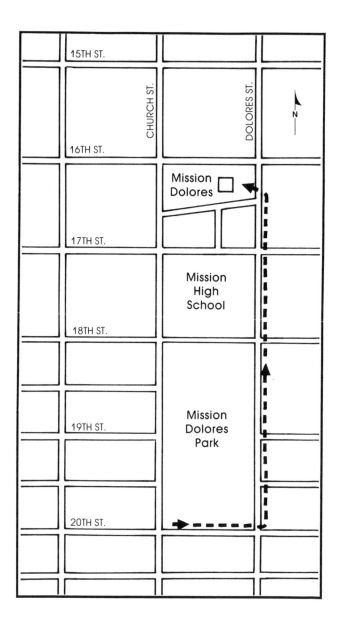

MISSION DOLORES

WALKING TIME: Allow a morning.

DISTANCE: Five city blocks.

PUBLIC TRANSPORTATION: Metro J Church streetcar comes out of a trench on the west side of Mission Dolores Park.

PARKING: Impossible on Sundays.

CLOTHES: Whatever.

> *Bells of the Past, whose long-forgotten music*
> *Still fills the wide expanse*
> *Tingeing the sober twilight of the Present*
> *With the color of Romance. . . .*
>
> —"THE ANGELUS," by Bret Harte

Bret Harte was writing about Mission San Francisco de Asis, commonly called Mission Dolores, when he penned his bittersweet lines about the dying glow of Spanish glory.

General Mariano Vallejo, who visited the Mission in its heyday, around 1826, later described the pueblo, or village, of Dolores as that portion of land between Church and Guerrero streets from west to east and between 15th and 17th streets from north to south. The pueblo, he wrote, "had one church, the residence of the reverend fathers, granaries, warehouses for merchandise, guardhouse for the soldiers, prison, and orchard of fruit trees and vegetable gardens, cemetery, the entire rancheria or Indian village, all constructed of adobe houses with tile roofs, the whole laid out with great regularity, forming streets, and a tannery and soap factory." The surrounding mission-owned *potrero*, or pastures, stretched down the peninsula as far as Point San Pedro.

Of this vast estate, only the indomitable old mission, rebuilt in 1782 near what has since become the corner of Dolores and 16th streets, is unchanged.

To get the full flavor of the Mission, the walker should know that it is one in a chain of twenty-one missions established by the Franciscan friars along the California coast from San Diego to Sonoma. Although the Spanish captains and kings have departed long since, you still hear the same Mass that on June 29, 1776, Father Francisco Palou, founder of Mission Dolores, first celebrated next door at the basilica in what is now the city of San Francisco.

Mission Dolores Park.

For historical perspective and an overview of the valley that was considered the finest on the peninsula of San Francisco by its first European settlers, begin this walk at the southwest corner of Mission Dolores Park, 20th and Church streets.

If it is a clear day, the panoramic view across the park, which encompasses downtown San Francisco, the Bay, and parts of the East Bay hills, will take your breath away. Look uphill to the southwest to see Dolores Heights, long the swankiest part of the Mission district.

Closer at hand, notice the gold-painted fire hydrant on Church Street, just south of 20th. Regilded annually because of its valiant performance after the earthquake of 1906, the hydrant is credited with stopping the ensuing fire from sweeping up the hill.

Walk east on 20th, under that imposing row of mature magnolia trees, a testament to the area's warm climate. Looking across the park, try to imagine a time when this was a little rural valley with cattle grazing near Laguna de Nuestra Señora de Dolores and a shallow lake that stood where Mission High School now stands. At a later time, the Old Plank Road, now Mission Street, linked the Mission settlement and the San Francisco of the Gold Rush. Once, the San Francisco and San Jose Railroad huffed through this valley. Ultimately, the city simply enveloped the pueblo.

At Dolores Street, which really should be called a boulevard for its parklike median strips, you have reached El Camino Real, the King's Highway, which began as a nine-foot-wide footpath linking the chain of twenty-one missions, each located one day's walk from the next. Turn left, downhill. If you had walked down this slope a hundred years ago, what is now Dolores Park would have been a different kind of open space, occupied by two Jewish cemeteries. Temples Emanu-El and Sherith Israel bought the land on the outskirts of the city in 1861 and used it for burials until 1894, when a city ordinance began phasing out interments within the city limits.

At 19th Street, you reach what was once the entrance to the cemeteries. Now it has been converted to a concrete plaza surrounding a replica of Mexico's Liberty Bell, a gift from the Mexican community in 1962. The statue uphill on the west represents Mexico's liberator, Miguel Hidalgo y Castilla. Mission High School, downhill at 18th Street, was built in 1926 to the design of architect John Reid, Jr., inspired by the nationwide fad for Colonial Spanish Revival architecture.

Continue down Dolores Street. As you near the Mission, watch for a crook-shaped pole holding a replica of a Mission bell in the median planting strip. In 1920, the California Women's Club marked the entire route of El Camino Real with such signposts to encourage automobile travel. Many of the poles have since been victims of car crashes.

The walker may surprise one of the faithful placing flowers before the Lady of the Wayside shrine in the Mission wall, which screens the little Mission cemetery. Like the tour buses parked outside, the shrine heralds that one has arrived at the original building of San Francisco. An entrance in the wall is the way into the Mission, via a small shop.

Before going in, walk past the entrance to look at the Mission's solemn old face. Flanked by Doric columns that support pillars rising from a wooden balcony, it was built by the Ramatush Indians of the Costanoan. Its interior ceiling is especially beautiful. When architect Willis Polk renovated the building in 1918, he restored it faithfully. The main entrance is surmounted by the "Bells of the Past," which Bret Harte found so romantic. His contemporary, Bayard Taylor, may have had a better ear for music. He found the bells "discordant."

Of all the missions, this is the only one almost overshadowed by the neighboring complex of sympathetic institutions. Most commanding of them is the recently renovated Basilica. Architects describe its ornate facade as "chirrurgueresque," from the Latin word for surgery, which in turn is derived from the Greek for "handwork."

A donation is requested for the Mission preservation fund in return for the privilege of browsing the Mission and its cemetery. It's worth it. The Mission is a museum in itself, and its display space has recently been expanded beside an attractive little garden court.

There has also been major garden renovation done recently in the cemetery, which was five times larger when native son Roy Burrowes, now in his sixties, attended school nearby. Buried in the cemetery along with pioneer William Leidesdorff, several victims of the vigilantes, and any number of early Irish residents are Father Palou, founder of the Mission, and Captain Luis Antonio Arguello, first Mexican governor of Alta California.

Any modest donation seems little enough to pay to step back more than two hundred years in time and savor, for a few precious moments, the peace and measured pace of a leisurely world foregone.

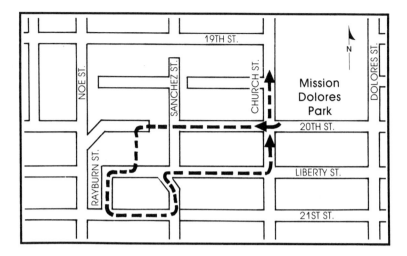

DOLORES HEIGHTS

WALKING TIME: A morning.

DISTANCE: One and one-half miles.

PUBLIC TRANSPORTATION: Metro J Church streetcar.

PARKING: So-so.

CLOTHES: Casual.

The Mission district has been called crowded, dowdy, rowdy, declining, rejuvenated, indifferent, lively, troublesome, and trouble-free. Both its detractors and supporters credit the Mission with a benign climate, but neither dwells on its beauty, charm, or serenity. Yet there are places in ''The Mish'' that have all these qualities. A fine example is Dolores Heights.

Begin at 20th and Church streets, at the southwest corner of Mission Dolores Park. You are standing in Horner's Addition, according to the official city map of 1861, drawn by Vitus Wackenreuder, a topographer for the Whitney Geological Survey of California. At that time, 20th was called Napa Street, and, on paper at least, the grid pattern of streets ascended the hill with no regard for the contours of the land.

Start walking west uphill on 20th Street, enjoying the rich mix of houses in Victorian, Mission Revival and farmhouse styles. At Sanchez Street, named for José Antonio Sánchez, a soldier of Juan Bautista de

Anza's exploring party, cars reach a dead end, but the walker can keep right on going.

Cross Sanchez and continue up the concrete steps. When Dolores Heights was being urbanized, around 1913, it became known as "Battle Mountain" for the way residents fought bitterly over the location of streets as the city prepared to cut into the hill. Every homeowner wanted the street cut at the level of his house, rather than that of his neighbor, which might be twenty or thirty feet higher or lower. The scars of this neighborly altercation are still visible in the high retaining walls and steps outside some homes.

At the top of the steps, pause at the upper dead end of 20th Street and walk out to its concrete wall for a vast view of the city. Mission Dolores Park is the welcome swath of green in the middleground, with Dolores Street defined by the green of its boulevard and Phoenix palms. Frame houses and apartments, punctuated by church steeples, give the Mission a neighborly look compared to the distant downtown towers. On a clear day, the East Bay's Mount Diablo, Roundtop, and Mount Hamilton can be seen peeking over lower East Bay hills.

Look for a metal stair rail and concrete steps that climb up the steep cliff on the south side of 20th Street. Although unmarked, this is a lane through a former goat pasture. Royal Miller, who was born nearby in 1884, once wrote to tell me how he flew kites on this slope as a boy. As late as 1900, from Dolores Hill west, there was only a foot trail to Castro Street.

At the top of the staircase, you reach one of San Francisco's early planning successes. The brick row houses on your right were all designed in the 1960s, after many meetings between the developer and community representatives. The result is a row of handsome houses, compatible with the community. Go out onto the little green square on your left to share their glimpse of the East Bay, framed by tall trees.

Leave the lane on Liberty Street and turn right. At the west end of the street, pause at the Liberty Street steps to look down on one of the city's finest groups of houses in the Art Moderne style, sometimes called art deco. All were built in the 1940s, and sharply contrast the peak-roofed and Victorian houses visible beyond Noe Street below.

Turn left on Rayburn Street, where the classic single-car garages are perked up with shingles. In the days of the Model A Ford, progress along this one-block street was often impeded by young men "tinkering" with their "Flivvers."

At 21st Street, turn left again. As you walk past these pleasant family homes, try to envision a time when this hilltop was a resort where vacationers from San Francisco came to enjoy the beneficial waters of Dolores Heights wells.

When gold was discovered in the craw of ducks swimming in the backyard pond of the house on the southwest corner of 21st and Sanchez, it set off a miniature Gold Rush. No one found a lode. The gold had come from a hole in a miner's poke. After the lady of the house fell in and drowned, the pond and well were filled. Springs lower on the hillside supplied water to refugees from the fire that followed the 1906 earthquake as they huddled in tents in Dolores Park.

On the northeast corner of 21st and Sanchez is an equally notable house, a slate-roofed stucco Tudor that is reputed to have been the hideaway of former Mayor "Sunny Jim" Rolph, although present owners deny it. In Rolph's time, a sculpture of Leda and the Swan that once stood in a public square in Florence, Italy, bathed perennially in the alabaster bowl in the middle of the brick front walk.

Inside, the house is equally splendid, with handsome hand-pegged random-planking floors, built by shipwrights from Sunny Jim's own shipyard. A massive fieldstone fireplace is made of stones said to have been unearthed during the Hetch-Hetchy excavations. The garden was planted by John McLaren.

Legends about the house are many. One is undeniably true: it's possible to "keep an eye on City Hall" from here, and vice versa. The house has sweeping views from its three decks. As you head down Sanchez Street to Liberty, you will glimpse much of the same panorama.

The bilevel streets on sections of Sanchez and Liberty are part of the compromise from the "Battle Hill Wars." Take the steps near Sanchez and follow Liberty back to Church Street, where the boulevard ends.

Once back on Church, walk north to 19th to find a footbridge that leads over the streetcar lines below into Dolores Park. At its end, trees frame a statue of Miguel Hidalgo, liberator of Mexico, which was presented to the city by the Mission Mexican community on September 16, 1962.

Linger in the park as long as you like. To end this walk at the place where you began, take the path back to the sunny southwest corner of Dolores Park. Before you leave, take a last look at the Mission no one talks about, the one abounding in beauty and charm.

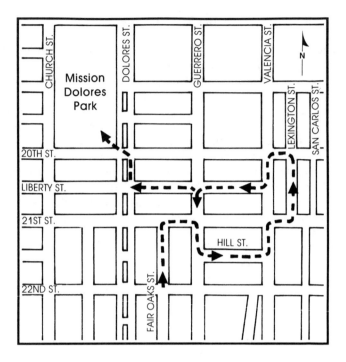

LIBERTY/HILL HISTORIC DISTRICT

WALKING TIME: Allow an hour.

DISTANCE: One and one-quarter miles.

PUBLIC TRANSPORTATION: Metro J Church streetcar; Muni bus 13.

PARKING: So-so.

CLOTHES: Second best.

What constitutes a neighborhood? People living near one another, first of all. Vicinity is almost a synonym, but my old *Webster's Collegiate* says neighborhood commonly implies a closer proximity "and, also, usually, friendliness."

It's hard to tell with Webster whether that "usually" was meant literally or ironically. No matter. Friendliness is the key to a real neighborhood: neighbors who know and speak to one another, sometimes socialize, help one another out in a pinch, and are concerned for the common good. Such neighborhoods are the strength of a city. A genuine one in San Francisco is known as the Liberty/Hill neighborhood—named for two streets on the slope of Dolores Heights. It is an area of well-maintained Victorian homes, which has been described as "a significant representation of nineteenth-century middle-class housing and developmental practices."

The homes within this neighborhood range from small mansions to "workingmen's Victorian cottages." Two of the houses in the neighborhood are registered historic landmarks. Another was once the home of Lotta Crabtree, darling of the footlights. It was built when much of the area was still owned by Don José de Jesús Noe, original grantee of Rancho San Miguel and last Mexican *alcalde* (mayor) of Yerba Buena, the village that became San Francisco.

To enjoy a walk around this east-facing slope of what was once known as Noe Hill and today is called Dolores Heights, transport yourself to the corner of 22nd and Fair Oaks streets.

Start walking uphill on Fair Oaks, which seems almost as rich in greenery as a country village. Credit the charm to lot-by-lot development, which gave the houses irregular setbacks. This also makes for more light inside houses than the usual shoulder-to-shoulder alignment.

Almost immediately you will be abreast of Lotta's cottage. Look for the gable at number 90–92. The modest cottage to which San Francisco's then highest-paid actress retreated to end her days was subsequently lifted up and a new ground floor constructed. Noe's cattle grazed on the slope below when the second floor of number 92 was built.

Continue up this charming old street to discover another oddity at number 2 Fair Oaks. It was slid into place under the eaves of number 68, the gingerbread ornamentation and veranda of which are unique. Look, too, at the Queen Anne touches at number 8 Fair Oaks, which has remained a single-family home while other nearby houses were divided into flats and duplexes.

Fair Oaks ends at 21st Street, where a line of elegant homes shares one of the finest panoramas possible of downtown San Francisco. Turn right on 21st Street to pass through the heart of a development that began in 1861. Known as the San Francisco Homestead Union, it was a community concept originated by Washington Bartlett, the first "gringo" mayor of San Francisco and the man who gave the city its name.

If the purple-leaved plum trees are in bloom when you reach Guerrero Street, you won't notice anything else. The rest of the year, the scene-stealer across the street to your left, number 827 Guerrero, is the Kathy and Leroy Looper landmark house. Now a home for the handicapped, the Looper House was built by John McMullen. A city landmark, it is also listed on the National Register of Historic Places, in such grand company as Ghirardelli Square, City Hall, and the Haas-Lilienthal House. The view from this corner gives a good perspective on its turret and Moorish entryway.

Also listed as a city landmark on this block is the house next door, number 811–813 Guerrero. Save both for closer inspection a little later, if you will, and turn right for one block to Hill Street, then left on Hill. En route you will pass other Victorians in Queen Anne, Italianate, and Stick styles. Since 70 percent of the homes in the neighborhood are Victorians, San Francisco's Landmarks Preservation Board has named the slope for special protection as an historic district.

At Valencia Street, turn left to 21st Street. Valencia was part of the route of the city's first street railroad, which began service in 1860, first with little locomotives known as steam dummies, then with horse-drawn cars, and later with cable cars. Public transportation along the street turned it into a commercial corridor.

At 21st Street, turn right one block to reach Lexington Street, a real-estate development built on speculation, in which every house is a little flat-front Italianate. San Carlos Street, half a block farther, is equally unusual, featuring slanted-bay Italianate houses. It is also notable for its marble curbstones. Walk through the street of your choice, then turn left on 20th Street and left again on Valencia to reach Liberty Street.

Climb Liberty Street and you will pass some grander homes, though nothing so imposing as the Flood Mansion. Gnarled old plantings soften almost every aspect. You may see neighbors here chatting on the sidewalk, Agnes Pritchard tending her garden, or meet Father Kermin McCormick of St. James Catholic Church riding his bicycle to a parish call.

At Guerrero, if you want a closer look at the two landmark houses, detour to the left, but return and continue up Liberty to Dolores Street and turn right.

You'll soon find you have reached an upper corner of Mission Dolores Park, a sunny oasis where you can rest from the climb. When Lotta Crabtree lived nearby, she could see Laguna de la Manantial, a lake long since filled, but the skyline wasn't nearly so spectacular in her time.

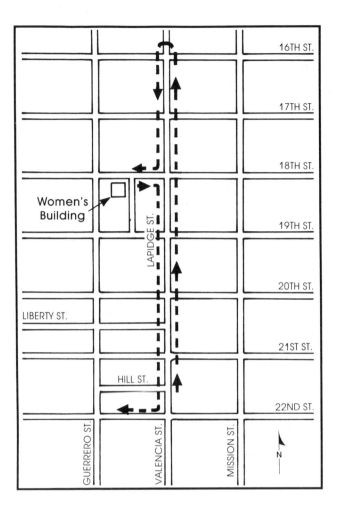

16TH ST.

17TH ST.

18TH ST.

Women's
Building

LAPIDGE ST.

19TH ST.

20TH ST.

LIBERTY ST.

21ST ST.

HILL ST.

22ND ST.

GUERRERO ST.

VALENCIA ST.

MISSION ST.

N

THE WOMEN'S DISTRICT

WALKING TIME: Allow an hour.

DISTANCE: Nine city blocks.

PUBLIC TRANSPORTATION: Muni bus 26 Valencia.

PARKING: So-so.

CLOTHES: Jeans are welcome.

Almost every waking hour of every day, every room of the four-story Women's Building, at 18th Street just off Valencia Street, is filled with concerts, plays, poetry readings, art exhibits, dance rehearsals and performances, health and exercise classes, seminars, political discussions, child-care lectures, or language instruction. There are committee meetings of forty or more organizations quartered in the Women's Building.

This is only part of the cultural activity in the community. Around the corner on Valencia, at New College, a fully accredited four-year alternative-education college and graduate school, the schedule is equally lively.

Along Valencia Street, the local focus for the Women's Movement, much of the energy goes into culture. An increasing number of businesses are women-owned or -operated. After dark, some of the action is discreetly lesbian.

To see for yourself, consider a leisurely walk along Valencia between 16th and 25th streets. This emerging Bohemia serves a mix that includes Mexican, Central American, South American, Native American, Caucasian, African-American, and other ethnic groups, as well as active gays of both genders.

Begin this walk after 11 A.M., for Valencia Street awakens late, yawning and stretching sleepily. At first glance, it looks like Lower Nowhere.

Look again. You'll get a different impression by dropping in at either Old Wives' Tales, a feminist bookstore at 1009 Valencia between 21st and 22nd, or, in the next block, at 968, Modern Times, a bookstore specializing in leftist literature that also carries both feminist and gay material. Look around at the remarkable number of books one rarely sees elsewhere; then, before you leave, pick up samples of the many free handbills, leaflets, and newspapers, to get a sense of the area's diversity.

The friend who introduced me to this walk steered me down the street to point out Osento, a women's bathhouse, and near it, Hispano Unidad Servicio Recuperación. We paused to see the working model of the mid-nineteenth-century gold-ore boat *Antelope* in the window of the Retired Teamsters Local 85, and smiled as we passed the "Rage," which sells, says the sign, new and used clothes "In the Heart of the Trans-Mission." The array of garages across the street explains the pun.

Scattered along the street are a few modest workingmen's Victorians, some nicely renewed, some in hideous asbestos shingles, others whose paint is flaked like rolled oats. In front of two are big blooming Bells of Ireland bushes, whose flowers are green.

When you are abreast of Liberty and Hill streets, both of which end at

Valencia, look uphill for unexpected views of Twin Peaks. Behind nice street trees are some of the most exquisitely refurbished Victorian homes in the city.

La Rondalla, as one whiff from the door will tell you, prepares its own tacos and burritos daily and is everybody's favorite Mexican restaurant along the street. Upstairs/Downstairs and Now and Then, on the other side of the street, have antiques from the same era as many of the nearby houses, while Harlow's is exclusively an art deco emporium. Just beyond the mini-park, Fickle Fox is a pleasant small restaurant.

We stopped in at the newsroom of *Coming Up*, a free, nonprofit lesbian/gay monthly paper. Men and women both toiled at the typewriters under a collection of colorful posters lining the walls. In the same shop is a typesetting establishment called Cu!t (spelling theirs).

"You'll never find a place to park if you come to Valencia after 5 P.M.," one of *Coming Up*'s editors warned us, "especially near Amelia's or Esta Noche, a Latino bar near Sixteenth Street." The basement of Amelia's features dozens of pictures of cult heroine Amelia Earhart.

New College, at 777 Valencia, is housed in what was once a mortuary. The gaudy, hot-pink building across the street has the same kind of converted-mortuary architecture; it houses Valencia Rose, containing a cafe, coffeehouse, and cantina. Both Garbo's and Penny Lane are barbershops, owned and operated by women, but serving both sexes.

When you reach 18th Street, digress westerly to Lapidge Street to find the Women's Building, once the Norwegian Club. The Dovre Bar, a dark pub frequented by the militantly Irish, is located in its northeast corner. Just beyond the shared wall, on the ground floor of the building, is a fine auditorium. At least eighty women in leotards were on the floor warming up in dance exercises when we peeked in.

There are four places you won't want to miss. The first is Eye Gallery, and the extension of New College. The second is Sports Palace, loaded with gymnastic equipment, where a group of serious, well-muscled men and women work out.

Artemis Cafe, at 1199 Valencia, is a third stop; sample the cappuccino. Next door are feminist law offices, the Women's Information Exchange, and the West Coast Women's Music Festival. On the corner of 22nd Street, Hibernia Bank, Lucca's Ravioli, the Happy Greeks, Minichello's, and Mama Vittoria give the street an international flavor.

To end this walk with a chuckle, a sigh, or a snort of indignation, depending on your own mental baggage, the fourth spot to seek out is Good Vibrations, a small shop devoted to a different kind of women's movements. It has a museum of old battery-operated vibrators and sells ostrich plumes, rabbit's fur cozies, and those taboo sex toys euphemistically known as marital aids.

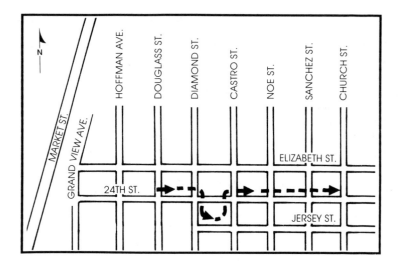

NOE VALLEY

WALKING TIME: Allow an hour.

DISTANCE: One-half mile.

PUBLIC TRANSPORTATION: Muni buses 13 and 48.

PARKING: Iffy.

CLOTHES: Downplayed but trendy.

> *Noe Valley, Noe Valley, you are ringing in my ears*
> *like a slow sweet piece of music for the long forgotten years.* . . .
>
> (WITH APOLOGIES TO JOHN MASEFIELD)

In a city once known for its neighborliness, it may well be that Noe Valley was the leader, for it is still neighborly. People speak to one another on the street, pass the time of day over the back fence, and, now and again, borrow a cup of bulgur. Salespeople in the 24th Street shops pride themselves on their helpfulness and courtesy. The Noe Valley section of the East & West of Castro Street Improvement Club, Inc., gets together to paint over any graffiti left by interlopers. Walk the streets that nestle in that pocket east of Twin Peaks and south of Market and the esprit de corps is readily apparent.

To make this walk, transport yourself to the corner of Douglass and 24th streets. The lively construction in the center of the lawn next to Noe Valley tennis courts, which looks like a frozen waterfall or a piece of contemporary sculpture, is actually playground equipment, the gift of the Friends of Noe Valley. Look south uphill on steep Douglass Street, where the green niche, formerly a quarry, is the Douglass Street Playground.

Twin Peaks and this slope were part of Rancho San Miguel, granted in 1845 by Governor Pio Pico to Don José de Jesús Noe, last Mexican *alcalde* of San Francisco. To avoid the humiliation of surrendering the town to General Montgomery, he retired to his then distant rancho at Twin Peaks, where he passed the rest of his life. The city charter line of 1851 stopped in those days at his Castro Street border. After 1862, horsemen paid a twenty-five-cent toll to reach the beach via the new five-and-a-half-mile Mission and Ocean Beach macadamized toll road.

Start walking east on 24th Street, originally named Park Street by John M. Horner because it led to the park surrounding Pioneer racecourse. Horner and his brother bought forty-three-hundred acres of San Miguel to lay out Horner's Addition, one of the city's earliest subdivisions. Elizabeth Street, one block north, and Jersey, one block south of 24th, still retain the names Horner gave them, but John, which he named for himself, is now 22nd, and Horner Street became 23rd.

When you reach Diamond, walk a block south to Jersey to see a "tower house," as Queen Anne–style houses were known when they were built in the 1880s. According to a little leaflet prepared on Victorians in 1975 for Stanford Research Institute, "depending on how fancy the tastes of the customer, cottages were $290 to $360 per room, residences cost $320 to $420 per room, and a villa could cost from $450 to $700 per room to build." Today, one could not build the front door for that price.

Bear left on Jersey to number 451, the Noe Valley Branch Public Library. For architectural buffs, the library is "Spanish, with nice ceramic moulding and the classical Beaux Arts axial symmetry." If it is open, go inside to see the library's archival photo display, a handsome piece of sculpture by Ruth Asawa, and the community garden, which surrounds the building.

Once you leave the library, look for the Stick-style Victorians along Jersey. Artist Mel Moss, journalist Rasa Gastaitis, gerontologist Gerry Murphy, and publisher Donald Allen of Grey Fox Press are typical of the residents who find this old neighborhood friendly. "Come in here," said Don Allen, who conducted me on this walk, steering me into Small Press Traffic Bookshop at 3841-B 24th Street, a block over. "It is exclusively devoted to publications on poetry, drama, fiction, and literary criticism. They have more than two thousand titles in stock from three hundred small presses in the United States, Canada, and England. Most of the books are printed right here in the Bay Area. If there is a new literary frontier emerging in this country, the small presses are in the vanguard of it."

Next stop is Star Magic, 3995 24th Street, devoted to "eclectic objects of Science and Spirit," including some remarkable telescopes, microscopes, ion generators, and other adult toys. Down the street at Ver Brugge Meats, the clerk pointed out that the fish was caught fresh daily on the butcher's own boat. Books Plus, Noe Valley's general bookstore, is also on this block.

A Cut Above Castro turns out to be a barbershop, Quiche and Carry is just what it sounds like, and Kidstuff has both new and used toddler's clothing for sale. The Frog Shop sells—surprise!—frogs, largely ornamental, while the Meat Market is a coffeehouse. At The Philosopher's Stone, another bookstore, the clerk may invite you to come back for a poetry reading.

The diversity is so great, both in shops and people, today, that the walker can find almost anything civilized along this vintage street, so end it where you please. The best discoveries are the ones you make yourself.

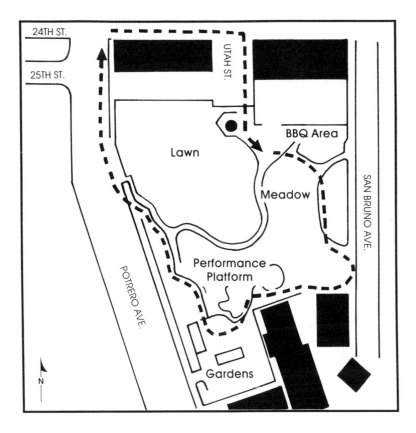

Map labels: 24TH ST., 25TH ST., UTAH ST., Lawn, BBQ Area, Meadow, SAN BRUNO AVE., POTRERO AVE., Performance Platform, Gardens, N

POTRERO DEL SOL

WALKING TIME: A pleasant hour.

DISTANCE: Six blocks.

PUBLIC TRANSPORTATION: Muni buses 9, 17, and 33.

PARKING: If you're lucky, at the dead end of San Bruno Avenue.

CLOTHES: Comfortable.

A more unlikely site is hard to imagine, yet San Francisco's newest city park, Potrero del Sol, nicknamed "Raza Park," is tucked between Potrero Hill and Bernal Heights. It stands just south of Hospital Curve in a wedge of previously forsaken land where the Army Street Interchange joins the James Lick Freeway, Route 101.

Good planning—the product of two years of monthly meetings—

and clever design have made Potrero del Sol a surprisingly quiet place of unusual charm. The park, completed in 1982, has a Latin feel. Residents of "Nicador," as writer Frank Viviano nicknamed the surrounding barrio, include many Salvadoran and Nicaraguan refugees. This park reminds them of home, and they love it.

In one sense, Potrero del Sol is a reincarnation of its first civilized use, which was also recreational. Until about 1850, this land was part of Rancho Rincon de las Salinas y Potrero Viejo, which translates roughly as the Farm at the Corner of the Salt Marsh and the Old Pastures. Precita Creek, sometimes called Serpentine Creek, meandered in great curves through the valley and toward the Bay. Army Street now surmounts it.

Long before this land was part of San Francisco, the Bernal family held their parties and barbecues in the creekside dell at the south end of what is now Utah Street. Later, residents found the dell so idyllic that they named it Eden Park and called the two bankside walks Adam and Eve.

Until 1923, when the first road was put through the area, Eden Park was a place where birds flocked, cows came home, and boys could put a raft into the water and float out to the Bay. Knudsen Dairy was a last vestige of the area's rural use. One of the first places in the city where the fog lifts, Potrero del Sol is appropriately named. It means Sunny Meadow. To see for yourself, begin this walk at Potrero Avenue and 24th Street, where there is a stoplight to aid the walker. The brown-shingled building on the west side of the street is the Good Samaritan Community Center, operated by the Episcopal Church. Cross toward the attractive factory building of Plant Brothers and continue east on 25th Street. As you walk, notice the carriage house midblock on your left, whose haymow door, painted barn red, still has its built-in hoist.

Then look through the porthole at 2789 25th Street to see a fine display of antique tools and a hitching post in the foyer. The stairs lead to several offices, among them those of architects Esherick, Homsey, Dodge, and Davis. With excellent common sense, the San Francisco Park Department selected this firm, whose offices have long overlooked the park site, to design Potrero del Sol.

At Utah Street, alongside Buena Vista School (also the Mission Education Center), turn right and walk half a block along the tree-shaded approach to Potrero del Sol's main entrance. In a moment you are in a tiled plaza surrounding a classic-tiered Spanish fountain, surrounded by massive benches in a muted terra-cotta color that is almost salmon pink.

Trees surround the plaza, hiding the Buena Vista School playground on the east and Plant Brothers' parking lot on the west. Look at the topmost level of the Plant Building to discern a handsome metal bas-relief sculpture on the wall of pioneers with oxen and a prairie schooner.

Then take the walkway that leads downhill between berms. The pine-shaded hill on the right has been nicknamed "Little Fuji" for Japanese-American landscape designer Sat Nashita, who planned the plantings. Sycamore trees grow on the left.

When you reach the long bench overlooking a great oval bowl of lawn, look down at the natural amphitheater facing a colonnaded stage. Continue walking east. On the left, you will see monolithic picnic tables and benches. The tables have checkerboards on top, and the largest semicircular bench has barbecue pits built into each end.

Head easterly along the walkway bordering the amphitheater oval, but pause when you are abreast of an entrance, the first of two you will pass, and look across San Bruno Avenue. Urban archaeologists can find at least three eras of the neighborhood's past visible side by side. One is the little cottage built when this land was rural. Another is a corrugated metal shed that bespeaks light industry, a land use still in evidence beyond the freeway. A third, indicative of our own time, is an overlarge billboard that urges youngsters in the schoolyard or park to smoke a cigarette that shall be nameless here.

As you descend the walkway toward the stage, another group of picnic tables and barbecue pits will be on your right. Circle them and go out onto the stage. Wisteria planted at the base of each column festoons the stage from the trellis above.

As you look out on the expanse of green lawn, which fills with people on occasions like the Cinco de Mayo celebration, try to imagine this area as a desert of concrete and broken bottles. That is the way it looked after the Knudsen Dairy left the area.

Conceptual artist Bonnie Sherk may have been the first person to realize the site's potential as a park. It became her dream to create a crossroad farm with sheep grazing in a meadow. One morning in 1973, freeway motorists were amused to spot what seemed to be a procession of cows coming home from Potrero Hill on the footbridge. The cows were made of board—Sherk's creation. Later, the Trust for Public Land bought the site pending city acquisition under an open-space bond issue.

Not everyone in the neighborhood saw the potential park as a farm. Many of the community meetings ended with everyone's feathers ruffled. The final design is a happy compromise. Some city maps still designate the area as Knudsen-Bloom Park, named for former owners of the land. Neighborhood kids call it Raza Park.

Unless there are mariachis practicing, walk off the stage on the west side. Almost immediately you are in a charming little garden, with a pond on your right. Past the pond, the rock garden is a special project of park gardener Mike Kosturos. It also hides a large community vegetable garden and the farm building.

The adobe-style building beyond serves as a gardener's shed–cum–rest rooms. Schoolchildren come during the day to see the little farm's chickens and goats. Culture-minded visitors enjoy the art gallery in the upper level of the barn. By night, it has a different character: jazz and rock bands perform in the building. The farm is ideally situated as a site for loud musical performances, since there are few nearby neighbors to be offended. Unfortunately, punk rockers sometimes vandalize the park.

Look through the driveway alongside the gardener's shed toward busy Potrero Avenue, beneath the freeway on ramp. The patch of green beyond is an older oasis, Rolph Playground, which has basketball and tennis courts, a baseball diamond, field house, and tiny-tots playground.

Step out onto the Potrero Avenue sidewalk and the noise of passing traffic will offend immediately. Don't be tempted to cross Potrero here to reach the playground. Instead, retreat back into Potrero del Sol and walk north within the quieter park. The berm of earth on your left shuts out most of the noise. Another, smaller bowl of lawn is on your right, on the slope of Little Fuji.

Soon you reach another entrance with benches. Go out under the trees of Potrero Avenue toward 25th Street. You have completed a loop walk and can end here if you wish.

If you want to try the tennis courts at Rolph Playground, or find yourself yearning for that spicy South-of-the-Border food, cross with the stoplight. Go south for Rolph Playground or north to find at least a dozen good restaurants on 24th Street, offering almost as many variations on Mexican and Central and South American cuisine.

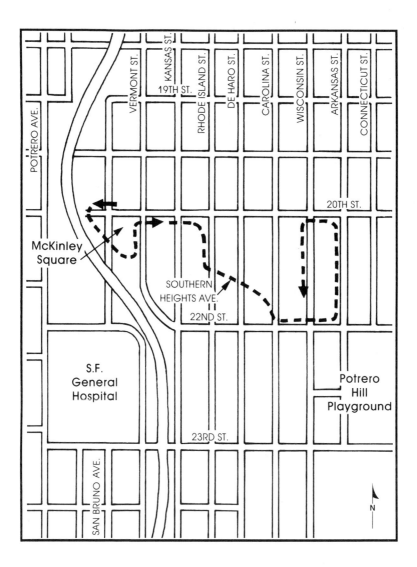

POTRERO HILL

WALKING TIME: Allow an hour.

DISTANCE: About two miles.

PUBLIC TRANSPORTATION: Muni buses 48 and 53.

PARKING: Crowded on Sundays.

CLOTHES: Whatever.

Tomatoes glowing red as a toper's nose. Great squash and pumpkins nestling like elfin treasure on the warming turf. Velvety green beans dangling like earrings. That's harvest time in the seventy community gardens of San Francisco.

For a pleasant autumn walk to see two of the more remarkable gardens under the aegis of S.L.U.G., the San Francisco League of Urban Gardeners, and enjoy some panoramic views of the city, consider Potrero Hill.

One of the city's most cohesive neighborhoods, Potrero Hill is an island marooned by industry. The same distance from Union Square as Pacific Heights, it has long been an isolated country town populated by artists, nonconformists, and Russian émigrés of the *Molokani*, or "milk-drinker," sect.

On its west side, the torrent of traffic on the James Lick Freeway, more commonly known as the "Bloody Bayshore," surges relentlessly against the hill. On the south and east, Interstate 280 adds to the roar of the clanging, banging, jangling sea of heavy industry that lies between the hill and the Bay. To the north, the scene is equally hectic as Southern Pacific prepares to develop around Mission Creek, and closer at hand, old factories are being transformed into a fashion center. High over this turmoil, the Potrero Hill community of cottages, Victorian townhouses, and an ever-growing number of new apartments enjoy dramatic views. The hill often basks drowsily in the sun while the rest of the city shivers.

Begin this walk at 20th and Vermont streets, across from "Baby Park," as the local residents have nicknamed McKinley Square. Walk west alongside the park one block to San Bruno Avenue, where the Potrero Hill Community Garden has half of San Francisco as a backdrop. Before you go through the ranch-style gate, pause to notice its roses, agaves, cannas, and the sandpile and mulch heap.

Richard Wagner, who told me he had been gardening on the hill for nine or ten years, said, "When I managed to hear the freeway noise as a Sierra river, gardening here became a meditation for me."

Enter and bear left along the brush-chip pathway. Window boxes and vines almost conceal an odd little cement-roofed shack on your right. Built illegally as a refuge by a gardener with domestic problems, it soon became a community toolshed. Notice the warning "Don't Add Bermuda Grass" on the compost pile on your left. Continue past cosmos, onions, and lettuce to the end of the path for a superb cityscape of Twin Peaks, sometimes clutched in the fog formation known as the "Hand of God." In the foreground is an eagle's-eye view of both old and new parts of San Francisco General Hospital.

Turn north, away from Hospital Curve, passing the lush vegetable beds (and older stool shacks) until you are at the northeastern corner of the garden. At the fenceline, three benches have been placed so a viewer can enjoy the downtown skyline with Mount Tamalpais and Buena Vista Hill as counterpoints. Gardeners may want to linger all day, visiting the plots that specialize in herbs or are planted in the French-intensive method. Stay as long as you wish. When you have made the complete circuit of the garden, return to San Bruno Avenue and turn right.

The garden, planted on park-department land, abuts McKinley Square. Just past a lovely young pepper tree, look for a stairway that climbs up into the square by way of a children's playground. Turn right at the sandbox and follow the line of old cypress trees halfway. Cut diagonally across the lawn toward the field house. Follow the sidewalk at its east end about fifty feet for an overview of the "wiggly" block of Vermont Street, which snakes downhill like the better-known curlicue of Lombard Street. Planting here was done by residents.

Return to 20th Street and walk east to Rhode Island Street. Turn south to pass Chiotra's Grocery, which has been serving the hill for more than sixty-six years. Both church buildings at 884 and 904 Rhode Island Street have Russian congregations, but the churchlike building on the east side of the street contains apartments.

At Southern Heights Avenue, veer left to reach a charming new mini-park, as yet unnamed. Planner Marie Carlberg, a hill resident, was the force behind the community effort that brought about this exquisite viewpoint. Pause a moment here to see the Bay Bridge and Yerba Buena Island beyond De Haro Street.

Alcalde Francisco de Haro, for whom the street is named, was the first mayor to live on the hill. He held the Spanish land grant known as Potrero de San Francisco or Potrero Nuevo—"New Grazing Ground"—which was then nearly surrounded by water. Early accounts say De Haro died of grief after his twin sons were slain by Kit Carson on the orders of General John Frémont.

The distinguished building on the northeast corner is the Potrero Hill Neighborhood House, designed by architect Julia Morgan in 1908 and registered as historic landmark number 86. A beehive of activity under the director Enola Maxwell, it has programs for the old, the young, the disabled, for addicts, alcoholics, photographers, knitters, chess players, artists, work hunters, bingo and blackjack players, dancers, Ping-Pong players, gardeners, and parents. Go in to see the charming fireplace, always ablaze when the day is chilly, if the building is open. If not, walk past it on Southern Heights and turn left beyond the last tree in its yard to climb up a new deck, just off Neighborhood House's theater, for a view over the Bay.

Return to Southern Heights, which cuts diagonally to Carolina Street. Look across the concrete wall to locate the Russian Molokan Church at 841 Carolina. Austere as the building seems, it is a church where the fancy piroshki are prepared for wedding feasts. Funeral processions, which also begin here, once went to Colma on foot. The casket was carried on the shoulders of friends as the procession retraced the deceased's path of lifetime habit.

Many of the *banya*, or steam baths, that once stood behind Russian homes on the hill have been converted to mother-in-law apartments.

The lush street divider on Carolina at 22nd Street was planted and is maintained as a community effort. Turn left on 22nd to pass the cliffy block that contains a reservoir and water tower. When you reach the firehouse labeled Engine 48, although it is now the home of Engine Company Number 37, pause a moment to admire the view north and south. Then cross Wisconsin Street, where a staircase descends the eastern slope of the hill in this steep block. As you go down, you can thank Tamara Patri for the leafiness. She planted these trees in 1967.

At the foot of the steps is the flowery Arkansas Friendship Garden, just across Arkansas Street. Unique among community gardens, it is tended to by both physically and mentally disabled people and has more flowers than vegetables. Abutting it on the south is the steep slope of Potrero Hill Playground. The path leads downhill to housing projects and a railroad tunnel that goes under the hill at Sierra Street and emerges at 19th and Arkansas streets. Martha Pavloff of 709 Carolina Street once told me: "We played in the tunnel as children and flattened against the wall when trains went through."

If you are game for a little hill-climbing, go north on Arkansas, left (or west) on 20th Street, and left again on Wisconsin, where the southeast corner has a tropical garden that includes thriving bananas, pandanus, philodendrons, palms, and bird of paradise plants. You will pass a rich architectural variety of houses that includes Italianate, Stick, Edwardian, Mission Revival, art deco, and contemporary styles.

By the time you leave the broad sun-filled streets, the neighborliness, the easy informality, the lofty views, and the friendly gardens may make you feel you've been in a time warp. If only it weren't so noisy . . . .

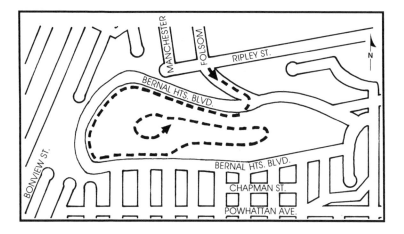

BERNAL HEIGHTS PARK

WALKING TIME: An hour.

DISTANCE: An uphill mile.

PUBLIC TRANSPORTATION: Muni bus 67 to Ripley and Folsom streets.

PARKING: West end of Bernal Heights Boulevard.

CLOTHES: Casual.

"Where can I walk my dog?" readers ask with increasing frequency as park after park excludes pets. For San Franciscans, one of the best answers is the forty-acre undeveloped crest of Bernal Heights.

The bare knoll just east of the summit of Bernal Heights is not only one of the best dog walks in the city, it is rich in springtime with wildflowers. Encircle the windshorn summit itself, bare of plantings except for some rangy Monterey pines and acacias that try unsuccessfully to screen the "ears" of a big disfiguring telephone microwave relay station, and you can enjoy a 360-degree vista.

Before beginning this walk, put on a windbreaker and flat-heeled walking shoes, preferably lug-soled. From the corner of Ripley and Folsom streets, climb tree-lined Folsom Street to Bernal Heights Boulevard, which loops the crest. When you reach the automotive barrier, turn right and walk on the closed road. It will bring you, safely sheltered from traffic, around to the south side.

If you had arrived at this level area, the site of an old red-rock quarry, on June 11, 1973, you would have found it alive with children, clowns, face painters, bagpipers, guitarists, and picnickers under a canopy of huge carp, writhing eels, and other fancy kites and balloons as the community of Bernal Heights celebrated the San Francisco Recreation and Park Department's acquisition of the land.

Through the years, neighbors have often gotten together for baseball, hunts, art fairs, block parties, wildflower plantings, and other festivities.

Most famous of all was Jack Lally's wake. In the late 1880s, when $15,000 was willed to Lally, he celebrated too hard and fell to his death in a ditch. His widow, Rosie, spent half of the inheritance on the keening, tying guests into chairs if they looked like they would fall out before the party was over. It lasted for a month. When the party was over, Rosie married a German waiter, and the wedding celebration lasted another four days before they took off on their honeymoon on local drover Tim Welch's dump cart. How much was left of the $15,000 is anybody's guess.

As you pass the automotive barrier to the roadway leading uphill, pause to read the sign that says, "This gate is at the request of the Bernal Heights people to prevent dumping. For the good of your neighborhood, please help us to keep it together." Neighbors turn out on the third Sunday of each month to do a park cleanup.

Notice the sheer cliff off to the left, a remnant of quarrying. Fossil *Radiolaria* in it are too small for the naked eye to see, but the layers of convoluted shale in this layer of the old Franciscan formation make a beautiful pattern.

Follow the road uphill. Betty Kilich, a longtime Bernal Heights resident who makes this climb daily with her dog, Yonya, likes to come at sunrise. "It is surprising how many joggers and other dog walkers are out on the trail at that time of day," she says. Young families use the hillside later in the day. One youthful father sometimes walks with a babe in arms as he sings "*Cielito Lindo*" in Spanish.

As you climb the 325-foot hill, try to imagine all the surrounding 4,446 acres as bucolic as these flower-filled slopes. The original land grant, Rancho Rincon de las Salinas y Potrero Viejo (the Farm at the Corner of the Salt Marsh and the Old Pastures), reached from Army Street to San Bruno Mountain. It was granted in 1839 to Cornelio Bernal, grandson of Don Juan Francisco Bernal, one of the soldiers who came to San Francisco in 1776 with explorer Juan Bautista de Anza. The family home stood on the site of what is now St. Luke's Hospital.

Cornelio's cattle grazed on the slopes until 1860, when this land was sold to John S. Cobb and Harvey Brown. They had the land surveyed by Vitus Wackenreuter to establish one of the city's earliest neighborhoods. Irish, Scots, and Scandinavians built on the lower slopes, raised vegetables, and kept poultry and dairy cows. So many of them also kept goats that Bernal Heights became known as Nanny Goat Hill.

Another of the great Irish neighborhood stories passed down in the oral tradition on Bernal Heights concerns the dogcatcher, a private concessionaire who was allowed by the city to keep what fines he could mulct from citizens whose animals wandered. When the poundsman imprisoned the Widow O'Brien's cow, Effie, he went too far. Her son and one hundred husky boys stormed the pound and freed Effie and all other impounded animals. Neighbors gathered on the hill that night to watch the old pound burn. It wasn't rebuilt until a Humane Society was founded.

Look south as you climb to see McLaren Park in the center, backed by San Bruno Mountain. In between lie steep streets and hillside cottages. As the road swings, the industrial area that borders the Bay dominates the view. If the day is fair, Mount Hamilton may be visible to the southeast. A little higher up, one sees the East Bay cities backed by Mount Diablo. At the hairpin turn, the downtown skyline of San Francisco suddenly takes your breath away. If you haven't looked at the city for a while, the growing density apparent from this angle may appall you.

This is also where a path takes off on the eastern knoll just beyond the roadside bumper into dog heaven. If you brought Fido, step over the barrier and head east along the footpath that is worn through the grass of the red-rock ridge. Owners often seem to position themselves at fifty-foot intervals along the knoll while their pets romp.

If you came sans man's best friend, continue on the roadway until you reach the telephone company barricade. Step over the bumper on the right side of the gate and follow the path that skirts the chain link fence around the private acre on the apex. Every step reveals more of the city as you walk. The Bay Bridge, the San Francisco skyline, Angel Island, Marin County, Golden Gate Bridge, the Pacific Ocean, and San Mateo County all present their outlines.

Eleven kinds of native wildflowers bloom here, including ceanothus, lupine, poppies, blue-eyed grass, convolvulus, cowslips, cranesbill, and amole, the soap plant Indian women used to pound in Serpentine and Islais creeks below, long before those natural waterways were buried under Army Street and Alemany Boulevard.

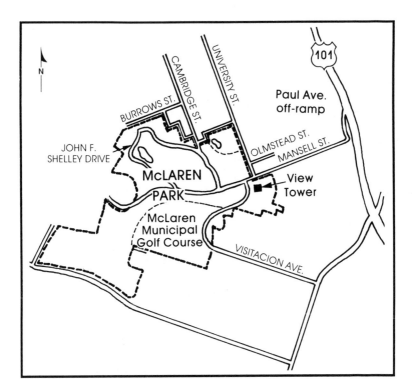

McLAREN PARK

WALKING TIME: A morning.

DISTANCE: A rambling mile or two.

PUBLIC TRANSPORTATION: Muni bus 29 to go; get off at Mansell and Visitacion streets. Return via 52 from Prague and Brazil streets.

PARKING: Plenty at Mansell and Visitacion.

CLOTHES: Stout shoes, warm sweater.

CAVEAT: Go with friends and your dog.

AUTO ROUTE: Bayshore south to Paul Avenue exit.

Little by little, the emerging image of McLaren Park approaches the great vision "Uncle John" McLaren held for it. One recent addition is the spectacular McLaren Overlook.

It was the magnificent topography that inspired McLaren. The

3,215-acre park, flung like a great mantle along McLaren Ridge, was the place McLaren, the legendary San Francisco park superintendent, felt Golden Gate Park should be situated. McLaren Park's heart still encompasses the open space he treasured, rich with wildflowers and marshy creeksides.

Around its perimeter, neighborhood demands for playgrounds, community gardens, golf courses, tennis courts, softball diamonds, soccer fields, and vista points constantly increase. Happily, the San Francisco Recreation and Park Department is shaping its efforts toward neighborhood needs.

My favorite of the newer areas is a stunning McLaren Overlook at Mansell Street and Visitacion Avenue. Lofty already, it has a remarkable tower that lifts a walker another thirty feet to reveal an unparalleled 360-degree view.

To discover this remarkable place, take a picnic and your dog, if you wish, and transport yourself to McLaren Park at Mansell and Visitacion. Notice the bicycle trail toward the west, but cross instead to the southeast corner and begin walking to the Overlook on the walkway that cuts diagonally through twenty acres of plantings of ceanothus and rockrose toward a stand of old wind-sheared Monterey pines. Nice sturdy picnic tables well set on circular pads of paving dot either side of the walk.

Shortly, one reaches a triangular bed planted with gazanias. Bear left around a circle of wildflower-strewn lawn. About a third of the way round, concealed by trees from this approach, is the view tower, a sturdy Bauhaus-inspired lookout designed by landscape architects Theodore and Gordon Osmundson.

Resist for the moment the temptation to climb the tower. Instead, go around to the east side to find a remarkable compass inlaid underfoot, sheltered behind a semicircle of tiled bench. It is big enough for hang gliders to read from an elevation of a thousand feet. From this vantage, downtown is true north.

Stroll around the balustrade to locate Mount Tamalpais, Fort Mason, and the "ship masts" of Sutro Tower. Bernal Heights is identifiable by its communications apparatus. Look east; Roundtop and Diablo stick up above the South Bay, with Swan River daisies and California poppies immediately below the parapet. Bayview Park, Candlestick, Hunters Point, and ships in for repair, an animated scene on weekdays, seem oddly remote with the waving grass in the foreground.

When you are halfway around the balustrade, cut back to the tower and climb it if it is open. With each turn of the staircase, more of the area comes into view as you rise. Looking south of India Basin, the greening Brisbane ex-dump with its lagoon is visible. Oyster and Coyote points stick out into the South Bay beyond it.

Seventy-seven tons of debris were removed from McLaren Park in the last year, some of it blown here to the ridge by strong winds, more just chucked by thoughtless motorists or moving householders. Now gardeners actually garden here, instead of wasting their skills and time gathering trash.

You may find gardener Bette Hered on her knees, trowel in hand, or see an Anna's hummingbird perched in the topmost branch of a young cypress tree. Audubon Society member Sheila Davies conducts regular birding trips through McLaren Park, because so many species frequent its unspoiled and varied terrain. Members of the Native Plant Society have identified some of the wildflowers that pop up here: bicolor lupin, blue flax, and spring beauties bloom in May.

The walkway visible below the waving grass is a section of a perimeter trail that will one day loop the entire park. New young trees have been planted in strategic places to create the windbreaks of the future. The old trees are a legacy from the time when this was cow country.

From this part of the Overlook walk, one can see Visitacion Valley below, with apartment towers standing among smaller townhouses. The most distinctive landmark is the Cow Palace, looking like a tremendous fifty-gallon drum laid on its side. When the Grand National was first held in the Cow Palace, horsemen exercised their prize mounts by riding them up to McLaren Park. Part of McLaren's dream was to link San Bruno Mountain with McLaren Park by a riding and hiking trail. For lack of it, cowboys and rodeo riders must now trailer their horses from the Cow Palace to McLaren Park.

When you reach the triangle, bear left again. New construction on San Bruno Mountain's lower flanks and excavated terraces will command the eye as you return toward Mansell. If you are up for more walking, cross Visitacion and follow the dirt paths westerly along the ridge.

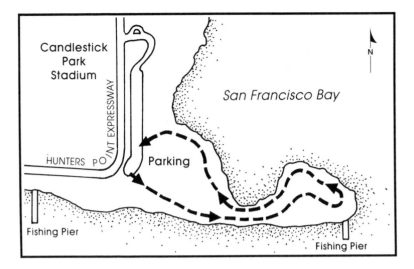

CANDLESTICK POINT

WALKING TIME: An hour.

DISTANCE: Two miles.

PUBLIC TRANSPORTATION: Muni bus 56 Rutland.

PARKING: $2, unless there is a game at the stadium, when it sometimes triples.

CLOTHES: Casual and comfortable.

DIRECTIONS: U.S. 101 south to the last of three Candlestick off ramps. Follow signs for stadium but hug the shoreline until you are on Hunters Point Expressway on east side.

Of all the wastelands that have been rescued from misuse or abuse during the last fifteen years, perhaps the most remarkable effort in San Francisco is four miles of Bay shoreline that has emerged as Candlestick Point State Recreation Area.

Thirty-seven of the 170 acres of this former garbage dump are now stabilized, planted, fitted with trails, and usable. The fishing is good. The bird-watching is sometimes sensational. The picnicking is pleasant, and the strolling unique.

A walk out to the end of Sunrise Point, the southernmost of the two points of land in the park, offers a fresh perspective for view collectors.

From the corner of Alana Way and Thomas Mellon Drive, cross the street about half a mile along a pleasant shoreline trail of decomposed granite, especially prepared for joggers. After you pass an old fishing pier, look for an open grassy meadow.

Sunrise Trail, paved in asphalt and level enough for tot strollers and wheelchairs, takes off just past the unisex toilets. (Rest Rooms. Comfort Stations. Choose your own euphemism.) Follow this broad walkway, and in a few minutes you will become aware of something that looks like a high board fence on the right. Look inside to discover that this is a suntrap, containing sturdy picnic tables and a barbecue pit. The windbreak shuts out the afternoon westerlies that roll through nearby Visitacion Valley, about the same time fog begins fingering the Golden Gate Bridge.

Visitacion Valley sounds like a name recently made up by a fast-talking realtor. In fact, it originated on a land grant called Rancho Cañada de Guadalupe Rodeo Viejo y Visitación made in 1841 by Governor Juan Bautista Alvarado to Jacob B. Leese. Leese was the second citizen to build a home and shop on the border of Portsmouth Square within the Pueblo of Yerba Buena, which subsequently became San Francisco. Continue east.

As you walk, the shoreline on your right will also be the county line. At the isthmus, the water on your left is in San Francisco; farther out on your right, it is in San Mateo County. The land, however, is all within San Francisco, completely situated on landfill created during World War II for a U.S. Navy shipyard. Shipyard cranes, including the world's largest, are visible beyond the water to the north at the AAA shipyard at Hunters Point.

When you reach the new cement fishing pier at the end of the point, walk it out over the waters of San Mateo County and look toward Sierra Point. Salmon, sturgeon, striped bass, perch, and starry flounder have all been landed here by lucky fishermen. Flotillas of migrating birds often pepper the water. At low tide, the remains of two shipwrecks are also visible.

Follow the path around the point and you will be looking north. Nice lawns here are dotted with Monterey cypress and pines. As you swing around a little bay, willets, avocets, and stilts may fly up ahead of you. Brown pelicans and great blue herons also fish here.

Mudflats, marshlands, and rock oyster beds along this shore provided clean air and food for Ohlone Indians long ago. Later there were Chinese shrimp camps in the area.

Beyond South Basin, the next cove north, there was once a racetrack called Bay View that provided amusement for devotees of "the sport of kings." The sharp, needlelike rock called Candlestick that gave the park its name is now a memory only, lost long since under the fill on which the stadium stands.

Bear right on the granite path when you reach the next junction. It brings you past another group of picnic tables well sheltered from the wind, alongside a man-made beach. You are heading toward Candlestick Point itself, which lies between Sunrise Point and Hunters Point. On at least one early map, it was named Garratt's Point.

Soon the granite path joins a paved one. Continue to the right for about the length of a city block. The recreation area was opened in September of 1983.

Bear left on the next granite path, which takes you up over a berm. Suddenly, you are back in view of the stadium and a few hundred feet from the parking lot. If you brought along your fishing gear, maybe you want to go back to that pier and throw out a line.

INDEX

Index entries in **boldface** refer to highlighted walks.